LEARN
BETTER

LEARN BETTER

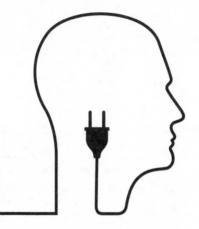

Mastering the Skills for Success in Life,
Business, and School, or, How to Become an
Expert in Just About Anything

ULRICH BOSER

RODALE.

3 1398 00485 3173

RODALE *wellness*

Live happy. Be healthy. Get inspired.

Sign up today to get exclusive access to our authors, exclusive bonuses, and the most authoritative, useful, and cutting-edge information on health, wellness, fitness, and living your life to the fullest.

Visit us online at RodaleWellness.com
Join us at RodaleWellness.com/Join

Rodale books may be purchased for business or promotional use or for special sales. For information, please write to: Special Markets Department, Rodale Inc., 733 Third Avenue, New York, NY 10017.

Printed in the United States of America

Rodale Inc. makes every effort to use acid-free ♾, recycled paper ♻.

Book design by Carol Angstadt

Library of Congress Cataloging-in-Publication Data is on file with the publisher.

ISBN–13: 978–1–62336–526–4 hardcover

Distributed to the trade by Macmillan

2   4   6   8   10   9   7   5   3   1   hardcover

RODALE.

We inspire health, healing, happiness, and love in the world.
Starting with you.

*For my parents,
who helped spark my
love of learning.*

CONTENTS

AUTHOR'S NOTE

IN THIS BOOK, I've used text that has previously appeared in other articles, reports, or blog items that I've written. I also edited quotes for clarity and shared some portions of the text with sources to gain their feedback. If I use only a first name to describe someone, then the name is a pseudonym. If there are any errors of fact, citation or clarity, I'll list them on my website: www.ulrichboser.com.

With regard to citations, I've found the use of footnotes in e-books distracting, and so I wrote up a notes section, which includes source material, notable asides, and further reading. With regard to conflicts of interest, I have some—don't we all?—and I've done work for different organizations and foundations that I mention in this book. Again, see the notes section.

When it comes to writing about my own history, especially as it relates to events that occurred years ago, I wanted to write "to the best of my knowledge" at the end of every sentence. I did not, but please consider the caveat.

INTRODUCTION

THE ELEMENTARY SCHOOL stood at the end of a cul-de-sac. It was a low-slung red-brick building some ten miles north of New York City, tucked away among ribbons of suburban streets, surrounded by solid ranchers and brawny Colonials. It was January 6, 1986, a cold morning, just above freezing. Parents pulled in front of the school in a convoy of cars, their children slipping out, laughing, talking, letting out the occasional raucous scream.

Shortly after 10:30 a.m., a young boy tucked himself into a chair in one of the school's classrooms. He was green-eyed with a big bowl of dirty blond hair. It was a few days before the boy's 11th birthday, and he almost certainly wore a turtleneck sweater and corduroy pants. Pages of schoolwork stuffed his backpack, most likely mixed together with some *Dungeons & Dragons*–inspired drawings.

The green-eyed boy had a difficult time learning, and that morning was no different. Class began with the teacher discussing how to subtract one fraction from another, and the boy strode to the blackboard to answer a problem from his homework. But the boy wrote down the wrong equation and had to redo the problem.

Then the boy became distracted, twisting around in his seat, contorting like an aspiring Houdini, and the teacher scolded him: *Please focus.* The other children answered questions. They solved problems. But the green-eyed boy remained bewildered. So rather than work through the math problems, the boy simply cheated, copying down solutions from a friend sitting nearby.

Then, some twenty minutes into the class, the teacher called on the boy to answer a division problem: *What's 770 divided by 77?* The boy didn't know. Another division question. Another confused grimace. Eventually, the class wound down. The teacher discussed homework assignments, while the green-eyed boy nattered on to a friend—sports, books, recess, who knows. The teacher scolded the child one last time before the class let out.

In many ways, the boy with the green eyes is everyone. A lot of kids make a mess of their homework. It's easy to get distracted. But that child was me. I lumbered along in my classes. My grades were weak. I floundered on exams. Teachers complained about my inability to learn, one telling my mother I would probably become a cook. So one morning, in January 1986, a school psychologist slipped into my 4th grade classroom to observe me in class.

While I've tried to recall the day, I don't have the slightest scrap of a memory. But for decades, I kept the psychologist's detailed report—a single-spaced black-and-white typewriter-created document. It describes how I managed to cheat, neglect my work, and forgo all focus during the one hour-long class. "Frustrated," "inattentive," and "distracted" are among the words of the school psychologist used to describe me.

Kindergarten was probably my first academic challenge. I was the youngest in my class, and I ended up repeating the grade because I couldn't keep up. In elementary school, teachers sent me for special testing, and I filled in the bubbles of a long list of unpronounceable psychological exams that sound today like a bit of Psych 101—the Bender Visual-Motor Gestalt Test, the Zeitlin Coping Inventory, the Projective Figure Drawing exam. For a few years in middle school, I spent a few hours each week in special education, a holding pen for cranks and misfits, social oddities, and academic outliers.

Different theories about the cause of my difficulties floated around, vague potential explanations. One account held that I was slow to learn because my immigrant parents spoke German at home. Others claimed that I had an auditory problem, that my brain wasn't wired correctly when it came to listening. Still others believed I lacked intelligence, that almost magical ability to think through issues and solve problems.

There's a bit of accuracy to each of these theories. My parents have lived in this country for decades, yet they still sometimes slip into German while speaking English. I do, indeed, have a learning disorder that makes it difficult to follow auditory details, and I still have a hard time following verbal directions. And let's be clear—I'm no genius.

There's another perspective on what happened, though, and when I look back now, it seems that I didn't know how to learn. I didn't have ways to think about my thinking. I didn't ask myself questions or set goals or even know what it meant to know something. The ability to learn appeared beyond me, and it left me "lost," as the school psychologist wrote in her evaluation.

With the help of some teachers, I eventually developed a few basic learning strategies. I would ask myself questions like: Do I really know this? Did I understand the underlying logic of what I was learning? I also came to terms with the idea that people learned at different rates, that I might need to put in more effort than my peers. Over the years, I discovered better ways to focus, becoming a devotee of anything that promoted silence, and even today, I buy earplugs by the box.

Eventually, my academic confidence began to tick upward, and so did my grades. Student government became an interest. So did sports—track, basketball, cross-country. I did well on my college admissions exams, and then, with a bit of luck—and a lot of work—a thick envelope from an Ivy League college arrived in the mail.

My academic experiences are not the basis for this book. In fact, if you compare my experience to the experiences of those stuck in dead-end colleges or bad corporate training, I had it great—supportive parents, well-funded schools, generally caring teachers. Plus, my auditory disability makes me less than representative.

But in the end, my experience drove an interest, one that developed into a career, and today I believe that a lot of people are like an early version of me—they don't think much about the best way to gain new knowledge and skills. People will often reread material, for instance, even though it's a weak approach to learning, or they'll use highlighters, which have a very limited research base. People also won't reflect on their skills or track their progress, despite the library of evidence on these learning approaches.

This happens despite the fact that most of us are constantly developing our skills and knowledge. Someone gives you some new software? You'll need to master the application. (Be sure to explain key ideas to yourself so you really understand them.) Land a new client? You'll want to present your ideas in a way that's engaging. (Don't put too many graphics on a PowerPoint slide; it overloads working memory.) Need to remember a phone number? (Use your fingers; they're a great way to store numbers for a short period of time.)

Not long ago, I grabbed coffee with one of my old special education teachers. We sat in a Starbucks, spinning out recollections. As we discussed some long-lost moments of elementary school—my issues with homework, certain teachers, other students—it made me feel like a kid again. At least my experience of being a kid—the odd shame, the addled confusion. At one point, I tried to share with her what I had learned since middle school, everything that I knew about learning.

But the words never quite tumbled out. I felt embarrassed. I didn't want to seem preening. So while I wrote this book for all sorts of reasons—to reframe the education debate, to hone my own thinking—one of my main drivers was to provide a guide to that green-eyed boy with the big blond hair—and to everyone else who might need one.

An experiment took place some years ago at an all-girls school in New York City. It was an old Catholic school, with some crucifixes hanging from the walls, looking somber and stern. The girls were in their first two years of high school, teenagers wearing polo shirts and pleated skirts, and the young women would later receive a little gift for agreeing to enroll in the study.

As part of the experiment, the girls were taught how to play darts for the first time, and the two psychologists conducting the study divided the young women into some groups. Let's call the members of the first group Team Performance, and they were told that they should learn the game of darts by trying to throw the darts as close to the center of the board as possible. In other words, the researchers informed the women that the best way to win was to rack up some points.

The psychologists also pulled together another group of young women. Let's call them Team Learning Method, and they learned to play darts very differently. The researchers had these girls focus on the process of gaining expertise, and the women started by working on how exactly to throw the darts, mastering some basic processes like "keep your arm close to your body." Then, after the women showed some proficiency, they were encouraged to aim at the bull's-eye, slowly shifting from some process goals to some outcome goals like hitting the target.

Finally, there was the control group. Their instructions? The researchers told them to simply "do their best." In other words, these young women could take any approach that they wanted to learning darts. Let's think of this group as Team Conventional Wisdom.

To learn more about the experiment, I met up with Anastasia Kitsantas, who ran the study together with psychologist Barry Zimmerman. While the experiment took place some years ago, Kitsantas still had the darts stashed away in her office at George Mason University, and on a rainy afternoon, she pulled out the little yellow missiles from an office cabinet to show them to me, laying the darts out like an important relic from some forgotten South American tribe.

Kitsantas held on to the darts because of the study's surprisingly large outcomes, and by the end of the experiment, the young women on Team Learning Method dramatically outperformed the others, with scores nearly twice as high as Team Conventional Wisdom. The women also enjoyed the experience much more. "Several of the students asked me to teach them more about darts after the experiment. They kept asking me for weeks," Kitsantas told me.

The takeaway from the dart experiment is a straightforward one, one supported by a growing number of studies, because learning turns out to be a process, a method, a system of understanding. It's an activity that requires focus, planning, and reflection, and when people know how to learn, they acquire mastery in much more much effective ways.

Indeed, the learning process turns out to be one of the most important predictors of learning. One recent analysis—or a study of studies—showed that learning methods dramatically shifted outcomes in just about every field. Another analysis found that the process of learning works in lockstep with GPA. Follow-up research by Kitsantas and Zimmerman replicated the dart study in other fields, finding that dedicated strategies boosted performance in everything from volleyball to writing.

Within the typically somber community of cognitive science researchers, the recent spate of learning-to-learn studies have sparked a glee that's typically associated with the Second Coming. Some researchers have dramatically labeled their papers with titles like "How to Gain Eleven IQ Points in Ten Minutes." (The researchers recommend thinking aloud while problem solving.) Others become exhilarated during interviews. "We should be spreading this gospel," researcher Bennett Schwartz told me. (Schwartz argues for more self-quizzing.)

A lot of the excitement stems from the originality of the findings, and as an idea, a more focused approach to learning is only some twenty years old. For a long time, experts had assumed that the ability to learn was a matter of intelligence, dedicated smarts, and so researchers didn't really study the issue. They assumed, it seems, that either people had the skill of learning or they didn't. For them, intelligence—and thus the ability to gain mastery—was an immutable trait like having blue eyes, a genetic gift of the gods.

For their part, schools followed the science, and despite years of education, despite years spent in classrooms, most people have never learned to learn. Generally speaking, we don't have a good sense of how to improve our expertise in a field or subject.

As an example, consider the word "studying": It's a remarkably vague expression. Does studying mean rereading a textbook? Doing sample problems? Memorizing? All of the above? For another example, take the word "practice." Does practice mean repeating the same skill over and over again? Does practice require detailed feedback? Should the practice be hard? Or should it be fun?

There are a lot of other misconceptions. When it comes to learning, people believe a lot of things that aren't really supported by the research. Working with some of the nation's most respected learning experts, I recently conducted a survey to see what people knew about how to acquire a skill, and the results were remarkable. While an overwhelming percentage of Americans said that they knew the basics of effective teaching and learning, they harbored a lot of weak intuitions and false beliefs about how people learn.

Two-thirds of the public believed, for instance, that students should be praised for being smart, for instance. But the research shows the opposite, and people learn more when they are praised for their effort than their intelligence. Another 50 percent of the public said people learn effectively without much guidance. But study after study shows that learning is a dedicated, engaged process. And while there's no research supporting the notion of learning styles—the idea that someone learns better kinesthetically or visually—more than 80 percent of the public believe that learning styles exist.

There's also a lot of good news here, though, because it doesn't take much to develop the learning process. Many of the improvement strategies that have been tucked away in sterile research studies show large gains with little additional effort, and on the day I visited with Anastasia Kitsantas, she pointed out that even small tweaks would dramatically improve outcomes. In the dart experiment, for instance, about half of the subjects on Team Learning Method recorded their scores after each throw, and even that task was enough to boost performance. "It's phenomenal when you think about it," she said.

But, of course, most of us rarely do.

The value of the learning process extends far beyond the recent science. It also reflects the nature of society today—and the shifting nature of expertise.

Recall for a moment the last bit of information that you typed into Google. Maybe you were looking for the address for a local pizza place or hunting for the hometown of pop star Michael Jackson. According to a series of studies by researcher Betsy Sparrow and her colleagues, you're more likely to remember where the information was online than the details of the actual information.

So if you searched for the hometown of Michael Jackson, you're more likely to remember the Wikipedia page of the King of Pop than the actual information (Gary, Indiana). If you found the address for the pizza place on a Web site, then you're more likely to remember the URL (greatpizza.com) than the actual address of the restaurant. "We are becoming symbiotic with our computer tools," write Sparrow and her colleagues, "growing into interconnected systems that remember less by knowing information than by knowing where the information can be found."

There are a few crucial implications from this line of research. For one thing, our brain—and its various quirks—are at the heart of learning effectively, and our brain will often "offload" information, storing it in places other than its own neural folds. In this regard, our smartphones, iPads, and laptops have become a type of "prosthetic brain" in the words of one writer, and recent research shows that we're less likely to remember a painting at a museum if we take a photo of the painting. Our brain, it seems, believes the image is stored on the digital device.

But there's a second, more important lesson here that gets to a broad truth about the Digital Age: Facts have lost a lot of their value. Details are no longer as important as they once were. For just about all of us, what matters today is not the data itself—what matters is how we can think better with that data. More exactly, how do we acquire new skills most effectively? How do we better grasp complex problems? And when should we store memories in our heads—and when should we store them on a computer?

If you lived just a few decades ago—or near the end of the Ice Age—it wasn't this way. Take the man known as Ötzi. He lived in the Italian Alps around 5,000 years ago at the start of the Bronze Age. He was a small man by modern standards—just over 5 feet tall, with a thick, matted beard carpeting his face. His forehead hung low over his eyes. His nose had once been broken, giving him the visage of an aging boxer.

Ötzi died deep in the Alps, trekking up a high mountain pass, falling behind a boulder, a sprawl of clenched fists and tired legs. An arrow had gored his shoulder, blood spilling from his back, killing him quickly. For centuries, Ötzi's murdered body stayed among the rocks until some wanderers found his corpse in 1989, perfectly mummified in the snow and ice.

Ötzi had developed an important type of knowledge, according to the archaeologists who've studied him over the years. A collection of half-built arrows hung around his shoulders, meaning that Ötzi had studied the foundations of archery construction. Filaments of metal coated his hair, suggesting Ötzi understood the basic procedures of metal smelting. And from the awkward attempts to mend his clothes with bits of grass, it appeared that Ötzi had developed rudimentary sewing skills.

But the knowledge that makes Ötzi so impressive is not same sort of knowledge that we need today. From the time Ötzi left the Alpine valley until just a few years ago, information was both highly static—and very expensive. For centuries, we sought out experts, who could pass along invariable details like how to build a bow and arrow, a form of technology that would not change for another 4,000 years.

At the same time, we worshiped data, which for a long time could be found only in rare, hand-calligraphed manuscripts and then, after the invention of the Gutenberg press, in faded books. When many of us were kids, writing school papers meant spending hours in the library going cross-eyed as we scrolled through microfiche. Acing tests meant studying page after page of details, memorizing dates, and learning equations by heart.

This view of learning continues to be implemented in most schools and colleges and training programs. Just pull any thick textbook from the shelf. I recently worked with curriculum experts Morgan Polikoff and John Smithson, and we showed that over 95 percent of one widely used elementary school math textbook focused on lower order thinking like memorization and understanding procedures.

But in the Internet Age, information is fire-sale cheap, and within tenths of a second on Google, we can figure out how proteins bind with plasma. Dinner-party disputes are quickly settled with a swipe of a finger on an iPhone. What's more, mastery itself is constantly shifting. The life cycle of expertise has become ever shorter—over the past ten years, for instance, the car-sharing service Uber shot from an obscure app to a household name.

This shifts both how and why we acquire new skills and knowledge, because practice alone doesn't make perfect anymore. We need to develop more than simple procedures in order to succeed, and the modern world requires that people know how to learn—and develop the thinking skills that matter.

It's easy to go too far here, so let's be clear. Facts still play a crucial role. Knowledge serves as the bedrock of learning. Memorization also remains a powerful learning tool, and what you know is often the best predictor of what you're able to learn. I call it the Knowledge Effect, and it's a theme that we will revisit often in this book because expertise demands fluency in the basics.

But knowing the facts is just the start, and when people engage in learning, they also need to understand relationships, to identify cause and effect, to see analogies and similarities. In the end, the goal of learning is about shifting how we think about a fact or idea, and when we learn, we aim to learn a system of thought.

So if we study microeconomics, we want to learn how to think microeconomically. If we learn knitting, we aim to learn to think like an expert knitter. Want to go scuba diving? Then try to learn to reason like a world-class diver. As educational psychologists argue, "Think of learning as figuring out the parts of an organized and intelligible system."

There's a lot riding on this new approach to learning—and the reason is sitting right there in your smartphone. After all, recent technological advances have decimated the jobs that require procedural knowledge. To a degree, this is an old headline. With the rise of online travel Web sites, the demise of travel agents is basically complete. ATMs have destroyed bank-teller jobs, while countless cashier spots are gone due to the advent of self-checkouts.

This shift is happening faster than even the most sanguine experts could have predicted. Some ten years ago, for instance, Harvard economists Richard Murnane and Frank Levy published *The New Division of Labor,* which made all sorts of predictions about which jobs will continue to exist in the future. For them, secretarial jobs would soon be gone—replaced by computers. Same with anything having to do with factory work—gone.

But computers will never be able to drive a car. For the two economists, piloting an automobile was simply too sophisticated, too complicated, to be done by any sort of device. Most of their predictions turned
out to be accurate—secretarial jobs have more or less disappeared.
Same with a lot of factory work. But on self-driving cars, the economists
clearly missed the mark: Companies from Google to Tesla have already
rolled out driverless cars, and self-driving taxis already roam the streets
of cities like Singapore.

Not long ago, I met up with Murnane at his house outside of Boston,
and when he came to the door, he seemed every bit the Harvard economics professor. He had a white beard and wore glasses and a National
Bureau of Economics Research sweatshirt. There was a small hole in
one of his socks.

As we sat in his living room, Murnane argued that the self-driving
car predication was the exception that proves the rule. Technology is
changing the world much faster than most people think, and he argued
that people needed "expert thinking skills" to succeed. In practical
terms, this means people need to know how to solve "unstructured
problems." If you're a computer engineer, you need to be able to tackle
technical issues not outlined in a technical manual. If you're a speech
therapist, you need to be able to help children who have not-easily-
defined language issues.

At the same time, people need to be better able to create understanding out of new information, according to Murnane. So if you work
for an advertising company, one of the key skills might be explaining
how a client can take advantage of what's in the news that morning. If
you're a stockbroker, it's making sense of how weather changes might
impact the sales of grain.

The audience for this book, then, is much wider than the nation's
students, and in the pages that follow, I also discuss ways to help people
engage more effectively in any type of knowledge work. For a tough
problem, for instance, people should look for analogies outside of their
field. If you have a film-development problem, for instance, examine the
music industry for innovative clues. If you have a difficult marketing
problem, look at journalism for some creative sparks.

POP QUIZ #1

What's the most effective way to learn key ideas?

A. Circling key points in the passage.

B. Rereading the passage.

C. Taking a short practice test on the material presented in the passage.

D. Highlighting the crucial ideas in the passage.

I also discuss how people can improve their ability to solve new problems, and when working on an issue, people should develop a pithy summary of the situation. By clearly defining a problem, we are often better able to crack a persistent riddle or issue. In this book, we will also cover various management ideas—like the value of peer learning and postmortems. After all, a lot of leadership boils down to helping people grow and develop.

More broadly, though, we have to realize that in a world filled with data, when facts and figures flow as freely as water, when even cars are driving themselves, we have to be able to acquire new forms of expertise quickly and effectively. Learning to learn is what experts call the "ultimate survival tool," one of the most important talents of the modern era, the skill that precedes all other skills. Because once you know how to learn, you can learn almost anything, and as a society, we need much richer forms of education, where information and knowledge work to foster the problem-solving skills that ultimately matter.

Still skeptical? Just Google it.

In many ways, my interest in the process of learning was rekindled with an email. At the time, I was laboring over a project that attempted to answer the question: What sort of outcomes does a school district produce relative to its spending? We aimed to provide the results for just about every district in the country, and it took months. The data was weak. There were statistical issues. If you want to figure out how effective a district is, for instance, how do you take into account that kids in low-income areas often arrive at school without having had any breakfast?

Late in the project, an email flashed into my inbox. My research assistant had flooded a statistical application with data and confirmed a pattern that we had been seeing all along: Spending did not line up with outcomes. In a few places, the relationship between spending and outcomes was so noisy that there was a small but negative relationship between money and test scores. In other words, if you were Billy Bean of *Moneyball* fame and looked at our data, it seemed like money spent on some schools actually predicted lower outcomes.

How is this possible? There are a lot of reasons, of course, and I'm not arguing that schools should get less money. Quite the opposite. But over time, I also came to believe that one of the biggest issues within education was the quality of learning itself. In too many areas, at too many levels, institutions were not set up to help people gain skills. Put more directly, in too many places, money is simply not being spent on what matters.

As concrete evidence, step into any lecture hall, with hundreds of students passively listening to a lecture. The research is overwhelming that the they'll-get-it-eventually approach is ineffective. Students in traditional lecture-based courses are 50 percent more likely to fail, according to one recent study. One Nobel laureate told me that he thought that traditional lecture courses were simply "unethical."

For another example, consider a practice like testing yourself. The evidence is conclusive that the strategy can dramatically increase outcomes, sometimes showing 50 percent higher outcomes. But students rarely use the approach, preferring to just leaf through their textbook again. (When it comes to quizzing, I tried to make this book an exemplar, and you'll find a lot of "pop quizzes" in these pages. I slipped the questions into the text to help you better remember what you've read. The answers are at the end of the book.)

To a degree, this book is a product of my work at one of the nation's leading think tanks. Since my confused days in elementary school—or, perhaps more accurately, because of my confused days in elementary school—I became fascinated with learning. After graduating from college, I aimed to provide students with better educational opportunities and worked as a researcher at the trade publication *Education Week*. Then I covered education—and other social topics—at *U.S. News & World Report.*

Eventually, I became a senior fellow at the Center for American Progress, a Washington, DC-based think tank. Working with a dedicated group of researchers and policy wonks, I examine education issues, and my research has had some impact over the years, from inspiring quips on *The Tonight Show* to sparking changes in education policy.

But more than that, this book rests on the work of the many scientists and researchers who've been studying the science of learning. Over the past few decades, the field has gone from an obscure topic to a well-established field. Still, most of the research findings have remained buried in dusty academic journals and obscure government reports. Far too little has reached the public. Far too little has changed how people learn.

This book is not another "what's wrong with American education system" tome. There have been enough of those sorts of policy stem-winders. Rather, I hope to outline the process of learning, to detail how we learn best. The rest of this book will map out this notion in greater detail, outlining a general method for gaining mastery that's come out of the research.

Not every learning activity requires a step-by-step approach. If you want to learn how to, say, change the tire on your car, you don't need to follow each idea outlined below, although it might help. But if a skill is worth knowing deeply, then it's worth knowing well, and we need to take a systemic approach to developing expertise, as follows:

> **Value.** It's impossible to learn if we don't want to learn, and to gain expertise, we have to see the skills and knowledge as valuable. What's more, we have to create meaning. Learning is a matter of making sense of something.
> **Target.** In the early part of gaining mastery, focus is key. We

need to figure out what exactly we want to learn and set goals and targets.

Develop. Some forms of practice make people more perfect than others. In this stage of learning, people need to hone their skills and take dedicated steps to improve performance.

Extend. At this point, we want to go beyond the basics—and apply what we know. We want to flesh out our skills and knowledge and create more meaningful forms of understanding.

Relate. This is the phase where we see how it all fits together. After all, we don't want to know just a single detail or procedure—we want to know how that detail or procedure interacts with other facts and procedures.

Rethink. When it comes to learning, it's easy to make mistakes, to be overconfident, and so we need to review our knowledge, reconsider our understanding, and learn from our learning.

Across these steps, there are some themes that we'll return to again and again. Learning is often a form of mental doing, for one, and the more someone is actively engaged, the more they learn. If you're reading some new text, ask yourself questions: What's this text about? What point is the author trying to make? Is there anything here that seems confusing?

At the same time, manage your learning. Have you gotten feedback? Have you benchmarked your performance? If you're giving a speech, videotape yourself. If you're writing an essay, ask a friend to read it over. If you're learning Spanish, talk with a native speaker. When it comes to learning, we need to target our learning and figure out what exactly we're aiming to know.

Also be sure to think about your thinking. Do you really understand? Have you accounted for the inevitable forgetting? In this regard, spreading learning over time is crucial. After all, we often fail to recall certain facts and details, and by some estimates, we lose about half of what we learn within an hour. This means that people should make sure to review what they know days, weeks, even months later. As we will find out, just making larger piles of flashcards—and thus doing more to space out our learning—can improve outcomes by 30 percent.

Emotions also play a crucial role. We often think that learning is purely rational, a matter of deep logic and focused reasoning, but our brains don't quite work that way. The process of gaining expertise is often just as cognitive as noncognitive. In this regard, we can't learn if we don't believe that we can learn. Like an engine that requires both oil and gas in order to run properly, our brains need both reason and emotion to perform at any sort of high level.

To gain expertise, people also need to look for connections, and effective learning often boils down to seeing relationships within a body of knowledge. So ask yourself: Is there an analogy that helps explain the idea? Are there links to other fields or subjects? If you're learning about something—like, say, the physics of a black hole—what conceptual similarity can you envision? Are black holes similar to sinkholes? A waterfall? A trash can?

In the end, there are better, more effective ways to learn, and we need to do much more to give everyone the skills they need to succeed. The goal in today's world isn't just to be smart or to memorize lots of facts. That simply is not enough anymore. Rather, the goal is to become an effective learner, one who can take advantage of all the tools of the 21st century. I hope this book shows you how—and sparks great change, so that we can all take full advantage of our deep capacity to gain new skills.

Chapter 1

VALUE

JASON WOLFSON ISN'T sure how many Lego sculptures he's created. Standing in the basement of his house, he's surrounded by dozens of his creations—a Lego dragon, a Lego airplane, a giant Lego moth with six-inch Lego wings. In boxes, in small plastic bags, on the table in front of Wolfson, there were still more constructions—a half-built lunar module, a Leaning Tower of Pisa, a cowboy—all made from Legos.

Some of Wolfson's constructions are finished—large artful works of bricks, part Warhol, part toy, part real-life fantasy. Other sculptures are half-built designs, creations in the making, like an artificial heart sculpted out of Legos. Along the walls, along the floor, pushing against the top of the room, are all of Wolfson's raw materials—hundreds of thousands of plastic bricks.

"Ah, these meteors are awesome," Wolfson tells me, plucking out a little gray meteor from the plastic box and showing it off to me in his palm like some sort of rare diamond.

Without question, Wolfson is an unlikely Lego devotee. He loves movies and vacations in Florida and does CrossFit on weekends. He grew up outside of Philadelphia and ran track in high school and helped head up his college fraternity. Today, he works as an engineer and lives with his wife, and he hangs a large American flag out in front of the house each Independence Day. Like many forty-somethings, his hair is thinning a bit. He often quotes films from the 1980s. I don't know if I've ever seen him wear anything but blue jeans.

But in many ways, Wolfson's interest in Legos makes all sorts of sense. When he toured me through his basement, he kept spinning out little stories, a way of explaining why each sculpture mattered. When Wolfson pointed out his true-to-size replica of the muppet Gonzo, he explained that his wife loved the Jim Henson–created puppet. As Wolfson showed me the blue police box made from the small bricks, he began to talk about his devotion to the TV show *Dr. Who*. Or the dragonlike Jabberwocky that Wolfson had once fashioned out of hundreds of Legos? Wolfson always loved *Alice in Wonderland*.

At first, Wolfson's stories seemed cute and charming, something to tell the writer in this basement. But the stories turned out to be a crucial part of his devotion. They made Wolfson's Lego sculptures something of value, something of substance, something that had meaning.

After all, Wolfson wasn't interested in any pile of little plastic bricks. He didn't care about some old box of dog-chewed Legos. Rather, he was fascinated by the pile of bricks that he had transformed into a scene from his favorite novel or an iconic phone booth from his favorite TV show.

To a degree, we're all part Wolfson. We may not have a burning passion for *Alice in Wonderland,* Muppets, or Legos, but in our mind, we all see the world through the frame of meaning. We engage in activities that we believe have value.

When it comes to learning, this idea is crucial. Motivation is the first step in acquiring any sort of skill. It's hard to learn something if we don't see any meaning in it, and we'll start this chapter by examining how value drives motivation.

But meaning is important for another reason—it's the very first step of understanding. If we're making a connection to a bit of expertise, we're starting to make sense of it. We'll cover this idea in the second half of the chapter and discuss the crucial role of uncovering significance in what we want to learn.

The value of meaning has its roots in the brain, and for all its rich complexity, our mind works as a type of storyteller. Like a film director, we're always creating some sort of narrative, some type of understanding, some sort of meaning. If you walk into a room for the first time, for instance, you will immediately formulate a value-laden story that explains the room's purpose. If it's a large space with a long, well-polished table, you might think: *a meeting room.* If there are a few barbells on the ground: *gym.*

The same thing happens in two dimensions with optical illusions. Sometimes we will see a beautiful young woman in a drawing, sometimes an older lady—but we're always seeing some sort of meaning in the image. It's never just a bunch of random, meaningless squiggles.

This is more than a cognitive quirk because meaning is something we have to create. People find their own value in the world, with meaning serving as a matter of perspective, a frame of mind, an attitude that makes something either wonderfully important or devoid of all significance. More directly, value is the ultimate fuel of our drive to learn. We're motivated to gain expertise because of the power of meaning.

Legos remain a good example. The bricks have become popular with adults because they make it easy to uncover a sense of relevance, and today many Lego expos will have tens of thousands of visitors, while glossy online magazines like *Brick Journal* chronicle the latest approaches. There are also Lego skills classes and books devoted to Lego techniques and a professor of Lego at the University of Cambridge.

Wolfson himself has spent decades perfecting his Lego skills for this reason. Because of the meaning that he finds in the brick constructions, he has learned how to create curved Lego structures—which is difficult given that the bricks themselves are square. To create a smooth look, Wolfson also developed the skill of building Lego constructions with the studs on the inside. For one project, Wolfson even developed a new programming code so that the Lego construction would play music when someone walked by.

Before I left Wolfson's house, he showed me yet another Lego construction, a dark blue moon land set. Wolfson had built the kit when he was five years old, sitting in his grandmother's dining room, perched alongside an eight-sided wooden table, his legs tucked into a low-slung chair. As we spoke, Wolfson gently held the construction in his hand, showing me the different details. The construction was an ode to his childhood self. It was something valuable.

When it comes to learning, meaning isn't something that finds us. It's something that we need to uncover on our own.

Take statistics, as an example. Without question, data analysis is a powerful tool. In fact, it's become nearly impossible these days to get far in many fields—banking, medicine, sports management—without some basic grasp of statistics.

Yet people generally don't have an intrinsic desire to master statistics. Condemn the elaborate nature of linear regressions—or the dust dry manner in which the topic is usually taught—but most people aren't powerfully inspired to spend their days reviewing statistics code or plotting histograms.

A psychology professor at the University of Virginia, Chris Hulleman is well aware of this tension. As a researcher, he has a statistics program like R or STATA loaded up on every one of his computers—it's basically impossible to publish a research paper without any sort of robust data analysis.

But at the same time, most of Hulleman's psychology students grouse at the mention of correlations. Many groan. A few whimper. For his students, statistics seems tedious—a painful, boring topic without any sort of relevance or value to their lives.

In college, Hulleman was an All-American offensive lineman, and today he still has the energetic, aspirational attitude of someone who has spent a lot of time playing competitive sports. And, some years ago, he decided to try and address this problem, to see if he could do more to spark his students' interest in statistics, and Hulleman had some psychology students write about why statistics was relevant to their lives.

Hulleman and his colleagues aimed to help the students find value in the data tools, and the researchers prompted the students with questions like: Can you see yourself ever using statistics in your life? Can you imagine using statistics in your career as a nurse, salesperson, or manager? The students then spent some time writing short essays, each filling a page or two of a notebook.

The outcomes were clear. By drawing a connection between their lives and statistics, the students became much more motivated in their studies; in some cases, the students came close to jumping a grade level, from a C average to a B average. In other words, the act of explaining why statistics mattered to them—in their future careers, their hobbies, the families they'd one day create—dramatically improved their levels of learning.

Since then, Hulleman has rolled out similar initiatives in various settings. He has had high school students write about the value of science to their lives, penning short descriptions of why science matters to them. Together with researcher Judith Harackiewicz, Hulleman has also provided pamphlets to parents to talk with their children about how science can shape careers, suggesting ways that the parents make science homework seems more meaningful.

Inevitably, a person or two will pen some snide remarks. "Man, quit wasting my time," wrote one high school student in a flash of defiance. But most people engage. Students will write about how they might need math once they have jobs at a company. Others talk about how the skills could help them in their personal lives. Many note that there's an intrinsic pleasure to having a skill.

Hulleman and I spoke early one afternoon, and he argued that there are lots of ways to create a sense of value. Rewards, novelty, context—they all make a difference when it comes to creating a personal sense of meaning. In this regard, intrinsic motivation—or inherent interest—is itself a type of value. We do something because we want do it. But in the end, Hulleman argued, people need to find their own relevance in a subject in order to be driven to learn that subject.

Psychologist Kenn Barron—who works with Hulleman—gives a different way to understand this idea. Not long ago, Barron wrote up a formula. "I tried to boil down 40 years of research to fit onto a cocktail napkin," he told me. The formula is motivation equals a mix of costs (or the amount of effort it will take to complete the task), a sense of expectancy (or the notion of self-efficacy, which we will discuss in the next chapter), and a feeling of value, or meaning. The last variable is often the most crucial, according to Barron, and it's a matter of "Do I want to do the task?"

There's something familiar about this argument, admittedly. After all, we've all had teachers who have proclaimed: "This is important." My parents said it all the time about my schoolwork, too: "You'll need this later." Now I hear versions of the idea from my company's HR department: "Your retirement account is central to your future."

But the crux of this line of research is different. In short, just telling people that something is important is not enough. In fact, Hulleman has found that simply telling people that information has value can backfire. When we're told how to feel or think, we can feel threatened or overly managed.

Instead, people need to find meaning in the activities themselves. In other words, value has to go from the person to the material, from the individual to the knowledge or skill. "It's about making that connection between what people are learning and what's going on in their lives," Hulleman told me. "Value is the mechanism. For people, the question is, 'Can I see why this is valuable to me?'"

Great public speakers often take this approach, and a good presenter will ensure that the material seems relevant to their audience. Former president Bill Clinton was well-known for this type of charm. If the topic of conversation was the Maldives, a skilled speaker like Clinton might subtly ask his audience if they had visited the nation. If the topic was a battle of some sort, he ask if someone had a relative who served in the military. Discussing a boring IT tool? Get people thinking about their own computer for a moment.

This idea also explains why that we're far more motivated to learn something if we have—or will have—some experience with it. When it comes to learning, we want to understand our world. We want to fill in our knowledge gaps, to see value. Meaning, then, can be self-perpetuating. The more that we know about statistics, the more that we want to know about something like statistics.

If I know something—like, say, that Venus is the hottest planet in the solar system—the more I want to know more about that: So why exactly is Venus so hot? Or if I know something about data analytics, I'll be more interested to understand Simpson's Paradox, in which trends are reversed within averages.

When it comes to Legos, this idea is oddly obvious, or at least it became obvious to me on the day that I stepped into the Lego convention known as BrickFair. The promoters billed BrickFair as the "grandest LEGO fan convention and expo in America." Wolfson had recommended that I attend it, and as I moved around the aisles, it was clear that people built things that held deep value to them.

One boy explained to me that he had once shot an M4A1 rifle, and so he built a recreation of the carbine to display at the convention. Another man, Bret Harris, had served in the Marines, and so he made military-themed things. And the person who created the picnic table-size recreation of the Vatican, including the two winged angels hanging next to the Oltramontano Clock? A Catholic priest from Scranton, Pennsylvania.

As I wandered around BrickFair, I ran into Brian Melick. Short with bright eyes and a booming voice, Melick had an unnerving amount of enthusiasm. While I talked with Melick, another man came by and jokingly asked his daughter, "Is your dad always this shy and negative?"

Melick is a drummer and has long been fascinated by using "found objects" to help students learn about percussion. So in his classes at local schools, museums, and libraries, Melick will first discuss some of the principles of drumming—things like shaking or rubbing. Then Melick will have people use whatever they can find—plates, pipes, even sticks—to make a shaking or a rubbing sound. The lessons help "connect us to our own environment," Melick told me.

Melick's approach stayed with me, and I ended up spending the whole day at the Lego convention, looking for ways that people connected to their bricks, making value out of their Legos. In the afternoon, there was a lecture about how to customize your Lego mini-figures. I also watched the Lego boat competition, where aspiring seafarers raced their Lego boats in the hotel pool. There was even a curtained-off room called Stay and Play, where people could create things that they saw as meaningful.

The strength of this very personal approach to motivation extends

POP QUIZ #2

True or false: Right-brained people are more motivated to learn.

far beyond Legos, and in the end, what's perhaps most interesting about the power of meaning is how easy it is to underestimate its power. For all sorts of reasons, we forget that people ultimately want meaning—and they need to discover that meaning on their own. In this argument, we know that meaning matters. We just forget that meaning is sort of a river, something powerful, something meandering, something that flows only in one direction.

The videogame Minecraft is a great case in point. When programmer Markus Persson first launched the online game some years ago, few believed that the program would ever succeed. After all, the game had no dramatic car chases or displays of daring-do. In Minecraft, there are not even points to figure out who is the winner.

Instead, the online game provides people with building blocks and allows them to create whatever they want in the online world. Using square blocks, people can build sprawling castles. If you love the Eiffel Tower—and want to build a facsimile out of blocks—this is your game. But, as the writers of Persson's biography argue, no banker wanted to invest in the gaming technology because it was "completely against what everyone thought people wanted" in a video game.

But despite the conventional wisdom—and a vast market built around shoot-em-up games—Minecraft has became one of the most popular games ever produced. There are more than 100 million users around the world, and Minecraft has outsold Tetris, Super Mario Brothers, even Call of Duty. Why? Because the program makes it simple to create something relevant, to find a personal sense of meaning. As Persson recently told a reporter, with Minecraft, "you can build anything you want to build yourself."

Some time ago, Yale management professor Amy Wrzesniewski conducted interviews of janitors at a hospital. At first, Wrzesniewski found exactly what you might think—the cleaning crew at the hospital seemed to be all about the money. The staff came into the hospital each day and scrubbed the toilets in order to make sure that they could write a check for the rent. It was the cash, in other words, that motivated the employees to sweep and broom and mop every day.

Over time, though, Wrzesniewski discovered that many of the janitors also viewed themselves as a key part of the hospital. Some of the cleaning crew would follow up on certain patients to make sure that they had enough visitors each day. Others would move artwork around to help engage the patients. One cleaning person told Wrzesniewski that "I'm an ambassador for the hospital." Still another called herself a "healer."

These inspired janitors were far more engaged in their work than their colleagues. Just as important, they were much happier about their lives in general. "It was not just that they were taking the same job and feeling better about it," Wrzesniewski once told writer David Zax. "It was that they were doing a different job." Put simply, the janitors saw more meaning and value in their daily toil, and it made them feel more fulfilled.

After the experience at the hospital, Wrzesniewski began studying the research, and it turned out that meaning was one of the biggest drivers of fulfillment. More than happiness, more than profits, people wanted their lives to have value, and people who report higher levels of meaning are less anxious, more healthy, and more satisfied with their lives.

To help people take advantage of this psychological habit of mind, Wrzesniewski and her colleagues spun out a career tool. They called the approach "job crafting," and it has a basic message: Shift your job to fit your interests. If you're an extrovert working at a library, craft your job so that you're a part-time tour guide for the library. Employed at a nonprofit firm and love data? Consider helping the marketing staff analyze trends as a way to boost donations.

Before Justin Berg became a business professor at Stanford, he studied with Wrzesniewski, and as part of his work, he interviewed educators who had gone through the process of job crafting. One teacher had a secret desire to be rock star, and so the educator began to include some Rolling Stones–like performances into his instruction, sometimes even walking on the tables like Mick Jagger. Another teacher loved computers, and so she took more of a tech role at the school. "It starts with a mind-set toward your job," Berg told me. "Can you see a way to make it more meaningful?"

There's an important analogy, and motivation for learning often requires something similar. Think of it as "learn crafting," and it's a matter of making what we want to learn more relevant. It's a way to find meaning—and thus motivation—in the skills that we're looking to gain.

A large part of the approach requires a shift in perspective. Are you gaining technology skills like Web design but are not much of a techie? Then make sure to see how the skill applies to your area of interest like couture fashion or badminton. Learning a financial concept like bankruptcy but dislike money talk? Then attempt to craft the topic to what's relevant to you, and think about how knowledge of bankruptcy might help your uncle who is teetering on the edge of insolvency.

This idea rests on a deeper and frankly pretty obvious truth: People are different. They have various interests, motivations, and personalities as well as diverse pastimes, backgrounds, and concerns. Yet we can't always choose what we want to learn. Sometimes we have to gain expertise in statistics. Sometimes we have to learn to drive—or master the company software.

A solution here is learn crafting, or hunting for meaning in the mastery that you've been assigned. In practical terms, that means asking yourself: How is this material valuable to me? How can I make it more relevant? How will I use the expertise in my own life?

This idea also explains why learners need some freedom. We often need space to find value, and a wealth of research supports the idea of giving students control over how they learn a subject. In one recent study, for instance, some high schoolers had some choice over their homework. Others had no choice at all. The results were clear: The students who had more autonomy showed more motivation—and far better learning outcomes.

Some schools and training centers have taken up the cause of learn crafting, although they generally don't use the exact term "learn crafting." At St. Andrew's Episcopal School outside of Washington, DC, students are often provided a choice in how they'll demonstrate their learning, from taking a conventional exam to creating a video.

Teens at the school will often opt to create some sort of independent project to show off their skills and knowledge, even though it can take three or four times as much work as taking a traditional test, according to Glenn Whitman, director of the school's Center for Transformative Teaching and Learning. "They see a lot more meaning, relevancy, and personal ownership," Whitman told me.

Even something as seemingly playful as Legos sometimes needs a bit of learn crafting. I once visited Cam Meyer's Junior Brick Builder Association's camp, where there's one overarching rule: no instructions. For Meyer, that means no Lego booklets or repackaged kits. The students have to decide on what to build—and how to build it.

This is not how the Lego company sells its bricks, to be clear. Just about every kit comes with a detailed list of procedures. But Meyer takes a different approach, and on the morning that I swung past his classroom, he started off by telling the students that there would be no directions. They would have to rely on their own creativity.

It took a few moments for the idea to sink in, and some of the students—mainly 10-year-olds—sighed loudly with frustration. In previous years, some had broken down in tears. But the students soon quieted down, and a hum descended over the room as the kids became absorbed in their Lego builds. One girl made a fierce-looking reptile. Another built an animal from a video game. It was clear that they were far more engaged than if they had simply followed a set of instructions.

"Would you rather have the instructions?" I asked one boy dressed in a blue T-shirt.

He shook his head. "It's more fun this way."

"I'm thinking about getting rid of the instructions so even my mom can't make what's in there," added the girl sitting next to him.

There's an important caveat here. Whether it's Legos or law school, instruction is important. We learn most effectively when expertise is broken down into discrete chunks, as we will see. But to stay engaged, to stay motivated, we also need choice. We need to have a hand in crafting our learning. When I spoke to Wrzesniewski's colleague Justin Berg, he told me, "Many of us could benefit from tapping further into our callings." Berg was talking about work, but learning is no different. When it comes to gaining expertise, we need to tap further into our calling.

There's an important question that we have not addressed, and that's why we even need a sense of meaning. The answer speaks to something important about who we are as a species, and in many ways, our desire for meaning is about our desire for discovery. We are often motivated to learn because we want to learn. People seek value because they evolved to seek value.

This isn't as circular as it sounds. Each time that I open an Internet browser, I'm struck by the urge to discover. Just this afternoon, I clicked on BuzzFeed's "21 Pictures That Will Restore Your Faith in Humanity." I know. I shouldn't have, and I quickly spun through the images. Two men saving a sheep from drowning. An oxygen mask on a cat. A homeless girl landing a new pair of shoes.

Then my eyes caught a glimpse of another headline—"16 Mountains to Climb for Beginners"—and I soon spun off into another corner of the Internet. I forgot the exact nature of the next hyperlinked rabbit hole—maybe a YouTube channel or a Wikipedia page or a gif of a snake eating an alligator.

Psychologist Jaak Panksepp has long argued that we're wired to seek in this way, describing seeking as "the granddaddy of the systems." For Panksepp, our emotions run on this urge to search, and he believes that feelings often serve as a type of seeking barometer, something that tells us how well we're doing in all the things that we're supposed to be discovering.

For Panksepp, this idea explains why people feel a surge of happiness when they try out something new. Our feel-good levels of dopamine jump at the experience of looking for something original. The converse is also true: Depression often boils down to a feeling that the world has no meaning, and it's typically marked by a lack of seeking behavior.

In this sense, seeking is like eating and sleeping, sex and love, a behavior that comes with our DNA, and without question, our emotion-driven urge to discover has a long evolutionary history. After all, new things often hold the most danger—and the most reward. New ideas, new people, new animals—these are the things that could help us or potentially kill us. Over time, they began to have their own special type of value.

Nor has life changed all that much since ancient times, and the emotional act of discovery is still at the very heart of what we do all day: Get up in the morning, and sleepy-eyed, you immediately start to look for some news and some clothes. Then you habitually root around for your breakfast—*where is the box of raisin bran again?* Next comes the feeling of the need to ferret out the car keys, and by the time you've left the house each morning, you've already been instinctively searching for dozens of different things.

The takeaway here is that motivation—or value—is often as much raw feeling as clear reason, and we engage in seeking constantly because that's who we are as *Homo sapiens.* We're a species of searchers. Spending an hour pecking through Web site after Web site, going from Wikipedia to TMZ to the *Washington Post* isn't a simple waste of time (although often it is). It also brings us a type of short-term pleasure.

This type of seeking, this sort of discovery, often serves as the first step of learning. To develop a sense of value, a feeling of desire, we tinker and explore, wondering if something matches our interests and values. If we want to learn engineering, we might tinker with Legos. If we want to learn about President Washington and the battle of Trenton, we might review the Wikipedia page.

In a way, we're getting a sense of what exactly we need to know. We're building a sense of desire. In the language of researchers like Suzanne Hidi and Kenn Barron, we've developed a type of situational motivation. Think of situational motivation as mind bait, and we're all pretty familiar with what it can take to spark this dopamine-infused drive: flashy images, bright sounds, or maybe just a couple cat videos.

This motivation can be enduring, and it might take an entire morning until we've exhausted all the links in an article devoted to the "40 Things That Make You Feel Old." But more typically this motivation is fleeting. It fades as soon as it arrives. Our attention has already run off to the next loud bell or high-pitched whistle.

In contrast, there's what might be called deep motivation. This sort of motivation is more profound. If situational motivation is mental bait, then deep motivation is a sort of trap. It snags on a fundamental part of who we are—a richer kind of value—and it's this type of motivation that pushes individuals to spend decades studying organic chemistry or perfecting their épée-style fencing skills.

So how does situational motivation become deep motivation? The answer goes back to the idea of value—and in the end, it's a sense of worth that keeps the motivation trap closed. Meaning is the dividing line between the drive of the situation and the drive of the personal, and when we find something meaningful, it becomes a much more intimate motivation.

Psychologists like Hidi and her colleague Ann Renninger have shown how this happens. In the first stage of motivation, it's typically all about situational interest. So, for instance, maybe you come across a YouTube video devoted to Occam's razor, or the idea that the simplest explanation is often the best. The video is powerful and snappy. So your attention is drawn in.

In the second stage, people will begin to see some sort of value in the topic. So as you watch the YouTube video, you begin to understand how the principle of Occam's razor can help you win arguments—and solve problems. Now you keep on watching the film clip because the clip has value to you.

In the third and fourth stage, motivation often becomes more and more intrinsic, and if we give enough attention to a topic, the interest can develop into a richer form of motivation. If you know a lot about Occam's razor, then you'll find value in different interpretations of the idea, and be curious about how the notion applies to different fields like medicine or sports.

This doesn't always happen, of course. Personality, experience, background, culture are all at play. At the same time, we have to support our seeking system, our desire to know. Practically speaking, this means sometimes letting yourself loose in the wilds of Wikipedia to uncover new ideas or spending some time watching a documentary because it's interesting or even just making time to experience new things and ideas.

At the same time, we have to realize that we need emotional support when the learning becomes hard. In other words, we need to manage our seeking system in order to get things done. For my part, I've come to view motivation as a fire. It needs an emotional spark in order to flame up, but without management, it can quickly die down—or grow out of control. Too little seeking, too little excitement, in other words, and we lose our desire to know. Too much seeking, however, and an entire day can be spent on BuzzFeed's page, "People Who Have No Idea How Fire Works."

The success of Web sites like BuzzFeed hints at yet another way to create value and drive for learning—our social side. After all, a lot of the popularity of BuzzFeed—or TMZ—has to do with our group-ish ways, and the Web sites aim to create material that we want to share with friends. We read articles like "People Who Have No Idea How Fire Works" and then tweet them off to friends and family.

In this sense, our peers promote value. They help us see meaning, particularly when it comes to learning. For a different example, take someone like Langston Tingling-Clemmons. While he graduated from college more than a decade ago, Tingling-Clemmons still remembers raising his hand in chemistry class at Bucknell University.

Short and thin-framed, Tingling-Clemmons was sitting near the front of the class at the time. It was his freshman year at the school, and he was almost certainly well-dressed. Tingling-Clemmons favors tie clips and paisley socks. Family members joke that he came out of the womb wearing a coordinated suit. Even when he plays sports, he wears matching outfits.

Tingling-Clemmons pushed his hand into the air on that day, and for a long moment, it seemed like every student in the room was staring at him. At the time, Bucknell had only a few hundred black students out of an enrollment of more than 3,000. Tingling-Clemmons himself was the only African-American in the course. Everyone else in the room was white, and as the seconds ticktocked away, as the professor finally answered his query, Tingling-Clemmons felt alone, with a quiet voice inside of his head whispering something along the lines of: *Should I really be here?*

Tingling-Clemmons eventually dropped the chemistry class. It wasn't the academics. Tingling-Clemmons graduated from one of the best high schools in Washington, DC. It was the feeling of being an outsider, a stranger—and it happened often during his time at Bucknell. "Since I was the only black kid in their classes, other people would recognize me over all campus," Tingling-Clemmons told me. "People would say hi to me that I didn't even know, and I was like *huh?*"

It's hard going off to college for just about everyone: You have to develop new friends and take more rigorous courses and live away from home for the first time. But it's even more difficult for students of color. In many cases, they feel like they don't belong. They struggle with fitting in. For them, the culture of college is very different than the culture of home. "I felt sometimes like I was an island unto myself," Tingling-Clemmons told me.

Some years ago, Deborah Bial decided to take on this issue. She started a program that helps students who were "overlooked" by colleges, helping them to succeed by giving them more social support in college. Called Posse, it sends typically disadvantaged students of color to colleges around the country in groups of 10. Each "posse" ensures that the students have a network of people to support them.

Tingling-Clemmons was one of the first Posse students to arrive at Bucknell, and despite his experience in chemistry, the program gave him a way to feel normal. With the other Posse students, Tingling-Clemmons would listen to music and go out for meals. They would talk about awkward moments in class—and play basketball to burn off steam. The group was small and tight-knit. One of Tingling-Clemmons's Posse friends later became the best man at his wedding.

Such emotional supports tilt the motivation scale, creating a feeling of value and meaning in learning. People in the Posse program are far more likely to graduate from college than their peers, with a graduation rate over 90 percent. Tingling-Clemmons left Bucknell with a double major in history and religion. During his senior year, Tingling-

Clemmons was student body president, and today he credits the Posse program with helping him graduate from the school.

Like many things related to value and meaning, our need for belonging is often overlooked. Part of the reason is that social cues are often subtle cues. They whisper instead of shout, and a feeling of togetherness, of social value, is typically indicated in all sorts of muted ways—accent, inflection, body positioning.

This means that small shifts in social dynamics can have a surprisingly large impact. In one study, for instance, Asian students with more "identifiable" Asian names like Vivek were more likely to have higher math scores than Asian kids with the names like Alex. Why? Because teachers assumed that students with more Asian-sounding names took math class "more seriously," and so they had higher expectations—and more targeted math instruction.

We also generally discover social identities only in relation to other identities. I never feel more American then when I'm in Germany, for instance. Being in Central Europe makes me realize all of the habits—too loud, too friendly—that make me red, white, and blue, and frankly, I'm much louder and more genial than most Germans. The converse is also true. I never feel more German than when I'm living in the United States, and I'm far more likely to be on time than most of my peers.

Despite all their nuances, social factors have a tremendous impact on our sense of value. Family and peers, friends and colleagues, they all give emotional meaning to learning, and when we're stressed or nervous or sad, we look to others. Test anxiety is a great example, and anxious test takers perform better if they have a closer relationship with friends. The support of peers, it seems, offers an emotional buffer against the mental strain of the exams. They make it easier to regulate our feelings.

Social networks are also a type of motivation, and if people feel like they don't belong, they're far less motivated and generally do worse academically. More specifically, people who take classes with their friends typically post higher test scores than people who don't have friends in their classes.

This idea also explains why public commitments can have such a dramatic impact. When people tell their friends that they're going to do something, they're far more likely to stay committed to that goal. If we declare something on Facebook or Twitter—*I'm going to learn to get my real estate license,* for instance—we're often more likely to go through with that promise. We want to keep our commitment to our group.

This is the positive side of peer pressure, of teams and tribes, clans and circles, and if one person dedicates himself to learning, it makes other people more dedicated to learning. We don't want to be the outsider or the misfit or the lazy one, and so motivation and meaning will spread within groups. A sense of drive can jump from person to person. As one recent study declared, "Mental effort is contagious."

When it comes to learning, our social ways are far more powerful than you think. Just imagine a highly selective school like Harvard. You might think that it's the school's programs that make the difference. The teachers, the curriculum, the facilities are all supposed to be the marks of excellence. After all, this is why Harvard is so expensive, at least according to their brochures—the school has to pay for the best instructors, the best materials, the best buildings.

It turns out, though, that other students actually explain a tremendous amount. Through a variety of social pressures, norms, and academic interactions, other students go a very long way to promote learning. In fact, in some selective schools, peers can explain as much as two thirds of outcomes. Put even more simply, a huge amount of Harvard's success has little to do with the professors or the curriculum or the buildings. Instead, it's mostly about the other people who attend Harvard.

Legos can provide some insight, with exhibit A again being Jason Wolfson. To keep up his interest in the bricks, he meets with a Lego club once a month. The group typically gathers at a local library, and as with every tight-knit clique, the norms are strong. Lunch is always at the local diner. Off-brand items like Playmobil are verboten. Touching someone else's construction without permission is reason to be shown the door.

When I visited one of the meetings on a Sunday afternoon, the group seemed like an extended family with everyone having clear roles. Wolfson was one of the gregarious ones, while Ken Rice was the de facto organizer. Micro-builds were Kim Petty's thing, and if you need to learn about military history and Legos, then Gary Brooks was the person to provide the lesson.

As Wolfson readily admits, the Lego group has had some rough spots, and ten years ago, some members split off from the group because "not everyone shared their enthusiasm." But largely, the Lego network provides value. It gives purpose, and Wolfson makes sure to attend just about every month. "My wife knows that on those days, she needs to do something else," he told me.

As for Langston Tingling-Clemmons, the Bucknell graduate, he's now married and has a young daughter. He works as a middle-school English teacher at an overwhelmingly black and poor school in Washington, DC. We once met up for a drink, and Tingling-Clemmons explained that he now applies the social lessons of Posse to his own classroom.

To cultivate more of a social connection with his students, Tingling-Clemmons will visit the home of each student every year. He also tries to mentor half a dozen students, visiting their sports games, taking them out to dinner, developing a closer sense of connection. He gives the students advice, too: *Find a mentor*, he tells them. If you want to stay in school, hang out with people who will stay in school.

As Tingling-Clemmons sipped a beer, he argued that he wants his students to feel a sense of belonging. He believes that these social ties are ultimately what's going to keep the students motivated to learn. As Tingling-Clemmons told me, "I try and use the credits that I gain in their hearts to help them do the right thing."

Meaning Is Learning

So far in this chapter, we've been talking about value and meaning as forms of motivation, detailing the ways that purpose and relevance serve as the fuel for our drive to learn.

This is important. But when it comes to the learning process, there's another reason to look for value—it's actually why we learn. We gain skills and knowledge in order to make sense of experience, to give explanation to the world around us.

This doesn't always happen. Not long ago, a community college student—let's call him Joe—wrote down the following answers to a set of math problems:

$$10 \times 3 = 30$$
$$10 \times 13 = 130$$
$$20 \times 13 = 86$$
$$30 \times 13 = 120$$
$$31 \times 13 = 123$$
$$29 \times 13 = 116$$
$$22 \times 13 = 92$$

Notice anything odd? More directly: Is the answer to 30×13 really 120? Or is the answer to 22×13 really 92?

In short, it appears that Joe did not have a good understanding of math. He didn't make much sense of the problem—or uncover any important patterns. Rather, it appears that Joe just recalled some isolated formulas and basic math facts and tried to punch out the procedures in order to provide some—incorrect—answers.

Now, this isn't a twenty-point headline. It's a lot easier to memorize facts, after all, and in many areas, people can get pretty far with a rote knowledge of a topic. Indeed, Joe himself managed to land a high school diploma—and enroll in a community college.

In many ways, the bigger issue is that people will often view expertise as a thing, something out there held by an instructor or codified in a book. So they listen to a lecture or scan a Web site or sit through a video, and they believe that the information will just migrate into their brains.

In this conception, learning is a noncontact sport, a process of taking a bit of data from one source and pushing it into our brain. Call it the "stuff" approach to education. We think there's "stuff" to be learned—a fact, some procedures, a formula or two—and we want to jam that stuff into our brain's storage bins and drawers like an old pair of socks.

This isn't how the brain works, though, and while people often talk about the brain being like a computer, that's not quite right. First, that notion makes it seem like if you just added some hard drive space, you'd be a lot smarter. Second, it conveys the idea that the brain just passively receives information.

Instead, we would be much better off thinking of the brain as a group of roads and highways, a system of streets and turnpikes. The road anal-

ogy reminds us, for one, that a simple pathway—a dirt road, for instance—
can be pretty easy to make. It's a matter of straightforward repetition.
Same is true for learning: Basic concepts or skills are often easy to master.

What's more, the analogy underscores that for the brain, expertise
is about making sense of things, an ability to see relationships within an
area of mastery. In other words, expertise is about having a deep network of connections within a skill or area of knowledge.

The work of psychologist Stephen Chew gives a different way to
understand this idea. He'll often do a little experiment with audiences
to help people understand the role of meaning in learning, to show that
expertise is about creating a type of mental link.

First, Chew will hand out a sheet of paper with some two dozen
words listed on it, and then he'll have half of his audience focus on the
letters in the words and count up the number of times the letter *g* or *e*
appears. Chew then has the other half of the class focus on the "pleas-
antness" of the words before asking them all to recall the words.

The classroom experiment is a replication of a much older study,
and without fail, the results of Chew's effort match the original: People
who rely on the more meaningful approach—figuring out if each word
was pleasant to them—recalled more words than the people who just
counted the number of times *g* appeared in the words.

The results are not even close. In the original experiment, people
who engage in a richer form of processing—the ones who made more
valuable ties to the material—remembered as much as seven times
more words than those who don't. Even in Chew's informal demonstra-
tion, people typically learn at least twice as much.

"If you think about information meaningfully, you are much more
likely to remember that information than if you think about it at a superficial, meaningless level," Chew told me. "And this is true regardless of
whether you intend to learn the material or not."

For people who're aiming to learn something, this idea is important for
another reason because meaning also provides learning with flexibility.
Understanding is what allows us to use skills and knowledge in different
situations. If we've made sense of an area of expertise—if we've shifted
our thinking—we can be successful in various contexts.

Take mixing up a gin and tonic, as an example. It's pretty easy to memorize the basic procedure: If you like your gin and tonic strong, add one part gin to every part tonic, and then add a lime, and the gin and tonic is ready to serve.

But to make meaning, to see value, to understand how to make a good gin and tonic, people should learn how the blend of gin, tonic, and lime work together to provide a distinctive *Mad Men*–like cocktail experience. Because it's this richer sort of learning that makes a difference if there's any sort of problem.

So, in the case of the gin and tonic, let's imagine that there's no tonic water in the fridge. A person with a more meaningful grasp of the drink would know that tonic water has a bitter flavor, and so she might substitute orange juice. Or if both the gin and the tonic bottles are empty, the person might pour together vodka and ginger ale, which provides an oddly similar flavor.

When it comes to learning, this idea is crucial, and so it's worth saying again: We learn for meaning, to shape our thinking. This is ultimately what makes it possible to apply our knowledge. So if you're a kid named Joe, it would allow you to take a different approach if you came across this problem again:

$$10 \times 3 =$$
$$10 \times 13 =$$
$$20 \times 13 =$$
$$30 \times 13 =$$
$$31 \times 13 =$$
$$29 \times 13 =$$
$$22 \times 13 =$$

You'd soon realize that there's a pattern, and you'd understand that the series of questions are more easily solved by relying on the power of thirteen.

The math approach, known as mental abacus, provides some insights into how we learn for meaning.

To get a sense of how mental abacus works, consider another math problem, and add up these numbers without any tool. No pen. No paper. No calculator. Just answer the problem in your head:

86,030
97,586
63,686
38,886

Any luck? More than that, could you complete the calculation in less than a second?

For most adults, our brain simply becomes overloaded by such a task. We can't hold the numbers in our mind for long enough. We try to add the six and carry the one and bring over the two and remember the seven and keep the five, and our mind quickly becomes a tangle of numbers, a cognitive shock of befuddlement.

The more important question is: Why not? I recently watched a high schooler named Serena Stevenson bang out answers to these sorts of math queries in rapid-fire succession.

On the evening that I meet up with Stevenson, she was sitting at a desk, wearing a Mickey Mouse sweatshirt. We were just outside of New York City in a small basement classroom, and her mental abacus instructor would read out some numbers, the figures tumbling into the air like coins thrown into the sky—

74,470
70,809
98,402

—and Stevenson would add the numbers in her mind in a matter of seconds, as fast as if she was recalling the name of some state capitals.

Stevenson didn't work through the problem like you or I might using short-term memory. Instead, Stevenson envisioned the abacus in her mind and then used her fingers to help her work through the problem.

I watched Stevenson for a while, and for each problem, she would close her eyes and ready her hands, and then, as she started to develop a solution, the fingers of her right hand would start to twitch and move, a slow progression of plucks and jerks, a collection of pinches and swipes. The movements were fast and exact, an attempt to find the solution using every hand gesture that she would use for a physical abacus, even though there was no physical abacus in front of her.

When I first saw Stevenson's gestures, I thought they were a pretentious affect like people who wear polka-dot bow ties or insist on pronouncing Van Gogh as *Van Goch*. But it turned out that Stevenson's movements were at the very heart of the practice, and without the movements—and their associated mental imagining—accuracy will often drop by more than half. As Harvard psychologist Neon Brooks told me, "When you prevent experts from gesturing, they do a terrible job. They completely fall apart."

This isn't an accident. Learning requires effort. To create meaning, we have to actively make sense of a bit of expertise. Part of the benefit of mental abacus goes to the mind-body connection, as we will see shortly. The abacus approach also turns out to take a more relational approach to learning, which provides other learning benefits.

But just as important is the fact that mental abacus requires people to produce their knowledge. It makes learning a matter of doing, an active process, and a wealth of new research suggests that more cognitively engaged approaches to learning—like quizzing, explaining, even enacting—show much higher outcomes.

In recent years, psychologist Rich Mayer has written a lot about learning as a type of mental doing, and he is an unlikely crusader for a new way to gain expertise. A soft-spoken Midwesterner, Mayer is generally pretty avuncular. He won't say someone screwed up. Instead, the person falls "somewhat short of being exemplary." Mayer doesn't believe that people have bad intentions—only bad consequences of bad decisions. Some of Mayer's favorite advice? "Don't radiate negative energy."

But on the issue of learning as a form of dedicated cognitive effort, Mayer has become something of a firebrand, and in his lab at the University of California, Santa Barbara, Mayer has shown in study after study that we gain expertise by actively producing what we know. As he told me flatly, "Learning is a generative activity."

Mayer gives a pretty good description of how this works. First, people need to select information, figuring out what exactly they're going to learn—like maybe a bit of Soviet history or Buddhist philosophy. Then people need to integrate that information into what they know by creating some type of mental connection between their current knowledge and the information that they're hoping to learn.

So if someone is learning about the Soviet dictator Stalin, they would want to link what they know (that Stalin was a dictator) to what they want to learn (that Stalin grew up in Crimea) in an active way that makes the new information meaningful to them in some way.

The power of mentally doing—of creating value in an area of expertise—is clear in basic memory tasks. Want to remember the French word for home, or *maison,* for instance? People are far more likely to recall the word "maison" if a letter is missing from the word (e.g., "mais_n") when they read it. When people add the "o," they're completing the word. They're finishing the thought and in the most basic of ways, they've done some work to produce their learning—and thus make it more meaningful.

The benefit of more vigorous learning approaches also extends to more difficult cognitive tasks. Take something like reading. If we push ourselves to dream up some sort of mental image of what we're reading—if we imagine the text in our minds—we retain a lot more, as Mayer has shown. By creating a type of "mind movie," we're building more cognitive connections—and making the learning more durable.

For a different example, consider something known as "repeat backs." The next time a person gives you a set of detailed instructions, take time to repeat back the instructions in your own words. When you summarize the instructions, you're taking steps to generate knowledge, and you'll be more likely to remember the information.

Over the past few years, the research on learning as a type of mental doing has shifted a lot of the conventional wisdom around how people gain expertise. In a large and recent review of the research, Kent State's John Dunlosky and some colleagues found that highlighting was a weak approach to learning, for instance. Why? It seems that the activity doesn't do enough to push people to build their knowledge. Likewise, rereading showed limited effects, according to Dunlosky and his colleagues. Why? Again, it appears that the activity doesn't spark enough mental doing.

So what approaches did show outcomes in Dunlosky's landmark analysis? When I reached Dunlosky on the phone, he argued that the most effective techniques were more active learning activities like self-quizzing and self-explaining. "This is a fundamental feature of how our minds work," he told me. To learn, "we're not just copying the information. We are making sense out of facts."

Learning as a type of mental doing works in larger settings, too, and I once sat in on biology professor Jennifer Doherty's course at the University of Washington in Seattle. The course has long been praised for its high outcomes, and while the lecture hall for Doherty's class was big, with more than hundred students, Doherty continually pushed the students to learn through dedicated cognitive effort.

During the course, for instance, she often asked the entire class to answer quiz questions and would randomly call on students. Doherty also had the students pair up and then ask their small group for an answer, asking things like "How do plants get their food if not from the soil?"

I saw this myself, too, when it came to the practice of mental abacus. Some months after I first visited Stevenson, I purchased a few abacus classes for my elementary-age daughters and me. If I was going to be writing about the practice of hand gestures and mental calculations, I thought that I should develop some vague skill in it.

The classes were harder than I expected, and even my six-year-old daughter would sometimes point out my errors with a bit of glee. The approach required a type of mental strain, of cerebral effort. "Intellectual powerlifting" is how another student described the practice to me. But within weeks, the more active approach paid off in understanding. Math became easier. Like lifting weights in a gym, the more engaging the exercise, it seemed, the better the results.

I wasn't alone in this conclusion, and studies suggest that abacus provides much higher learning outcomes than more traditional forms of math instruction. Psychologist David Barner has studied the practice in a randomized field experiment, and when I met up with him, Barner

POP QUIZ #3

True or false: Students who "study" a text will learn less than students who make the text "meaningful" to themselves.

argued that the abacus could have a deep and long-standing impact on math understanding. "Based on everything that we know about early math education," Barner told me, "I'll make the predication that students who study abacus have higher SAT scores."

In light of all the evidence about learning as a form of mental doing, what's perhaps most remarkable is how little our schools and universities have paid attention to it. Walk into any library on any college campus, and students will be passively reading. (If you want to learn the material, do more to actively engage it.) Stride through any high school, and students will be mechanically highlighting every last page of text. (Self-testing is much more effective as a learning approach.) People often prepare for important meetings by skimming notes. (The superior approach? Going into an empty room and actually saying what you want to say.)

University of Washington's Scott Freeman has been studying learning as doing for years. In fact, Freeman helped create the biology lecture class that I attended at the University of Washington. Recently, Freeman and his colleagues have decided that the data is so conclusive, so plainly decided, that they now refuse to even conduct studies comparing lecture courses against more mental engaged types of classes. "If you're a professor and you refuse do active learning, it raises an ethical question," Freeman told me. "It's like a doctor giving you a less effective drug. You'd think it's an issue of malpractice."

Tom Sato came to the link between meaning and mental effort on his own. For years, Sato has been offering private abacus instruction. He taught the practice to high schooler Serena Stevenson, for instance, and over time, Sato realized that more engaged forms of learning sparked richer forms of understanding.

Sato soon began using more active approaches to learning in his own life, and he recently learned coding well enough to build an iPhone app. Not long ago, Sato also picked up a three-stringed guitar known as a samisen—and could now bang out songs.

When I met Sato, he had begun to practice the martial art known as muay thai, and early one morning, I went to watch him practice his boxing skills. On the day that I visited, it was cold. Snow blanketed the streets, and as Sato practiced, I sat in the back of the workout room, a narrow space covered in red mats, watching him as he learned a new muay thai punch.

"Like you're throwing a corkscrew jab," Jimmy, his instructor, yelled.

Sato tried the two-punch combination again. His first jab was supposed to yank down his opponent's left arm in a twisting motion. Then Sato's right hand was supposed to loop around for a strong hit, a slug to his opponent's temple.

Sato's attack appeared unsteady, at least at first. He couldn't quite pull down his opponent's forearm, and his large red boxing glove glanced off Jimmy's forearm, barely making contact. So Sato executed the combination again, moving in slow motion, focusing on each step in the punch.

"Perfect," Jimmy yelled, after Sato threw the combination for what might have been the twelfth time. "Perfect."

From a learning perspective, it was clear to see what was happening. By doing the action—throwing the punch—Sato uncovered a better grasp of how the new punch differed from other punches, like, say, a corkscrew jab. In other words, the effort of the punch made it a lot easier for Sato to grasp how the punch fit together with other blows and strikes.

This idea helps explain why learning by doing creates meaning. The approach helps us see complexity, to grapple with nuance, ultimately shifting how we think. More exactly, cognitive work doesn't just make learning stick. It also promotes a deeper level of comprehension.

Take, for instance, a child who is learning his letters. It turns out that students who manually practice writing out their ABCs develop a more systemic understanding than students who just study or type the letters. By physically penning their letters, the students gain a deeper sense of how the characters come together to make words—and studies show that the students learn to read at a much faster rate.

For a different example, take self-explaining. When we explain an idea to ourselves, we're mentally doing, and again, research shows that we gain a more networked form of mastery. So, for instance, if I explain a concept like gravity to myself, I'm connecting the idea of gravity with other ideas like the notion of mass. I'm also talking to myself about other historical facts—like maybe the discovery of gravity by Sir Isaac Newton—as well as juxtaposing gravity with other concepts like motion and weight.

To be clear, just working hard isn't enough. People can be active while learning and not gain very much. In other words, just throwing punches doesn't necessarily make expertise in something like muay thai. Nor do people need to be moving around to be mentally active. We can be sitting still in our seat and be deeply engaged. Researcher Dylan Wiliam makes this point well, and he argues that more active forms of learning are effective when people are thinking hard and thinking hard about expertise.

To a degree, we know this idea, or at least we know it in some very specific fields. Language attrition, for instance, has a pretty long history, and people will often lose their ability to speak a language if they don't use the language. This often happens to people who've learned a second language. Whether it's Chinese or Lithuanian, it becomes harder to express yourself if you don't actually use the language.

What's more surprising is that language attrition often happens to native speakers. Not long ago, for instance, I spoke with Yayoi Ota, who grew up in rural Bolivia. Ota's parents were Japanese, and she typically spoke to them in Japanese. As a kid, Ota also learned to write in Japanese and attended afternoon Japanese classes and spoke to many of her friends in Japanese.

After graduating from high school, Ota moved to Santa Cruz, one of

POP QUIZ #4

Which statement describes the role of facts in learning?

A. Facts hurt learning.

B. Facts are important to learning.

C. You can always look up the facts online.

D. Never get a fact wrong.

the largest cities in the country, and now she spends her days speaking largely Spanish. Few people around her know Japanese, and today Ota has basically forgotten her native language. She can speak a halting form of Japanese with her parents—and some old friends—but her writing skills are almost entirely gone, a mother tongue that's been essentially cut out.

This seems bizarre. Ota's first words were in Japanese. She spoke to her parents in Japanese for years. But this type of language attrition happens to native speakers a lot more than you might think. After being held for five years by the Taliban, Sgt. Bowe Bergdahl's English fell apart. Despite the fact that Bergdahl spent his entire childhood speaking English in Idaho, he lost his native language skills while being held captive in Afghanistan.

People like Ota or Bergdahl don't necessarily lose all knowledge of the words in their native language. Ota, for instance, can still recall—and write—some basic expressions. Instead, what disappears is meaning. People like Ota can't recall how the language comes together. They can't grasp the relationships and systems embedded in the language. As one researcher put it, language attrition is a slow "untangling [of] a complicated knot of interconnections."

In the end, we produce our knowledge, we generate our skills, because it helps create the networks of meaning. It supports the knowledge relationships that sustain value, that shift our reasoning. After his muay thai training, Sato and I went out for breakfast. He was tired. His face looked pale. We ordered some tea. The food came to the table as Sato explained that more engaged approaches supported deeper understanding. "The big question is: Do you just memorize certain things?" he said. "Or do you try and see how it all fits together?"

There's an important thing to understand when it comes to the idea of finding value in an area of expertise: We have to be on the lookout for it. Even if we're mentally doing, we will not learn something if we're not aiming to learn it.

Doctors, for instance, have had a lot of opportunities to study the muscles of the knee. Operations on the joint date back at least a hundred years, while more than a half a million knee surgeries take place each year in hospitals around the country. For many orthopedic surgeons, the sinewy knee muscles are like a second home—they know them like the inside of their bedrooms—and doctors will explore the tendons just about every day, pulling apart the meniscal cartilage or examining bits of synovial tissue.

Still, Swiss researcher and orthopedist Karl Grob managed to uncover a new tendon in the knee not long ago. Together with a team of researchers, Grob discovered a small, sinewy muscle right above the kneecap that had never been shown before in any anatomy textbook—or mentioned by any surgeons.

Grob is pretty humble about the discovery. "I'm just a normal surgeon," he told me. "Anatomy is kind of my hobby." Other experts were less moderate. "Introducing a new muscle is almost as elusive as the legendary Bigfoot," is how one medical blogger put it.

So how did this happen? How could so many doctors overlook a muscle in the knee, a tendon that's been operated upon hundreds of thousands of times each year? A good part of the answer lies in the nature of mind-set. Put differently, Grob found the tendon because he was looking for the tendon. He learned something about the knee because he wanted to learn it. With a different attitude, Grob saw value in a set of muscles where others didn't see any value at all.

Psychologist Ellen Langer has been studying this idea for decades, and on the afternoon that I slipped into her office, she argued that learning for meaning required mindfulness, an active search for value. For Langer, this type of attitude—this sort of perspective—was about more than just paying attention. It also required people to engage in experiences in a way that highlighted the newness of the experience. People needed to turn off the brain's "automatic pilot," she said, and actively search for expertise.

In many ways, this type of mindfulness comes down to context. Framing plays a crucial role in developing an engaged attitude, and we often need some sort of spark, a twist in perception, in order to draw our attention to the learning itself. This was oddly clear when I was talking with Langer. Sometimes, the conversation was irreverent. The mind-set was humor, and Langer teased me about forgetting something: "You're nervous!"

But then I'd ask a question, and the frame would change back to something a bit more educational. Langer would ask me pointed queries—"Do you understand what I'm saying?"—and suggest that I read a certain text. The discussion had become about uncovering something meaningful; it was about learning something new.

There are other factors that promote a more engaged attitude. When we see expertise as more open-ended, we're more mindful, according to Langer. It also helps to see issues from different perspectives, and when we shift our viewpoint, we typically learn more because it makes us more attuned to subtleties within an area of expertise.

But perhaps most important is meaning itself. One of the best ways to turn off the brain's automatic pilot is to look for value. In one early study, for instance, Langer had two groups of students read a passage in a textbook. She gave the two groups the exact same instructions but with one key difference. One group was told to "study" the text, while the other group was told to make the passage "meaningful to themselves" in some way.

The results? The "meaningful" group was much more engaged, and they showed better results. They understood and remembered more. Even more important, when the "meaningful" group had to write an essay about the passage, they produced texts of much higher quality.

For a real-world example, take language attrition again. It turns out that mind-set plays a key role, and people are far more likely to lose native language ability if they have a weak opinion of their native country. Research shows, for instance, that a native Spanish speaker is far more likely to forget Spanish if he thinks poorly of Spain. With a negative mind-set—and a more limited sense of value—people are less able to speak in their native language.

On one hand, there's something obvious about this. It's hard to learn Excel if you have a hateful view of Excel. But there's something oddly remarkable, too, because mind-set shifts our thinking in very subtle ways. In one of the language attrition studies, for instance, it didn't matter how much the person spoke their native language if they disliked their native country. If a person had a negative view of their native country, their native language skills eroded at a much higher rate, even after accounting for time spent speaking the language.

Langer offers some take-home advice on this issue: When people are acquiring a skill, they should be on the alert for nuances. In order to learn, we need to actively hunt for what's original and novel in an area of expertise. In this sense, we gain understanding by looking for differences. "Noticing new things is the definition of mindfulness," she told me.

Langer also recommends having an exploratory mind-set toward learning. So if you read a book for a class, don't constantly focus on the resulting grade—it can make the experience seem stomach-twistingly stressful. Instead, find material in the book that you're curious about, something that has value to you. The learning outcomes are often higher—and the experience is far more enjoyable.

Similarly, surgeons shouldn't always look only to repair a torn ACL. They should also take a moment to search—and discover. After all, they might uncover another new tendon.

There's a problem with the idea I've been writing about in this chapter, and it turns out that making meaning has a dangerous side. By definition, learners are not experts, and we can come to weak conclusions, finding value where there's no value at all. To put this bluntly, we can be wrong.

In a way, the issue is that learning is a cumulative process. Mastery builds on itself. Meaning scaffolds itself on meaning, and people don't typically learn very well on their own, especially at the start of the learning process. Our skills are weak. There's no expertise. We don't know what we don't know.

If you put a five-pound bag of rocks and a five-pound bag of feathers in front of someone, for instance, and ask them to learn the idea of mass versus weight, they wouldn't gain much from the experience. Unless the person knows something about gravity, they simply are not going to come to the conclusion that things with the same mass fall at the same rate. (At least according to legend, Galileo demonstrated this fact by dropping two bags from the Leaning Tower of Pisa, showing that mass was, indeed, different from weight.)

In a more practical sense, learning requires instruction. To gain skills and knowledge, people need guidance—and support. Mentors, trainers, instructors all play a tremendous role. We will revisit this idea repeatedly throughout this book. For now, let's call it the Value of Educators.

Oddly, up until recently, no one had systematically studied the role of teachers and how exactly they promoted learning. Certainly, experts have been theorizing about the practice of instruction for centuries. The Socratic Method dates back to ancient Greece. The apprenticeship model goes back to medieval Europe. The Han Dynasty in China may have pioneered a high-stakes testing approach to schooling—it offered the first civil service exam.

Still, no dedicated researcher had tried in a reliable fashion to measure the difference between a great teacher and an average one using robust data like test scores, surveys, and videos. Some years ago, Microsoft founder Bill Gates became fascinated with this fact. He had come across a research paper on the topic of teacher quality—and crowded the document with notes and scribbles. Gates couldn't understand why one of the most basic questions in education had not been answered with modern research tools. "It was mind-blowing how little it had been studied," Gates later remarked.

Eventually, the world's richest man poured some $40 million into the research project, and it was massive: Dozens of researchers, hundreds of schools, thousands of teachers, almost a hundred thousand students. As part of the project, researchers developed a new type of video camera that would give a "panoramic" view of a classroom during a teacher's lesson. Every student in the project filled out surveys. Some 500 people were trained just to evaluate the videos of the teachers.

Known as the MET (Measures of Effective Teaching) study, the project lasted two years, and some of the findings include things we've briefly touched upon but in more dramatic fashion. For example, very few teachers in the study pushed students to create their own ideas. Student participation in tasks that required meaning making was rare.

But the more interesting results were something else, and it turned out that when it came to teaching, there were two main drivers of student outcomes, according to Harvard's Ron Ferguson, who helped study the data. First, there's what the researchers called "academic press," or the degree to which a teacher pushed a student academically. This was a matter of how much the educators encouraged students to work hard, to really engage with the material.

The second factor was "academic support," or the degree to which students felt motivated by their teachers. This second factor was about relevance, about a sense of personal connection between the students and the teachers.

What's interesting is that the conclusions of the MET research share a lot of similarities with the ideas outlined in this chapter. Specifically, effective teachers push students to engage in academic struggle, making sure that students do the hard work of making sense of a topic. In other words, great educators make students engage in learning as mental doing. At the same time, great teachers provide motivation and support. They help student find meaning in their learning. They provide autonomy—and a sense of relevance.

This isn't a freak discovery. Well before the MET study, Nobel laureate Carl Wieman concluded that people should think of teachers as "cognitive coaches." For Wieman, the issue was that the word "teacher" often made people think too much of someone who just hands out information. But that approach to learning gets it all wrong, he argued, and it makes it seem as if learning a topic like physics comes naturally to us.

When I reached out to Wieman, he explained that teachers needed to be more like athletic coaches. They should help students "learn a topic by breaking it down into the key elements of thinking required, then have the students practice that thinking," he told me. At the same time, educators should motivate students to do their best "to carry out this hard work." In other words, people need emotional support. We need to be cheered on.

For individuals, the takeaway is that we need educators to help us improve. Other people help us make sense of a topic. Plus, we can't forget the social side of learning, the need for emotional support and relevance. "When you're learning, you're going to need someone who's going to support you developing," Wieman told me.

Interestingly, the MET study suggests that students themselves often have a pretty good sense of who is an effective educator, and surveys of students were excellent predictors of future learning, according to Ferguson. All to say: If you want to find a great teacher or mentor, don't look at credentials (they often don't mean all that much). Don't care too much about number of years that the teacher has been in the field (again, it's not hugely predictive beyond the first few years).

Instead, ask other people. Did the educator challenge people? Did the instructor explain things clearly? Did the person learn a lot in the class? Also ask about academic support. Did it seem like the trainer cared about them? Did the person make the material relevant? How did the educator aid people who were struggling?

The idea of support is an important one, and we're going to look more closely at the idea in the next chapter. Because it turns out that meaning is often just the start of learning—and in the end, we also need to plan exactly what we hope to learn.

Chapter 2

TARGET

THE EDUCATION PROGRAM known as Success for All has long been known for its feel-good stories. Dillon Middle School, for instance, was in academic shambles for years. In the press, the South Carolina school was one of the poster children for the state's "corridor of shame," a group of high-poverty districts located in the state's northern corner. A documentary featured Dillon for its lack of academic struggles, and when President Obama visited during his first run for president, he described the school as not even "minimally adequate."

But the school managed to turn itself around, and one of the drivers was the reform initiative Success for All. Shortly after the school adopted the program, reading outcomes almost doubled. It helped, too, that Dillon made tremendous monetary investments, installing everything from air conditioning to new computers. While Dillon still has clear issues, the school now posts outcomes higher than many of its high-poverty peers.

While the stories are not always this dramatic, these sorts of results are pretty standard for Success for All. *The New Yorker* once argued that the program has the "best sustained record" in education, and when the US Department of Education recently reviewed all the research behind Success for All, officials declared it to be one of the nation's most effective educational initiatives.

The bigger question is: Why? What's the reason for all this success? What besides a fairy godmother can explain these sorts of Cinderella-like changes? Much of the answer lies with Bob Slavin. A professor at

Johns Hopkins, Slavin started the Success for All program together with his wife, Nancy Madden, in the 1980s.

Slavin is a researcher's researcher, and he'll often go off on long tangents on the best ways to measure effect sizes. His monthly newsletter is called *Best Evidence in Brief,* and to create Success for All, he drew up clear rules about what studies to use as the basis for the program. He ignored any research that had run for less than three months—too short to draw meaningful conclusions. Pre- and post-tests were required. Randomized controls were central, too.

The resulting program was revolutionary for its time. Given the data on cooperative learning, Success for All was one of the first to emphasize group learning. Because of the value of instructional time, Success for All blocked out a large chunk of each day for high-priority learning topics. Reading was taught by emphasizing the sound-letter connection, an approach that was controversial back then but is now widely practiced.

But perhaps more than anything, Success for All was highly targeted. The program's secret sauce was—and remains—targeting. Students are grouped and regrouped, to ensure they are learning exactly what they're supposed to learn. There's dedicated tutoring for any student who lags behind. The curriculum is organized, synced together like a lockset. The program even publishes its own books, hiring authors to write texts tailored to the specific needs of students.

Success for All's laurels rest, then, on a pretty straightforward idea— learning is not accidental. We need to prepare ourselves to gain a particular skill. In a way, this idea goes back to the notion of learning as a process, a system. To gain knowledge, we need to have a dedicated way to acquire that knowledge.

This approach is unusual, at least for most of us. When people typically try to learn something new, they often dive right in. They try to gain expertise on their own, and then, if the activity turns out to be harder than they expected, they think: *I never was really good at that anyway.* This belief in an exploratory approach to learning is widespread. In my survey of the public, more than half of people argued that "discovery learning"—or unguided learning—was a great way to gain new skills.

The point is not to make learning mindless—creativity and discovery remain key. So is the opportunity to create deep understanding. But when people are in the early stages of learning, they need to manage the process closely, and learning often boils down to a type of knowledge management. It's about setting goals and creating plans, about acquiring background skills and targeting expertise.

In this chapter, we're going to look more closely at this idea, examining two questions that are crucial to anyone trying to gain any sort of skill. What am I going to learn, and what sort of plan do I have in order to learn it?

These questions help us stay focused. Along with Bob Slavin, I once visited a Success for All school called Windsor Hills Elementary School. Tucked away in one of the poorest neighborhoods in Baltimore, the school has long struggled. Almost every student is poor enough to qualify for both free breakfast and lunch, and life expectancy in the area is lower than it is in North Korea. Instruction at the school had been weak, and one of the teachers at the school used to tell students: "If you put your brains in a bird, he'd fly backward."

In an effort to boost outcomes, the school had adopted Success for All, and on that morning, Slavin and I moved from classroom to classroom. We talked to various Success for All teachers, and Slavin pointed out different features of the program. Sometimes we just sat and watched a class. And while Windsor Hills had picked up Success for All fairly recently, the program had already gone a long way to target the learning at the school. Outcomes were slowly going up; same with attendance rates.

Teachers were also increasingly figuring out what students needed to know—and how students were going to know it. As I visited classrooms, I saw one teacher evaluate the performance of every student in her class against a set of specific reading questions. In another room, an instructor reviewed material with a student, going over every item that the student had gotten wrong on a computer program.

In still another class, a teacher had her students evaluate their own evaluations. So the students listened to a little girl read from a bit of text, and then the kids began debating how the child's speaking skills stacked up against a checklist of key skills.

POP QUIZ #5

What role do facts have in learning?

A. Facts can impede learning.

B. Facts can improve learning.

C. Facts have no impact on learning.

"I think that was a 90," one boy said.

"She made two mistakes. It should be an 80," another student said.

"Does speed count?" another child asked.

At one point, the fire alarm rang suddenly, and students flooded the halls. Slavin and I eventually made it outside, where we stood just beyond the schoolhouse door. Standing on a patch of pavement as the alarm continued to ring, Slavin pointed out that interruptions are normal in learning. Blueprints are never fixed. Sometimes a student might need extra emotional support or wander off topic or the fire alarm will go off.

For Slavin, these more social, more emotional aspects of learning only underscored the need for more targeted approaches. "When you're learning, you can't make it up as you go along," he told me. "You can change the plan as you go along, but you always need a plan."

Before we address how to target our learning, we should look at why we even need to take these focused steps in the first place. To understand that idea, let's talk about phone numbers. More specifically, let's talk about how hard it is to remember a new phone number.

You know the experience. Someone gives you their telephone number, say something like 231-555-0912, and within moments, you've forgotten it. At best, maybe you can recall the first three digits. *Was it 231?* But the rest of the digits have disappeared, a blank spot, a wisp of a memory.

Phone companies have long struggled with this issue. At first, the companies tried to avoid relying on the frailties of human memory, and when firms first rolled out telephone lines in the 1800s, people would just pick up the handset and tell the operator the name of the person that they wanted to reach.

As telephones became more common, this personalized approach became too complex, and phone companies tried to standardized numbers with a type of mnemonic memory device, relying on area landmarks. So if you lived in Porter City, your phone number might be PORter 3234. If you lived in Elmwood, your number might be ELMwood 4543.

But this numbering system also became a Gordian mess, with long and awkward combinations of names and letters. So in the late 1950s, the phone companies rolled out still another system, requiring all phone numbers to be seven digits long. This approach is now ubiquitous, and most people around the globe have a phone number that's around seven digits long.

Yet it turns out that this approach doesn't work all that well, either. In the argot of cognitive scientists, seven-digit numbers typically overwhelm the brain's short-term memory. Known as the brain's sketch pad, short-term memory is where people hold temporary information like phone numbers, and it's a pretty limited holding space, with our brains being able to juggle only three or four items at time. (In contrast, there's the brain's long-term memory, which is pretty expansive. This is where the brain keeps memories of old friends, childhood feuds, and any sort of expertise.)

To their credit, phone companies today appear to understand the severe limitations of short-term memory, and so important emergency telephone numbers are just three digits long. For most of us, these shorter numbers—like 911—are memorized with ease, fitting easily into the brain's short-term memory.

This idea has implications far beyond phone numbers, and researchers like John Sweller have shown that short-term memory is often where learning happens. If we want to learn ballet jumps—or microgenetics—short-term memory has to process the experience before it arrives in long-term memory.

The rub is that short-term memory is so, well, short. The brain's sketch pad is a small sketch pad, and in many ways, short-term memory works like a narrow doorway: It keeps out anything large; it blocks out big pieces of information. Or think of short-term memory like a dial-up modem, slow and uncertain.

This fact goes a long way to explain why we need to focus our learning. To gain mastery, we need to break down knowledge and skills into digestible parts and concentrate on discrete bits of mastery. In other words, people have to make sure that any new expertise can fit through the brain's doorway and become well stored in long-term memory.

This notion explains, for instance, why we can't multitask while learning. Music, driving, and computer programs all drag on short-term memory and thus keep us from understanding. Indeed, even a little music in a presentation prevents people from learning: In one study, people who took online classes without background music learned as much as 150 percent more.

The presentation of content makes a difference, too. Because of the limitations of short-term memory, we learn better in smaller doses, and people typically gain a lot more if there are fewer graphics on a page or PowerPoint slide. This idea also explains why short sentences are a writer's best friend. Fewer words—and more breaks between ideas—make it easier for people to grapple with new information.

Still, most of us are like the phone companies. We overestimate how much we can keep in short-term memory, and people often try to learn too much at one time, taking an overloaded, all-you-can-eat-style approach to gaining expertise. People will think, for instance, that they can learn from a speech while talking to their friend. (They can't.) Or people will try to understand a big, complicated idea in a single sitting. (They can't.)

When I reached psychologist Sweller, he gave the example of foreign language programs that try to instruct people in history or literature or math. By combining the two topics, people learn a lot less, he argues. "You're going to learn neither," Sweller told me. "It's cognitive overload."

Cognitive overload can also occur during protracted events. Long talks, lengthy meetings, prolonged lectures can all erode short-term memory, crowding the limited pathway to long-term memory. For this reason, experts like Ruth Colvin Clark argue that classes for adults should never go longer than 90 minutes. We simply don't have the mental stamina to continue learning for much longer.

Likewise, there are our own thoughts, and the limited capacity of short-term memory explains why anxieties can be so hurtful to gaining any sort of mastery. When we feel stressed—when we're scared or fearful—we can't focus. Our emotions fill up the brain's sketch pad. Psychologist Sian Beilock has shown that this sort of stress impacts even the youngest of children, and when first and second graders are busy fretting—*this is too hard*—they have significantly less cognitive power.

When I interviewed Beilock, I actually had a version of this experience. It was early on a summer morning, and Beilock and I sat down in a large atrium at the University of Chicago, where she's a professor. We talked about her work, discussing her recent studies. Then, about 10 minutes into the conversation, Beilock mentioned she'd just finished up a book titled *How the Body Knows the Mind*.

My brain froze for a moment: *Wait, what book? Should I have known that she just published a book? I probably should have read that book.* It's that sort of brain freeze, that moment of worrying about something else, that's dangerous for developing any sort of skill. Without my short-term memory doing what it was supposed to do— interview Beilock—I couldn't focus. I didn't ask thoughtful follow-up questions.

Effective communicators know that our brains are easily overloaded, and so they'll simplify their message so that it fits into the tapered confines of short-term memory. Apple's marketing success is all about targeted simplicity, for instance, and many of their ads are little more than an image in a sea of white space. Not long ago, Coca-Cola's slogan was just the word: "Real." Perhaps the best ad slogan of all time is just a dozen letters long: "Just do it."

There are other News You Can Use messages here, and people have to focus what they're going to understand. If someone wants to improve their marathon times, for instance, they'd be much better off targeting something specific like performing better on hilly terrain. Similarly, think of a playwright. To improve, he or she should focus on something very particular, something very focused, like getting better at emotion-filled dialogue.

The Value of Educators plays an important role here. Effective instructors create easy-to-gain chunks, feeding their students a bite-size type of mastery. More exactly, great teachers are highly aware of cognitive load, and they provide instruction in a way that's straightforward to understand. This means that if you often feel fully bewildered in a class, there may be too much new information coming at you at once, and you're probably not learning all that much.

At the same time, the nature of short-term memory underscores the value of attention, and when you're learning, stay clear of anything that adds to cognitive load. So when you're solving math problems, don't check Twitter. Likewise, don't ruminate on travel plans while listening to an important talk. Also, keep off Instagram if you're really trying to gain a bit of expertise. All of these types of distractions erode short-term memory and keep us from learning.

When it comes to the fragile nature of short-term memory, my favorite study looked at college students who used laptops in class and found that the students who were online didn't learn as much as their Wi-Fi–less peers. Okay, that's not news: The students with computers were distracted, and so they learned less.

But the laptop use also decreased the learning of the students who sat next to the computer users, even if the nearby student didn't actually surf the Web. In other words, the students were distracted by other people's distraction. Their working memory was compromised by other people's hardly working memory.

When it comes to the process of learning, we need to target a second, very important reason: knowledge. We understand things through the prism of what we know, and anything that we want to learn is based on what we've already learned. In other words, we're going to look beyond the role of short-term memory and better understand how long-term memory shapes the development of expertise.

Every few months or so, for instance, I'll be sitting at my computer, trying to master some bit of technical know-how. Maybe I can't print out some documents, or perhaps I can't find the external drive on the office's network. I've already rebooted the computer, hunted around online for a solution, and maybe even watched a YouTube video or three. Nothing.

Finally, I reach someone in my organization's tech department. More often than not, it's a desktop support technician named Horace Payne, and he'll walk me through the solution, showing me how I need to use a certain set of commands or maybe explaining to me the best way to fix some software.

As learning goes, Payne is providing a very basic form of tutoring— or one-on-one instruction—and it's hard to argue against the overwhelming body of data behind the practice. Some decades ago, psychologist Benjamin Bloom argued that tutoring was twice as effective as any other form of education. One government report dubbed it "the most effective form of instruction ever known." Whether it's tech help or French lessons or marketing strategies, pairing a student with an instructor is one of the most effective ways to learn.

Many organizations have come to this realization over the years. Some computer firms, for instance, now offer one-on-one tech services at their stores. Similarly, consider the concierge service you'll find at many high-end hotels: It's a type of a tutoring for travelers.

The rub, of course, is that tutoring is pricey. It requires a lot of people power. This is why computer companies like Apple try to make sure that all of their "hands-on diagnosis" appointments last less than five minutes—and why most low-budget hotels don't have a concierge service.

But in many ways, there's a more important point to consider, and what's why tutoring is so effective. A few reasons seem pretty clear. When people get one-on-one attention, they get a lot of feedback. It's also easier to motivate students—tutors know what things someone finds meaningful.

And then there's the fact that tutoring is tailored to a student's level of knowledge. It's highly focused. Payne, the tech guy in my office, for instance, knows what I know and don't know. When we talk, he'll ask first, what exactly has gone wrong, then he'll ask what I've done to fix it. Have I updated the programs? Do I know the software? Is this a new problem?

This is typical in tutoring. If someone in a one-on-one class has a misconception about fractions, for instance, the teacher will typically stop and explain the issue. Don't know about yeast but want to bake bread? The teacher will unpack the topic for you. Land in a new town but don't know the language? The concierge might help you learn the local phrase for "thank you."

Tutoring works, then, because it builds on what we know. The instructor is adapting the information to what we already understand. In the Introduction, I described this idea as the Knowledge Effect. It boils down to the fact that it's hard to learn something if you don't know anything about it.

This idea holds true for every field—math, art, wood carving. There is no learning without some prior knowledge. Facts and figures are the first step to richer forms of thought, as cognitive scientist Dan Willingham has argued, and we need background knowledge to understand just about anything.

As an example, consider a phrase like this: *Haben Sie heute gefrühstückt?* The text doesn't make sense if you don't know German. Or take the following sentence: "An improved dispersion strengthened lead-tin alloy solder is provided in which there is dispersed in the solder up to about 5 percent of small particles." Again, the text is nearly impossible to understand without some previous knowledge of material science.

Think of knowledge as the central building block of learning. It's the brick and mortar of understanding—and one of the best predictors of learning. There are countless illustrations of this idea. Mastery of long division helps people get better at algebra. Expertise in construction fosters architectural skills. If people have better understanding of basic Civil War facts, they're better able to grapple with the causes of Southern secession.

This happens because our brains create mental templates in order to store experiences in long-term memory. More exactly, our brains will "bundle" new information with previous information, using old knowledge to help us make meaning out of new knowledge. So after we receive information in short-term memory, it's shipped to long-term memory, where it rests within a broader context of understanding.

We can use this mental habit to help us learn. Say, for example, you want to recall the number: 1,945. One way to improve your memory of the number is to think of the date that World War II ended: 1945. If you're like most people, this makes recalling the 1,945 number easier because the new figure has become attached to a long-term memory.

For another example, imagine if I wanted to recall the names of my boss's three young daughters—Kiera, Beatrice, Penny. I would recall them a lot more easily if I linked the names to something that I know well, if I bundled the data into long-term memory. In this case, I might think of some basketball teams—the Knicks, the Bulls, and the Pistons—and use the first letters of the team names to help me recall the names of the three young women.

Similarly, take the classic mnemonic My Very Educated Mother Just Served Us Nine Pizzas, which stands for the order of the planets in our solor system (Mercury, Venus, Earth, etc). As a learning device, mnemonics are effective because of the nature of long-term memory: They hang new knowledge on old knowledge, even if it's just a phrase about mothers.

There's more when it comes to knowledge and long-term memory, though. It turns out that facts are not just some form of intellectual fuel for our ruminating engines. Rather, knowledge and thinking are mixed together within the structure of our brains, as Willingham suggests. Content and cognition turn out to support each other within our neural constructs. As Willingham argues: "Memory is the residue of thought."

There's a rich-get-richer aspect to this idea: If we have a network of knowledge, it makes it easier to add to the network. In other words, if you want to learn more statistics, the best thing to know is statistics. If you want to improve your Spanish, the best thing is to know is Spanish.

The converse of this idea is true, too: If you don't know any Spanish, it's best to start with learning the basic facts such as frequently used words like *hombre* and *cuarto*. If you're starting to learn guitar, memorize the basics like chord progressions.

For individuals, this starts with clearly identifying what background knowledge is necessary for expertise. Sometimes this is obvious. It's hard to learn to cannonball into a pool if you don't know how to swim, for example. But more typically, it's pretty subtle. So ask yourself: What skills do I need to acquire? Does this field have some foundational concepts that I need to master?

In this sense, knowledge really is power. The understanding of facts makes gaining expertise more effective. Speed reading is a good case in point. There's little evidence that speed reading works. Few experts believe in the practice, and in the end, you're much better off having some background knowledge about what you're reading. If you have some prior understanding, you'll be able to gain from the text at a much faster rate.

Think of content as more than king. It's also learning itself.

When people think about learning, they often envision something static. We acquire a skill—and then we're done. But the nature of learning, the nature of expertise, is dynamic. To acquire expertise, people have to learn at a level slightly beyond their skills. Put more directly, learning does not have a comfort zone.

During my first visit to Windsor Hills—the Baltimore school that adopted Success for All—researcher Bob Slavin and I once stepped into a classroom where students were being regrouped based on their performance, and I immediately focused on a boy named Nassir. A stocky fifth grader, Nassir was in a class with mostly second graders, many of whom barely reached his chest. He was a giant, it seemed, among overgrown toddlers.

For most of the morning, Nassir sat in the back of the classroom, perched on a small chair, wearing a Windsor Hills shirt. Despite the difference in size and age, he was learning the same material as the other children, with the teacher reviewing some of the basic phonic sounds that go into the vowel combination "ur." Later, Nassir sat with another boy, and together they scrawled out the word "fur" on a small white board.

The Success for All approach to regrouping dates back to the 1950s, allowing for more targeted forms of instruction. By grouping students together according to their levels of performance rather than their age or grade level, the teacher can provide instruction that's more directed. It makes it easier to deliver more rigorous—and personalized—instruction to kids like Nassir.

At Success for All schools, this sort of regrouping happens every morning. So at exactly 9 a.m., all of the students in the elementary school move to different classrooms depending on how well they can read. In Nassir's case, he trudges down from his fifth grade classroom to the second grade classroom so that he can get more tailored instruction. Then, after the ninety minutes of reading, he'll haul back up again.

Regrouping has its issues. Older students are often embarrassed to be in classes with younger students, for instance. But the approach pays off. Given Nassir's struggles, there's little question he would have floundered if he'd been in English with the rest of his fifth grade classmates. He was simply too far behind to engage in grade-level work. He would not have been challenged—he would have been academically lost.

Regrouping relies on a corollary to the Knowledge Effect. Because to learn something new, the skill or knowledge has to be, as Goldilocks famously argued, "just right." The skill can't be too far beyond our current level of skill, or we become lost in a haze of learning confusion. But the knowledge also can't be too easy, or we don't learn anything at all. The best place to learn, then, is just beyond what we can know or can do.

I once visited psychologist Janet Metcalfe in her offices at Columbia University to find out more about this idea. Over the years, Metcalfe has conducted hundreds of studies of students as they try to figure out what they should be learning, and she argued that people are often pretty bad at the practice. When people attempt to learn something new, they'll often target "either the things they know already, or things that are just too difficult for them," according to Metcalfe's research.

For her part, Metcalfe argued that learning is often about finding the best "window of opportunity" or engaging in material just beyond our understanding. For example, imagine that you want to improve your understanding of art history. Most people would start by reviewing some of the things that they already fairly familiar with—Rembrandt was a Dutch painter, Van Gogh was a post Impressionist, the art of painting dates back tens of thousands of years.

Learning happens, though, when people are pushed just a bit past what they can do comfortably. We need to stretch our knowledge in order to learn, and the most effective learning happens when people learn the easiest materials among the things that they have yet to understand. So more effective questions for the person learning about art history might be: Who was Giacometti? Why was Louise Nevelson such an important artist? Why is Degas considered the first modernist painter?

As Metcalfe argues, the window of learning is always moving. It's a target that constantly changes. As soon we learn one skill, we need to move up to the next skill. Well-designed video games do this well: Players are always just a bit beyond the range of their skill. Each level is slightly harder than the one before, and it's this ever-evolving lure of mastery that keeps people focused—and honing their skill in the game.

Nassir seemed to have a sense of this "just right" aspect of learning. Months after I first got to know him, I sat down with him as he ate his lunch. In many ways, he was a typical preteen. He proudly told me about his Nintendo game system and some of his favorite video bloggers. He complained about the school lunch, which on that day was a brown slop of a meatball sub that he never touched—he ate two bananas instead.

We talked about Nassir's family and friends and how he celebrated his birthday at Olive Garden. Nassir noted that school has become more difficult over time, that the academic expectations had been raised. "You gotta work hard," he advised, and in a way, that was the point. We all need to target our learning a little bit beyond where we are, to always be working a little harder than we did before.

Better Thinking

The notion of an effective learning zone goes beyond content—or even rigor—and even at this early stage in the learning process, we also want to develop connections, to hone our thinking skills. In this regard, we have to keep in mind that expertise—and memory—aren't linear sorts of things. Rather they function more like sprawling networks, a system of hubs and links.

Bror Saxberg knows this idea as well as anyone. One of the best learners I've known, Saxberg has a medical degree from Harvard University along with a PhD in engineering from the Massachusetts Institute of Technology. Saxberg has also landed a master's degree in math from Oxford along with two undergraduate degrees, and today he works as the chief learning officer at the education firm Kaplan.

It was early in his career that Saxberg first noticed that experts organize their understanding very differently from amateurs. Back then, Saxberg was a medical school student at Harvard, working with a team on a difficult case, a patient with a painful illness. Together with the group of students, Saxberg ran down the basics on the patient—blood pressure, lab results—without any luck in coming to a diagnosis.

Then Saxberg and his team began to hunt for more unusual illnesses, reading textbooks and hunting around in different medical manuals. They ordered more tests and exams. Again, no clear diagnosis. So the team called in one of the most senior doctors in the hospital—let's call him Dr. Wildenstein.

A serious man in a long white lab coat, Wildenstein walked into the patient's room and declared a diagnosis within a few moments. In fact, it took Wildenstein less than a minute to figure out what was wrong with the patient as well as to detail a path to recovery.

For Saxberg, the Wildenstein story offers a clear lesson. While Saxberg and his team had a collection of isolated facts, Wildenstein had a systematized type of expertise. The experienced doctor knew the concepts—and the connections—and so he had a much easier time figuring out what was wrong. As Saxberg argues, Wildenstein was a "walking data analyzer" because he had "pattern recognition to realize what was important and what was not."

In many ways, this is the hallmark of mastery, and just about every professional has developed what Saxberg calls "pattern recognition" skills. From airline pilots to architects, from baseball players to musicians, experts think in more connected, more relational ways. Their long-term memory is rooted in links instead of features, in systems instead of facts, and so like a diviner, like a "walking data analyzer," they can look past the surface features of a problem and identify core issues.

A number of experiments back up this idea. Cognitive scientist Art Graesser once pulled a group of people together into his lab, and the subjects learned about different devices—a toaster oven, a cylinder bolt, a dishwasher. Then Graesser gave the subjects various ways in which the household items could break down, and it turned out that people who understood the device asked better queries about what could have gone wrong. By seeing connections, by knowing relationships, they could more easily come up with reasons that the device didn't work.

It takes a long time to develop this sort of networked expertise, and in the next chapter, we will look more closely at the issue of how to practice in ways that support this approach to mastery. But there's an important lesson for people who are just starting to learn something—we need to target the underlying logic that ties together an area of understanding, to see how expertise comes together.

One approach is to write down what you know about a topic before you learn something new about that topic. So if I'm honing my grilling skills, I might note things like: *Choose steaks with a bit of fat. High heat works best. Use tongs, not a fork, so meat stays juicy.* If I'm learning about the Electoral College, I'd write: *The political process that helps get presidents elected.*

According to experts like Robert Marzano, the benefits of this approach is that it helps people focus on linkages rather than isolated facts. By writing down what we know, we're preparing our minds to make more connections within that body of expertise, creating a more systematized form of thinking—and understanding.

Another tool to better network our learning is a low-stakes assessment. Part of the benefit of tests is obvious—they provide a matter of clarification, a bit of feedback, a judgment of sorts. In other words, quizzes help us understand what exactly we don't know. This approach can go a long way—when we fail an accounting exam, for instance, we know that we need to get better at accounting.

But just as important, informal quizzes can help us better systematize our expertise. For an illustration, ask yourself a question like *why is Aaron Burr important?* or *why do people use crampons while climbing?* Inevitably you'll start thinking about related facts and ideas. For the Aaron Burr query, for instance, you might think about how vice president Burr oversaw the first impeachment trial and make conceptual ties to modern impeachment trials. As for crampons, you might think of them as hooves but for climbing boots.

Indeed, people who gain skills and knowledge effectively are often engaging in a type of quizzing in their minds. They'll ask themselves questions as they learn: Why is this true? How does this link to other ideas? In Graesser's study of the learning of household items, for instance, people who asked "why" and "how" questions showed much richer understanding of the items than those who didn't.

When I met up with Saxberg—the chief learning officer at Kaplan— he did this in conversation, too. As we talked on that afternoon, Saxberg ended just about every other sentence with the word "right?" and a little pause. In essence, Saxberg was asking: Why are we talking about this? How well do you understand this?

Saxberg has seen the value of helping people make connections at Kaplan, too, and with his help, the company has begun using a more targeted approach as part of its LSAT prep classes. In the past, the LSAT classes on reasoning had been taught with a video in which a professor excitedly lectures to students about how to solve a specific type of problem. But the firm recently developed a set of learning tools that presented the complex ideas in a more focused, more networked fashion, with specific examples that walked students directly through the skill set.

The outcomes were tremendous. Students performed far better in the posttest. What's more, it took students only nine minutes to master the topic. In contrast, the video-based lecture required students to learn for some ninety minutes. That's a difference of almost an hour and a half.

The issue wasn't that the video was bad or that the professor was weak. The issue was that more examples provided more robust ways to spot connections. It broke down the material in a more coherent way. It made the system of knowledge easier to learn.

Another way of thinking about this idea is that mastery is about more than content. Expertise is about more than accumulated facts. To really know something, people also need to develop a set of thinking skills. Interestingly, these thinking skills are often so intricate and complex that even the experts themselves don't really know how to explain them.

A version of this idea occurred to me some years ago when I met up with font designer Matthew Carter. Generally, Carter doesn't want you to notice the words you're reading. That is, you shouldn't be aware of the way the small horizontal line at the top of the *T* hovers near the *h* at the beginning of this sentence. Nor should your eye catch on the heavy down strokes of a *W* that give the letter its classic look. "If the reader is conscious of the type, it's almost always a problem," Carter told me. Letters on a page should "provide a seamless passage of the author's thoughts into the reader's mind."

Why does Carter have such strong opinions? Well, he is one of the world's most well-respected designers of fonts. Microsoft's Verdana font is one of Carter's designs. Carter also created the headline font of the *New York Times* and the Snell Roundhand font. Or just pick up any Verizon phonebook. The design of all of those letters and numbers come from Carter's hand.

I spoke with Carter at his apartment in Cambridge. Tall and aesthenic looking, with a ponytail of white hair, he explained how AT&T had asked once him to create the smallest legible type that could be printed on low-grade paper. Ideas for new fonts would sometimes come to him as he sauntered through graveyards, looking at headstones. He detailed how his creation, Bell Centennial, has flat, short curves on the sides of the *g* in order to increase the white space in the characters and make the letter more legible.

But as we talked on that winter afternoon, Carter also seemed to have a little difficulty describing what exactly made for a beautiful, easy-to-read font. When Carter talked about how an *h* and *t* should fit together in a word, for instance, he called the decision "purely aesthetic." As for the process of putting together a font, he told me it was plainly uninteresting, something not even worth discussing: "Watching me work is like watching a refrigerator make ice."

Without any equivocation, Carter is one of the best people in the world at creating typefaces, the Winston Churchill of font design. And yet still there was a vagueness about how exactly he executes his designs. It wasn't just me, either. In other interviews, Carter is somewhere between kindly humble and purposefully obtuse. He once told another reporter: "I'm more of a chameleon."

It turns out that it's pretty easy to overlook everything that goes into a specific area of mastery. Once we know something, it's hard to explain that knowledge to someone else. In his lab at USC, Richard Clark has examined this idea in dozens of different studies. He'll bring an expert into his lab—maybe an experienced nurse or a tennis pro or a skilled federal judge.

Then Clark will ask them detailed questions about their area of expertise. What are you thinking while you perform this step? Where is your right hand during that procedure? Tell me, step-by-step, how do you do that?

While these individuals are all highly regarded experts, Clark typically finds that they can identify only about 30 percent of what's needed to "solve a complex but familiar problem or accomplish a task." The rest is what Clark told me is "fully automated, unconscious." In other words, most of what experts know is simply beyond their actual ken. They don't really know what they know; they made it fully automatic.

What all this makes clear is that we can't just go to an expert and ask them to explain something to us. The experts often just don't have

POP QUIZ #6

True or false: When it comes to learning, metacognition (e.g., thinking about thinking) can be more important than intelligence.

enough awareness. Nor can we just read a Wikipedia article and come with a really deep knowledge about a field or area of expertise. In most Wiki pages, there isn't enough explanation of the thinking and reasoning skills that are embedded within the content.

But it gets worse. Remember the idea that we discussed earlier about how short-term memory can hold only a small trickle of information like the digits 911? Well, the small, narrow pipeline of short-term memory makes learning from experts even harder because we can't handle a lot of new facts at once. Even if someone could explain all of their expertise in one burst of explanation, we couldn't pick it up. If too much new information gets thrown at us, our brain becomes overloaded.

However, as learning progresses, we can plug more and more information into the holes of meaning. Knowledge bleeds into other knowledge. Skills support other skills, and over time, with the help of long-term memory, we can develop more and more mastery. Expertise "automates when it is used over time," Clark told me. "The automation process frees up 'thinking space' so we can take in more new learning without overloading our short-term memory."

But in the end, it's the Value of Educators all over again, and we need instructors who know their subject—and have ways to explain their subject. People, then, shouldn't choose educators just because the person is an expert in the field. They should also look for instructors who have experience teaching that subject, who understand how to explain key skills and ideas. Likewise, we need learning materials that unpack the thinking that's embedded in an area of expertise and explain it in a targeted way that makes it easy to grapple with.

Interestingly, this sort of focused knowledge development extends well beyond knowledge itself. It's also key for our emotions, which is the topic that we will turn to next.

Thinking about Thinking—and Emotions

Consider for a moment the book that you're holding right now. In the publishing industry, this book is known as a popular science book, or an effort to translate the findings of academic research for a wider audience.

You've probably come across these sorts of books before. Malcolm Gladwell writes a type of popular science books. *The Immortal Life of Henrietta Lacks* by Rebecca Skloot is a popular science book. Susan Cain, Daniel Coyle, Steven Johnson, and Atul Gawande have all written important popular science in recent years.

Generally speaking, popular science books follow a certain pattern. Almost all of them push a surprising theme or idea. In Gladwell's *Blink*, for instance, he argues that split-second decisions are better than deliberate ones. In the first *Immortal Life of Henrietta Lacks* book, Skloot discusses the origins of a cell line that's used in just about every science lab in the country. In Steven Johnson's *Future Perfect*, he outlines a new way to think about societal reform, arguing for a bottom-up approach to change.

Like any form of narrative, popular science books have shortcomings. The books will sometimes overstate their case. In their eagerness to present counterintuitive findings, the authors will gloss over key details. Talent can't be boiled down to a single type of brain issue, as Daniel Coyle argues in *The Talent Code*. Malcolm Gladwell's idea that expertise comes with 10,000 hours of practice doesn't stand up to close scrutiny.

Why does this matter? Because knowing what you're reading is key to understanding what you're reading. Context is often one of the most important parts of comprehension. Put differently, learning to learn is often a matter of knowing about what you're learning.

Take a look at this text, for instance:

There's a right way and a wrong way. Neither is clearly described. If you do it the wrong way, there could be a major error. If you do it the right way, though, you might also still get it wrong.

You can read and reread those four sentences all that you want. But it's nearly impossible to understand the words without knowing the context. The sentences simply don't make logical sense if there's no broader framing.

Think about all of the possibilities: Is the text part of a technical manual on how to defuse a bomb? A material sciences paper on crystal formation? A 20th-century spy novel with an unreliable narrator? A metaphysical poem on the nature of doing? The text could come from any of the above, and in the end, it's the context that gives the words any sort of actual meaning.

This idea has important implications for how we focus our learning because of a skill known as metacognition. Psychologists define metacognition as thinking about thinking, and in broad terms, it's about understanding how you understand something. It's about gaining mental perspective and a sense of cognitive awareness.

In some ways, metacognition comes easily. When you decide to close the instructional manual and begin piecing together an IKEA table, you've engaged in a form of metacognition. When you frantically review your lecture notes before a big speech? A bit of nervous metacognition. That nagging, tip-of-the-tongue feeling that you get when you can't remember the name of a kid you went to high school with? Metacognition.

Metacognition has two parts, according to experts. First, there's the planning aspect: How will I know what I know? What are my goals? Do I need more background knowledge? Second, there's the monitoring part: Could I learn this idea in a different way? Am I making progress? Why am I doing what I am doing?

This sort of metacognition often comes easily to experts. When a specialist works through an issue, they'll think a lot about how the problem is framed. They'll have a sense of whether or not their answer seems reasonable or not. They'll reflect on how they got to an answer.

The key is not to leave this thinking about thinking to the experts. The research suggests, in fact, that beginners often need this sort of metacognitive thinking just as much as the experts. In other words, the faster that we ask metacognitive questions, the quicker we can master new skills.

When it comes to learning, one of the biggest issues is that people don't engage in metacognition nearly enough. We don't do enough to understand the things that we don't know. At the same time, people feel too confident in what they do know. The issue, then, is not that something goes in one ear and out the other. The issue is that individuals don't dwell on the dwelling. They don't push themselves to understand.

In this regard, metacognition often comes down to a set of questions that we ask ourselves: How will I know what I know? What do I find confusing? Do I have a way to measure my understanding? These sorts of queries are powerful, and metacognition is often more important than raw smarts when it comes to learning.

According to researcher Marcel Veenman, for instance, students who have a rich ability to manage their thinking can outscore students who have sky-high levels of IQ. "We've found that metacognition often accounts for about 40 percent of learning outcomes," Veenman told me, while "IQ only accounts for 25 percent."

The act of writing is a good example of metacognition because when we think about composing sentences and paragraphs, we're often asking ourselves crucial metacognitive questions: Who will be reading this? Will they understand me? What things do I need to explain? This is why writing is often such an effective way to organize one's thoughts. It forces us to evaluate our arguments and think about our ideas.

Some like psychologist Doug Hacker describe writing as a form of "applied metacognition," and it happens to me all the time. Before I start writing, for instance, I'll have some sort of idea—a flicker of a connection, a sparkle of reasoning—and the notion or argument will seem irrefutable. Maybe, for instance, I'll want to email my wife to ask if she could watch the kids on Saturday night because an old college buddy is in town.

But then I'll start writing the email, and my logic simply falls apart. I realize that my argument is actually pretty weak since I saw my buddy last month. My intended audience will never buy it—and the email gets trashed. To use Hacker's words, I applied a type of metacognition and found my logic to be lacking.

We can do this ourselves. Imagine, for a moment, that you want to become a better travel photographer. Then ask yourself metacognitive questions while you're starting to learn to shoot images: How would an expert think about taking this picture? What sort of assumptions am I making about light and composition?

For another example, imagine you want to improve your understanding of the notion of a leap year. So you ask yourself: What do I know about leap years? How would someone know about leap years? Why is it even called a leap year?

For their part, researchers recommend that people ask these sorts of questions well before they start learning something. By probing ourselves before we gain a bit of expertise, we're priming our metacognitive pump—and making our learning more durable. Indeed, psychologist Lindsey Richland and a colleague have showed that people who try to answer metacognitive questions before they read some text learn a lot more, even if they can't answer the metacognitive questions correctly.

Or consider this bit of metacognition: Have you noticed the pop quizzes interspersed through this book? I included a few of them in every chapter as a way to prompt a type of engaged thinking about thinking. My hope is that you attempt to answer each of the questions and think, *Do I know this about learning? Why do I know this about learning?* In the end, it will lead to a deeper form of understanding.

The power of metacognition goes beyond our thinking. It also extends to our emotions, and when it comes to the process of learning, we need to manage how we feel. If metacognition is about planning and monitoring our thinking, we need to do the same for our emotions, and as people learn, they need to ask themselves: How do I feel? Is this task frustrating? Scary?

What's easy to forget is that learning is a deeply emotional activity. Our feelings dramatically shape our ability to gain any sort of skill. People often associate this aspect of learning with children, and really, there's no question that some eighth graders will do anything except say that they need help in their algebra classes. They're simply too embarrassed.

But emotions play a tremendous role in the learning of adults, too. Feelings often determine what we're going to learn. A new line of research in psychology shows that emotions actually serve as a type of bedrock for our knowledge and skills. Our thoughts are woven together with feelings, and in the end, there's really no real difference between cognitive and noncognitive approaches to learning.

Take a now-famous patient named Elliot who walked into the office of Antonio Damasio in the late 1970s. At the time, Damasio was a professor of neuroscience at the University of Iowa, and Elliot had just had a large tumor removed from his brain. The growth had started just above Elliot's nose, right behind his eyes, and eventually, it grew to the size of an overgrown golf ball.

Before the surgery, Elliott had been an upstanding father and successful businessman. He was smart and funny and well read, a role model in his community. After the surgery, he still had a very high IQ, and on tests, he scored in the superior range. He could still talk about politics and the news and even make jokes. But Elliot was emotionless. "He was cool, detached, unperturbed even by potentially embarrassing discussion of personal events," Damasio writes in his book *Descartes' Error.*

Damasio eventually uncovered a number of patients who showed similar types of brain damage as Elliot, and they all showed similar symptoms. They seemed to have lost all of their emotions. They appeared to be purely rational. There's something about this idea that might appear attractive. Without emotions, it might seem like we can finally think clearly.

But it's not, and patients like Elliot had a terrible time making decisions. Without their emotions, they became lost in rational thought. They lacked an ability to think, to reason their way through problems. There were money problems, and Elliot lost a large sum of money to a swindler with a vague business scheme.

These patients simply couldn't get a feel for the overall nature of an issue. Damasio once asked a patient with similar frontal lobe damage about the next time that he planned to visit the lab. Damasio suggested two dates to the patient, who began reviewing his calendar.

For the next 30 minutes, the patient outlined all the logic involved in deciding between the two dates. He had previous commitments and later commitments. He mentioned the weather and the time and other potential meetings. The patient talked about anything that might possibly shape his decision.

"It took enormous discipline to listen to all of this without pounding on the table and telling him to stop," Damasio writes. "But we finally did tell him, quietly, that he should come on the second of the alternative dates. His response was equally calm and prompt. He simply said, 'That's fine.' Back the appointment book went into his pocket, and then he was off."

When it comes to learning—and thinking—it turns out that our emotions work as a first line of defense. They serve as a type of doorman, telling us if we should engage the skills of reason or not. This is what Elliot lacked: He didn't have a way to signal that he should embrace reason. He didn't know how—or when—to think. As Damasio argues, "Emotions was in the loop of reason."

There's an even deeper connection between thought and feeling, though, and the source of the issue goes back again to our brain. Our nervous system is not like a car engine with discrete and independent parts. Rather, a brain is a sea of connections, a mass of interwoven components, and people are constantly reusing the same neural parts for different purposes.

Social pain, for instance, runs on the same brain circuit as physical pain. Similarly, emotional anguish ignites the same neural systems as corporal anguish. In many ways, there's no neural difference between the pain of feeling alone and the pain of slashing your finger, and in the end, the dopamine-fueled happiness that comes from solving a math problem is ultimately not that different than the dopamine-fueled happiness that comes with connecting with a friend.

Put differently, the head is part of the heart, or said another way, the body is often no different than the brain. The lab studies that undergird this work are legendary—and frankly, more than a little weird. If someone is physically uncomfortable, for instance, they'll view other people's faces as angrier. Prompt someone to be forgiving, and the feeling of redemption will make them jump higher in a test of physical ability. My favorite? If people give a random object the middle finger, they have less positive opinions of that object, even if they have no experience with the object.

The deep connection between body and mind, between emotion and thought, helps explain some of the power of mental abacus, the math practice that we came across in the first chapter: When people move their fingers while doing the calculations, they're often sparking the same mental circuits that they'd spark if they were actually doing the math. As Harvard's Neon Brooks told me, the hands are helping the brain to "think" through the mental calculations.

There are some fascinating applications of this idea, and the next time you're faced with a geometry problem—or even an architectural drawing—research suggests that you should literally finger the drawing as a way to gain a deeper grasp of the issue embedded the problem. According to experts, the hand gestures promote learning by making the drawings easier to understand.

Psychologist Sian Beilock also recommends that people incorporate gestures to help remember a specific idea. So if you want to make sure to thank the host at the end of a big speech, make sure to associate the words of gratitude with a specific movement like a nod during practice sessions. Then at the speech, give the nod, and the movement will spark the memory of the words.

For my own part, I'll often use my hands to help me remember the codes for conference call numbers. Not long ago, for instance, I had to dial into a meeting line. The dial-in number had three fours in a row, and so I stuck out three fingers as a way to better remember the digits, basically offloading the memory to my hands, using my body as a form of intelligence. For a short moment, in other words, my fingers were my mind.

There's a downside to emotions. Strong feelings can also keep us from learning, and we can't gain skills if we feel emotionally uncomfortable. Our thoughts can't settle if we feel stressed, and study after study has shown that emotions can also drive down learning outcomes. Sadness, depression, even just physical discomfort can all make it harder to land expertise.

So how do we target the emotions associated with learning? How do we manage our feelings and plan for expertise? Let's start to answer these questions by considering Jim Taylor.

For a long time, Taylor was a good but not great slalom skier. While Taylor was ranked nationally, he often didn't finish races. Anxious about his performance, worried about his times, Taylor would miss gates. He'd make bumbling mistakes and misjudge a turn and crash in a pile of snowy powder. "A mess" is how Taylor described himself—"my own worst enemy."

After taking a college psychology class, Taylor tweaked his emotional preparation by using mental imagery to practice for his races. Before Taylor even stepped into the starting gate, he would imagine himself racing down the mountain, envisioning every gate, bump, and hip turn. It was a type of mental dream, a matter of watching himself perform "from the inside out."

Taylor calls the results of his little intervention "spectacular." By using mental imagery, he gained a much deeper belief in his abilities and eventually managed to shape how he felt about racing. "From doubt came confidence," Taylor argues. "From anxiety came intensity." And within a year, Taylor became one of the top twenty skiers in his age group in the nation and eventually made the US Ski Team.

The power of mental imagery goes back to the interconnected nature of the brain. The deep ties between body and mind explain why mental imagery can produce such dramatic effects. There's simply not a big difference between imagining an experience and the experience itself.

Mental imagery allowed Taylor to gain something that psychologists call self-efficacy. It's a belief in one's ability, a feeling that one's going to succeed, and it turns out to be crucial in dealing with the emotional vagaries of learning. It's a way to manage our feelings, and when Taylor practiced mental imagery, he developed an important type of confidence: "When I arrived at a race, I not only knew that I was going to finish. I knew I was going to win."

Like many psychological theories, the notion of self-efficacy is both simple yet profound. Stanford psychologist Albert Bandura first developed the concept in the 1970s, and in a number of important research papers, Bandura argued that people need to have the expectation of success. Specifically, Bandura found that people are far more likely to engage in an activity if they know that they can accomplish the activity.

Self-efficacy, then, is different than an overall feeling of confidence. It's not a matter of self-esteem. Instead, the idea revolves around the belief that we can accomplish a very specific task, that we can achieve positive outcomes in what we aim to do.

This expectation of success brings all sorts of benefits. If we believe that we can accomplish a task, we're far more likely to put forth effort. With a greater sense of self-efficacy, we're also far more likely to achieve our goals—and be happier with the results. Just as important, self-efficacy sparks focus. It makes us more targeted in our goals, and so we're far better able to handle diversions.

When I reached out to Bandura, for instance, he emailed back, writing that he was on a "production treadmill" for his new book. He was working "late into the night" and had no time for interviews. This is self-efficacy in action: With more confidence, we're more committed. We have a deeper sense of control, a richer sense of agency. Bandura had a book that he wanted to write—and he was going to achieve that goal, regardless of the emails in his inbox.

In this way, self-efficacy operates as a buffer for the inevitable frustrations of learning. When we know what we're going to achieve, we're better equipped to deal with setbacks and distractions, with the bruised feelings and dedicated focus that learning requires.

Bandura underscored this point when he eventually made time for an interview, telling me that when people learn, they need ways to cope with various nagging feelings: Am I good enough? Will I fail? What if I'm wrong? Isn't there something else that I'd rather be doing? For Bandura, these sorts of thoughts and emotions can quickly rob of us our ability to gain expertise. They disrupt our short-term memory. While some of these feelings are typical, too many of them and "you'll get totally wiped out."

There are a number of ways to manage these thoughts and emotions, and we have to write out plans, map out long-term strategy, to help keep ourselves motivated. In this regard, learning to learn often boils down to a type of project oversight. It's about creating objectives and then figuring out ways to reach those objectives with clear and achievable benchmarks.

The research is overwhelming on this point, and literally hundreds of studies have shown that people with clear goals outperform people with vague aspirations like "do a good job." By setting targets, people are better able to accomplish what they want to accomplish. To be clear, learning goals should not be New Year's Eve–like aims like master the tango. Overly ambitious learning targets can backfire, Bandura argued, because they seemed too vague and distant.

Instead, Bandura's research shows that people are more likely to succeed if they have easy-to-accomplish benchmarks. So instead of something like master the tango, people should detail smaller targets like attend tango lessons once a week or practice dancing at home on Wednesday evenings and Sunday afternoons. These sorts of goals can be extremely helpful—and often serve as one of the best ways to manage our emotions.

At the same time, we need to keep ourselves emotionally motivated. In this regard, self-talk matters, and we need to avoid black-and-white thinking. So rather than tell yourself, *I'm the worst,* tell yourself, *I'm struggling.* Also make sure to find moments of progress and reward even small accomplishments like noting, *I worked for three hours today.*

To help keep us inspired, we can also make bets with ourselves. Some years ago, for instance, programmer Francesco Cirillo developed a helpful approach to creating a sense of efficacy. At the time, Cirillo was a college student, and he often found himself sidetracked, distracted by everything. So Cirillo placed "a bet with himself": He set a kitchen timer—called a pomodoro in Italian because it looks like a tomato—for ten minutes.

The pomodoro technique worked, and Cirillo soon began experimenting with different lengths of time. Eventually, he found that the best approach was to study for twenty-five minutes and then take five minutes off to enjoy a few minutes of aimless fun like Facebook or

POP QUIZ #7

True or false: Quizzing is an effective way to learn.

Pokemon Go. Cirillo called it the Pomodoro Technique, a way to set goals for accomplishing work while respecting our need for breaks.

I've used the Pomodoro Technique for years. It's as a way to promote my own sense of efficacy, to manage my own seeking ways, and it's made me realize that the mastery requires management. We need a way to overcome the inevitable distractions—and raw mistakes—that come with engaging expertise. Skier Jim Taylor puts it well. Learning, he argues, is often about "feeling success in your mind's eye."

The more social, emotional side of learning often came up in my interview with researchers. It usually happened when I asked the Question.

Just about every time that I interviewed a learning expert, I'd pose some version of the following query: How do you learn to learn? If you're trying to gain a new skill, how do you approach the task? What do you do with your own kids or students that most other parents or teachers don't do?

In a way, I simply wanted to know what the experts did in their own lives. In my mind, I called it the Question, and there'd often be a slight pause, a clearing of the throat. Sometimes I felt like I heard the person's perspective shift, from academic viewpoint to parent viewpoint, from expert mind-set to learner mind-set.

Not surprisingly, the answers often reflected the expert's point of view. If an expert focused on math, she would talk about math. If an expert worked on memory, he would talk about memory.

Yet time and again, regardless of the expert's background, the emotional side of learning would bubble up. We came across David Barner in the first chapter—he did research on the mental abacus—and when we meet up for dinner, Barner explained that he would often do math riddles with his young daughter so that she would have a sense that math was fun.

In other cases, the researcher would basically bring their work home with them. Grit expert Angela Duckworth told me that she taught her children about "self-control" experiments when they were still in preschool.

Perhaps the most provocative answer regarding our softer side came from cognitive scientist Lisa Son. She and I met up in a Starbucks one afternoon in New York City. We talked for a while, and when the topic of children came up, I asked a version of the Question.

Son smiled immediately: "I explain the things I can about my work to my kids as much as possible."

Son studies the role of memory in learning, and she believes deeply in the value of difficulty. Son's expectation is that learning will be hard, a struggle, something that causes unease. "What parents need to do is allow their kids to be okay with being uncomfortable, to be okay without knowing the answer," Son told me. "If students are never given the opportunity to struggle with their thoughts, then future struggles may become too frustrating."

Son gave examples of ways that she expects her children to really grapple with their learning. She'll often withhold a key bit of knowledge from her kids to help them learn. She'll be vague about feedback during science topics, for instance, or she will not correctly answer a math fact that her child had asked for.

Indeed, it seems that Son actually tries to cultivate a little academic pain. Son won't protect her young son from bumping his head on the kitchen table, for instance, unless it seems like he's really going to crack his head open. And when Son's daughter asked about the idea of time zones, Son would not explain the concept, even after her daughter asked about the idea for months. "As a researcher, I will never give my kid the answer. Never," she said. Only "hints."

Son's approach builds on the idea of learning as mental doing, and Son herself has seen similar effects in her own lab: If people have to put forth more cognitive effort, they gain more. For an example, imagine a young student—call him Moe—has written a short essay with a few spelling errors. As Son explained, most people would tell Moe the correct spelling of the words he missed. But not Son. She'd ask Moe to "look over the page and see if you spelled all of the hard words correctly."

If Moe didn't notice the specific spelling issues, maybe Son would point out which words Moe got wrong. But based on her research, Son would not give him the correct answer or spell out the words. Moe would have to discover the correct answer himself. "As the student reads more on their own, they'll see the word spelled correctly, and they'll never forget the right answer," Son told me. "People need to do learning on their own for long-term maximum learning power."

The expectation of difficulty is important to learning. It is an extension of the notion of self-efficacy. We need to believe that our hard work will pay off, and we need others to believe it, too. I saw this in my development. It was an expectation around the nature of work that had perhaps the greatest impact on my own experience.

I didn't always have a positive view of grindstoning, to be sure. My early experiences in school made me believe that I was a little slow. My teachers played a role—some nursed a pretty limited view of my abilities. One first grade teacher told my mother that I would most likely turn out to be a cook. Another asked if my grandparents were Nazis.

I acted out, too. In middle school, for instance, I landed an in-school suspension for torching a lab table, sparking a fire so large that it required a blast from an industrial-size fire extinguisher.

But my identity evolved. Because of my dedicated parents, because of some helpful teachers, I began to believe something different about myself and the nature of learning. I realized that while I had the same basic talent as others—just about all of us do—my brain simply required more time to work through the material. I needed to put forth more effort.

And over time, struggle became central to how I understood learning. It was the narrative that I lived by, the social contract that I signed. I promised myself that I would outwork everyone in my classes—and explained to friends that I was a learning draft horse, an animal that succeeded due to unmitigated effort. My social circle also slowly changed, becoming less rebellious and more geeky.

It helped that I'm from a family of elbow greasers. My father would often use a German phrase along the lines of *If you don't have brains, then use your brawn.* Being of German descent helped, too. The Teutonic obsession with diligence gave another layer of social meaning to my beliefs about the importance of hard work.

Other people began to expect more of me over the years—and I expected more of myself, sometimes to an extreme degree. Before my first class in college, I remember slipping into the empty university classroom to prepare myself emotionally. In the empty room, standing among the chairs and dust motes, I recalled the encouragement of my friends and family, muttering things to myself along the lines of *I'm not going to be outhustled. I'm going to work harder than everyone else.*

In hindsight, my pep talk seems overly dramatic, a bit of teenage dreamery. This was a college course, not a clash of civilizations. But at the same time, we need these sorts of boosts. When it comes to the emotional side of learning, we don't work alone, and in the empty classroom, I was reminding myself of who I was, fostering the social and emotional efficacy that college demands.

The practical takeaway here is pretty simple. We need to believe in struggle. We need to know that learning is difficult. What's more, we need the people around us to believe, too. To overcome the struggles and difficulties of learning, we need social support. Or recall the Posse program that we discussed in the previous chapter. Part of the reason that the program is so effective is that it creates a strong group expectation of success.

I've seen this in my own research. Together with some colleagues, I found that teachers' attitudes toward students make a tremendous difference in outcomes. In our study, for instance, high schoolers whose teachers anticipated that the teens would finish college were three times more likely to land a college diploma. In other words, a person is far more likely to receive a college degree if he or she has a high school teacher who believes that the person will, in fact, land a college degree.

This idea is at the heart of Lisa Son's approach. She's building norms around the nature of effort, the essence of struggle, the path to expertise. As Son told me, laughing, "I think I overdid it, but if someone gives my kid the answer, she'll kill you."

There's a final lesson when it comes to targeting our feelings, one that brings us back to Bob Slavin's Success for All program. More exactly, an odd paradox exists at the center of the emotional side of achieving expertise, and when we're learning, we often have to balance ourselves between social support and social pressure.

This idea often crossed my mind when I visited Windsor Hills, the West Baltimore school that had adopted Slavin's program. A good example is the morning that a young man told me, "You look just like Joe Flacco."

I was standing in the front office at the time. After my first visit with Slavin, I had continued to swing past the school, making four trips over the course of a year. I was curious to see how the school implemented the reform program, how the more targeted approach to learning would play out over time.

On that morning, I was waiting for a meeting with the school's principal, Corey Basmajian, and after the comment, I soon started Googling pictures of the Baltimore Raven quarterback Joe Flacco on my phone, thinking, "Wow, I look like a football superstar!"

But some ten minutes later, I saw Basmajian, who like me is white. The principal told me that people at the school also often mistake him for Joe Flacco, too, and that's when a moment of awkward racial insight dawned on me. Segregation, rather than my actual appearance, was probably the cause of my being an NFL doppelgänger.

This should have already been obvious. The school was deeply segregated, with no more than one or two white students, and after the riots over the death of Freddie Gray, the issue became even more salient. The Baltimore police had picked up Gray during a drug arrest, and he died in the back of a police van, pleading for help. Gray's death sparked a surge of anger, and on the night of the funeral, people burned cars and ransacked stores.

The riots took place just few dozen blocks from Windsor Hills. Some of the middle schoolers bragged about running through the streets, while one of the second graders was Freddy Gray's nephew and appeared on the front page of the newspaper. I visited the day after the looting had subsided, as police continued to caravan through the city, National Guardsmen still stood guard on street corners, and the sounds of helicopters *whoop-whooping* overhead made it seem as if this were some war-torn nation.

After riots, it's tempting for a school like Windsor Hills to expect less of students. Powerful emotions make it hard to learn, as we've seen. But emotional support can be a slippery slope. There's the danger of being too compassionate, too forgiving, and in the weeks after the riots, many of the teachers at Windsor Hills worked hard to navigate this catch-22.

On one side, the educators wanted to offer support. They wanted to help students develop emotionally. On the other side, the teachers wanted to be relentless on academics. They wanted to challenge their students. One afternoon, for instance, I slipped into Naomi Blaushild's classroom. It was late morning. She was teaching language arts to fifth graders on the second floor.

"You started a new book," Blaushild said. "Can someone tell me about the new book?"

A pause. A bit of talking, while one student mumbled, "What new book?"

Blaushild twisted her body—suggesting *this is a warning*—and then called on a student. "D'ante, go ahead."

"It's about, like, poisonous frogs and animals," the boy said.

"Thank you. Can anyone tell me anything different?" Blaushild asked and then called on another student. "LaMarcus?"

"It's about animals that are dangerous," the boy said.

Blaushild was far from stern. I would not even say she was strict. Her students would often give her hugs. Laughs came easily to her. The classroom wasn't quiet either, and Blaushild assigned lot of group work, with students pairing up to chatter noisily in corners. At the end of class—and sometimes in the middle of class—the students would do "brain breaks," with Blaushild dancing with her students.

Blaushild, it seemed, simply tried to navigate a middle path, and when it comes to learning, we can all gain from her approach. People need to set rigorous targets for themselves; we need to expect a lot of struggle and setbacks. At the same time, we need to make emotional space to support our deeply social ways. People can't learn if they don't feel like they can learn.

Awareness is key, too. Learning is about recognizing what we're going to learn and how well we're learning it. Are we ready to learn? Do we know what we know? Do we know what we still have to learn? What exactly will we learn next? This sort of targeted, metacognitive focus is central when we're beginning to gain mastery in a new field, and more structured forms of education work well for people who don't know much about a topic.

This is a forward progression, though. It's a forward progression emotionally, and as we gain more understanding, we feel more confident. Learning is also a forward progression cognitively speaking, and as we gain more understanding, we need more open-ended activities. With more expertise, people need to practice their knowledge and skills on more novel, unstructured problems, a topic that we will turn to next.

As for Windsor Hills, the school continued to post some clear successes. The principal increased the number of field trips and added a football team and a weeklong camping excursion. Still, the outside world intervened. Fights would break out in the lunchroom, with every walkie-talkie in the school blaring with alarm. A few of the teachers left, frustrated with the changes. In some classrooms the air conditioning didn't work, and the month of June would feel like a rain forest.

On one of my last visits to Windsor Hill, I left the school and walked slowly to my car. I had parked not far from the school's main entrance, and as I got to my car, I turned around. At that moment, under the sprawling sun, kids' voices rolling across the playground, the school looked large and regal, an academic castle perched up on the hill. It seemed like there was a clear path to the future.

Chapter 3

DEVELOP

THE FIRST SIGN was probably the three-pointer. It was an hour or so into the basketball game, and my T-shirt sagged with sweat. Blood thumped in my ears. Adrenaline, the hormonal Red Bull, ran clear and strong. I caught the pass on the wing, and my defender gave me a long moment at the three-point line.

I was not supposed to launch a shot. For years, I had been one of the worst players on the court, barely good enough to make a layup. Other players would often overlook me on offense. Opponents would target me for steals, a bit of easy basketball pickings. Even among a group of slow, weak, middle-aged basketball players, I was slow, weak, and middle-aged.

Still, I was by myself, wide open, so I tucked my elbow and fired the ball with a brawny sort of aim. The ball lofted toward the basket, an orange orb, hanging in the air, a small slice of eternity, and then, surprisingly, the basketball slipped into the bottom of the net, with a loud snap.

"That was a three," someone yelled out.

Did that actually go in? I thought. And then, later, a follow-up notion: *Were my basketball classes behind this?*

The story of my basketball career is a short one. I played a lot as a kid, and in my middle school days, posters of Magic Johnson hung in my bedroom. But in my late teens, I gave up the sport. Other interests took my attention. Schoolwork pulled me into its orbit. For a long while, I stepped onto the court once a year, largely to play a hacking street ball with my brother.

A few years ago, though, I started playing in a Wednesday night pickup game, and I fell in love all over again: the exhausting workouts, the pride of a well-placed shot, the post-game trip to the bar. But I was the guy that no one wanted on their squad. On some nights, I might play for some two hours without landing a bucket. My only redeeming quality, it seemed, was the dedication with which I fouled my opponents.

Then one afternoon I found basketball instructor Dwane Samuels on Craigslist. During his twenties, Samuels had played basketball at some big-name colleges, notching up minutes in summer leagues against NBA All-Stars like Benjamin Wallace. Later, Samuels found a spot playing for the Washington Generals, the Harlem Globetrotters' perennial opponents.

While Samuels was now retired from any sort of professional basketball, he was still a human velociraptor, large and muscular, and during our first session, he had me running sprints and jumping rope and dancing through an agility ladder. Eventually, Samuels tossed me a Spalding and had me review the most basic of basic moves—dribbling through a set of small, orange cones, shooting layups, taking two-foot jumpers.

Samuels had moved to the United States from Jamaica as a teenager, and in his Caribbean-tinged accent, he always kept up a slow steady patter of advice and encouragement as I repeated some of the same drills that I had once did in elementary school: "Keep your elbows in" and "aim for the top of the backboard," he said.

Shy, embarrassed, I didn't tell anyone about the classes—not friends, not family, certainly not anyone that I played basketball with. A lead-footed forty-something should not be going to basketball classes. Tennis classes? Maybe. Golf lessons? Fine. But basketball is a young person's game, fast and quick, and most of Samuels's clients were children who were about the same age as my own.

Within weeks, though, my jumpers started falling in more regularly. I hit three-pointers. Other people began to notice, and a friend asked me for advice on his form. "You were Mr. Lights Out! with the shooting," someone else emailed me. Indeed, my game improved so much that a teammate jokingly asked me if I had been taking steroids.

How could a few lessons have such an impact? Was Samuels some sort of mad-genius instructor? Or was there something about the nature of practice that I had missed after all these years?

The answers bring us to the value of developing our skills and knowledge, the next stage in the learning process. Once we figure out what we're going to learn—and how we're going to learn it—we have to start to develop that mastery. More exactly, we have to enter ourselves into a feedback loop, to hone our skills in a structured sort of way.

In this sense, what many people call practice isn't really practice. They're not engaged in a dedicated way to improve, not using any sort of learning method. There's a good amount of research on this idea, and the raw amount of time spent practicing often bears little relationship to the actual amount of learning.

Or just consider that some first-year college students will have clear misconceptions about basic physics, even after they solved more than 1,500 basic physics problems. So while the students had banged out Newtonian problem after Newtonian problem in high school, the students still couldn't really explain Newton's third law.

The Knowledge Effect plays an important role here, and whether we're playing against the Globetrotters or improving our Latin, it's hard to figure how to develop a skill unless we know something about the skill. In this sense, every beginner lacks the metacognitive ability of knowing what understanding that they need to develop. That's, after all, why they're beginners.

I can't, for instance, get better at something like urban planning because I don't know enough about the topic. For another example, consider that birding experts can tell the difference among the 300 different types of doves. I'm an amateur, so, frankly, they all look like pigeons to me. Not surprisingly, this fact makes it hard for me to get better at spotting the difference between a wood dove and a collared dove.

There's a lot of culpability to go around, and we often don't look for ways to improve our skills, to better ourselves. Handwriting is a great example. After grade school, we tend not to practice our penmanship with

POP QUIZ #8

True or false: Sugary drinks make people less able to learn.

any focus, and so our *g* will look more like an *s*. Sentences will look like a set of tiger claw marks. In fields like medicine, this happens despite the fact that weak handwriting skills cause some 7,000 deaths each year.

When it comes to developing a skill, evaluations are also crucial. We need targeted feedback. Training expert Anders Ericsson argues that many practice sessions are useless because there's not enough dedicated monitoring and focused criticism. When most people try and develop their skills, "they don't have a clear idea of what they should improve, and so they're just wasting their time," Ericsson told me.

On this point, I was sinner number one. Before I signed up for classes with Samuels, I would go to the local court to train my skills. I'd shoot around for a half hour, throwing up long jumpers. I didn't really focus my efforts, though. I didn't get any feedback on my footwork or hone certain moves. For a long time, I didn't even track the number of jump shots that fell in.

The experience with Samuels was quite different. We worked on very detailed aspects of the game like a short jumper from the block or a one-dribble pull-up. Between trainings, I had discrete homework like lying on my back and practicing my shooting form. We once had a conversation about how my middle finger should roll off the ball, with my index finger leaving the ball with a downward motion as if I was dipping it into a glass of water.

With Samuels, targeted criticism was a constant. During our practices, I wasn't practicing layups as much as I was practicing hitting the ball high off the glass. I wasn't developing my shot as much as I was making sure that my feet were well placed. Sometimes Samuels would hold my shoes or move my hips to get me into the proper position. "Details first," Samuels would often say, "Details first."

As for my first three-pointer, I reached out to Samuels the following day. In the email, I explained that I had swished a twenty-footer. He shared my surprise—and enthusiasm. An email fired back from him within the hour: "The sky is the limit now!"

In many ways, development in an area of expertise starts with feedback. Once we have a sense of what we want to learn and start to do that learning, we need some information on how we're performing.

My favorite example is Mark Bernstein. A brain surgeon in Toronto, Bernstein once wrote down every single mistake that occurred in his operating room over a ten-year period. If a tube fell to the floor, Bernstein made a note of it. If a suture didn't stick, he'd record it. Even just a bit of miscommunication between Bernstein and a nurse would go into his database, tagged with various details like the date and age of the patient.

Later, when Bernstein and his colleagues looked closely at the data, it turned out that the effort to record errors had a tremendous impact. By writing down mistakes—by creating a feedback system—Bernstein and his team made far fewer gaffs. The effects were immediate—think of it as a performance steroid—and his team's surgical error rate plummeted over the first year. What's more, the effect continued to hold for more than a decade, with Bernstein's error rate eventually declining from more than three mistakes per month to just around one and a half errors per month.

Bernstein was engaged in one of the most basic forms of feedback, a practice known as monitoring, and according to researchers like Ericsson who have written about Bernstein, the practice often comes down to a form of awareness. In order to track outcomes, people have to notice what's going on. In Bernstein's case, this was about attending to mistakes, looking for slipups, reviewing gaffs, and his team's oversights were often pretty obvious. If a machine didn't work right—or a scalpel clanged to the ground—there was an error.

But generally speaking, Bernstein's mistakes were more subtle, small things like a poorly positioned sponge, a delay in anesthesia, a misheard word or command. And it's in this regard that monitoring is so important. To find errors, we need to track errors, to observe our gaffs, and after each surgery, Bernstein would log each mistake in a database, noting the severity of the error, the type of mistake, and the degree to which it could have been prevented.

To help monitor performance, other people will use journals or diaries. For a long time, for instance, I've kept a file in which I'll reflect on my writing performance. Like many people, I frequently make grammatical mistakes, often confusing "which" and "that," and in the document, I'll give examples of my slipups as well as pen some notes about how to avoid errors—or boost performance—in the future.

Still others swear by video as a way to track outcomes. In football, for instance, former NFL coach Jon Gruden has a massive library of football games. Today Gruden works for ESPN, and he still keeps up the data set of footage, including videos of practices going back more than two decades. "I break down the tape like I'm a quality-control coach," Gruden once told a reporter.

Part of the benefit of this sort of monitoring is that it pushes us to be more aware. When we're tracking our performance, we're more focused on improving, and in many areas, people often pay almost no attention to their performance.

Driving is a good example. Few of us make any effort to get better at navigating a car. Indeed, most of us still park as poorly as we did as when we were seventeen, or we brake too much going into curves. I've watch people drive straight for miles with their blinker signal still on.

Public speaking is similar. Most of us often have to give talks in front of large groups of colleagues. We're called on to present in front of bosses or clients. But people frequently make the same mistakes over and over again, like a broken wind-up toy. They speak too quickly, or they don't make eye contact, or they twist a ring on their finger nervously.

What's easy to forget is that we're all part automaton. Whether it's playing football or doing brain surgery, it doesn't take much for a task to become a mindless habit, an unthinking custom. This helps explain why monitoring can be so powerful. We are stepping out of automatic mode and asking ourselves: Am I doing this correctly? Did I make a mistake? How could I do better?

When we track performance, patterns of behavior also become

more clear. In Bernstein's case, he found that an overwhelming percentage of his team's surgical errors were preventable, things easily avoided like the contamination of a scalpel. Surprisingly, Bernstein also discovered that more patients generally led to fewer errors, not more. He also showed that adding new staff members to his surgical team didn't lead to any noticeable uptick in mistakes.

Granted, this sort of close monitoring has its downsides. Tracking outcomes can be embarrassing. For me at least, it remains shaming to admit that I still mix up "which" and "that," even though I'm a professional writer. Worse, Bernstein's team once dropped a piece of someone's skull "about the size of play card" onto the floor during a surgery. "Mortified" is how Bernstein describes the experience.

Yet, this type of focused awareness boosts outcomes. Increased observation of our performance makes us better at just about everything. Over the years, for instance, there's been a lot of debate over the best approach to lose weight. Every day, it seems there's a new approach to dieting, from the Atkins diet, which bans carbs, to the Paleo Diet, which demands that your meals looks like they did some three thousand years ago. And that's not to mention all the dramatically named supplements and shakes that line grocery store aisles.

Not long ago *Vox* writer Julia Belluz rang up twenty of the nation's most respected diet experts to figure out what actually worked when it came to losing weight. Belluz limited herself to top researchers and thinkers, people who really care about solid, research-based evidence. "What do your patients who lose weight and keep it off have in common? Where do people go wrong?" she asked.

So what was one of the top recommendations? Surprisingly, it wasn't about any sort of specific approach like Weight Watchers or Atkins. No mention of three-hour gym works out. Instead, Belluz found that effective dieters who keep off the pounds over the long-term are "are good at tracking—what they eat and how much they weigh."

In other words, people who lose weight—and keep it off—monitor their weight constantly. They jump on the scale weekly at least—and follow every calorie. The University of Ottawa's Yoni Freedhoff recommended a food diary, in which individuals write down everything that they eat each day. Food diaries "aren't sexy or fun, but before you start a diet, you need to know where you're at to know what you should change," Freedhoff told Belluz.

In this regard, learning isn't any different, and Freedhoff's advice applies to expertise just as much as it applies to diets: In order to develop any sort of skill, you need to know what you know—and what you need to change.

There's actually a more powerful form of feedback than monitoring, and it typically requires some sort of external evaluation, some outside criticism. Indeed, more than anything, it was external feedback that boosted my basketball skills.

This fact was clear in my early practices with Dwane Samuels. Like a type of soothsayer, he could see things that I could not see, and in many areas, I simply had no sense of the scope of my weaknesses.

Take something like squaring off to the basket while taking a jump shot. As far as basketball goes, the idea is canonical, the first commandment of the shooter's bible, and I had come across the idea many times before my basketball classes.

But without realizing it, I would fire off the basketball at a diagonal slant to the basket, twisting like a preteen ballerina. Samuels pointed out the issue at our first practice, and I soon changed my footing. It took a few more weeks for the adjustment to stick, but the change made my shots far more likely to go in.

The value of this sort of feedback goes well beyond basketball, and a big part of the reason is that it's hard to uncover our own mistakes. Even if we monitor, we can't uncover all of our errors. This is the nature of learning, the nature of knowledge, another reminder of the Value of Educators: We need outsiders to offer targeted criticism, to give outside judgments.

Take writing this book as another example. When I submitted a draft to my editor, I had read the text countless times, reviewed each sentence with the devoted care of a 17th-century monk. Typos? I thought there weren't any. Gaps of logic? I assumed that I had addressed them all.

But my editor, Marisa Vigilante, found rough spots—obvious gaffs, limp reasoning, unsteady prose and structure. Even before I submitted a draft, Vigilante told me that this happens with just about every author, famous or not famous, new or experienced. "It's impossible to edit your own work for this very reason, no matter how smart or skilled you are," Vigilante told me, "I'm your second reader."

This idea also explains why outside criticism is often a little humiliating. After all, it's hard to hard to hear that we're doing something wrong, especially when you know you could be doing better. More exactly, it often pained me to see Vigilante's edits, because they were so on target.

Without question, there are issues with feedback. It can go too far, for one, and good feedback doesn't tell people what exactly to do. People still need to produce their learning—they need to do—and generally speaking, helpful feedback provides guidance. It gives us a way to direct our development.

Let's say, for example, that you thought that the Spanish word for rooster was *pollo*. A weak form of feedback would have just given you the answer. ("You got that wrong; the correct answer is *gallo*.") Or it might not provide any feedback at all. ("Please go to the next question.")

The best feedback mixes an observation with a structured way to produce the proper outcome. In the rooster example, for instance, the most effective feedback would indicate that the answer was wrong—and then would provide some slight hints. ("The correct translation for rooster starts with a *g*.") If someone still doesn't provide the correct answer, then perhaps another tip ("think *ga*") until the correct answer (*gallo*).

This sort of structured feedback is important early in the learning process, and thoughtful criticism and guidance can have a tremendous impact for beginners. But over time, feedback should fade—and people should do more to produce their own answers, to engage in more mental doing, to creating understanding. "Simply re-presenting a fact or concept, whether as feedback after an error or not, is far less effective than having people 'generate' the information," psychologist Bob Bjork told me.

The role of feedback also explains why curriculum is so important, and textbooks and worksheets and other forms of practice turn out to have a huge impact on what we learn. I've seen this in my own research with my colleagues Matt Chingos and Chelsea Straus, and the effects of a high-quality curriculum are about the same as the effects of a high-quality instructor, even though high-quality curriculum is often cheaper.

To put it differently, if you're a student who has a bad teacher and a bad curriculum, you're better off fighting for a better curriculum. The outcomes are about the same, but the cost is lower—and frankly, it's often a lot easier to get a new textbook than to find a new teacher.

So what does shoddy curriculum look like? Well, it gives bad feedback, and the practice sheets and textbooks will often simply provide answers to students without pushing them to build their thinking. Weak textbooks also tend to be shallow in that they'll cover lots of different topics in very cursory ways so that students don't get extended practice in an area.

Despite the evidence on feedback, it seems that people generally have to come to this conclusion on their own. We need to discover our own desire for outside advice. Not long ago, the doctor and *New Yorker* writer Atul Gawande hired a coach to help him develop as a surgeon. It was difficult at first. Like priests, doctors often work behind irreproachable doors, and Gawande felt embarrassed. No one had observed his work in the operating room for almost a decade. "Why should I expose myself to scrutiny and fault-finding?" he asked.

Even for someone at the top of his career like Gawande, though, the effects were noticeable, and he gained insights into his practice, developing new skills and approaches. Over time, Gawande also provided better support for other doctors, letting his residents grapple with key ideas before helping them. But perhaps above all, Gwande writes, "I know that I'm learning again."

When it comes to feedback and the process of learning, there's one more important point—people need explanations. To learn, we need to understand why we're wrong—and get feedback on our thinking. This is crucial when it comes to developing expertise because we typically gain skills and understanding in order to have a new way of reasoning through a situation.

To address this issue, some educators have rolled out programs known as cognitive apprenticeships, and I once met up with psychologist Gary Klein to find out more. In the field of psychology, Klein is pretty well known. His research on the power of gut decisions revolutionized how people understand the role of emotions in expertise, and Malcolm Gladwell's book *Blink* depended in large part on Klein's research.

Klein recently developed a bit of software called ShadowBox, which uses a cognitive apprenticeship approach to learning, and on one afternoon, I watched a video from the training program, which began with a YouTube clip of a police officer stepping toward a young skateboarder.

"Give me the board now," the officer said.

The scene was a suburban town just outside of Boston, and the officer was short and broad with the square chest of a lineman. The young skateboarder was maybe sixteen or seventeen. He was taller than the cop but much skinnier, and he clutched his skateboard like a four-year-old holding his favorite toy.

"I'm a legal citizen of the United States," the young skateboarder said.

"Give me the board now."

"Can I have a reason, please?"

"Because you've been warned," the officer said, stepping closer to the young man. "Give me the board *now.*"

I hit the mouse pad, pausing the video, the two men now frozen in time, nose to nose on the computer screen.

At the time, Klein and I were perched in his living room. The iMac in front of us had a large screen. Klein had turned up the volume, and it felt like we were watching a cell phone video that would soon go viral.

As part of the training program, I was supposed to note every time that the officer was escalating—or de-escalating—the situation and then provide a detailed reason. So with the film clip paused in front of me, I typed out some sentences in the blank box on the screen, indicating how I thought that it would be a good time for the officer to defuse the situation.

For Klein, this was one of the most important aspects of the program. Specifically, it was a way for me to get insights into my reasoning, to compare my thinking to the thinking of experts. Before showing me the video, Klein had a panel of law enforcement experts review the clip and provide advice on how they might handle the situation. Klein and his team then compiled the expert line of thinking, so I could match up my reasoning against the reasoning of the law enforcement experts.

The clip started up again, and I made a few more notes about moments of escalation—and de-escalation—and then, at the end, a dialogue box popped up: "Consulting with the experts," it said.

No surprise, I flunked the assessment. I identified only one of the crucial moments. Even worse, I didn't even see some of the things that the experts had flagged. For instance, the experts in policing had noticed that the officer had put his hand on the young man's skateboard. But that gesture was far beyond my ken. I also didn't make much of the fact that the police officer was pointing at the skateboarder, while the experts had argued that pointing was unnecessarily aggressive.

But this was the idea: I was getting feedback on feedback. Like an instructor, Klein narrated the experience, explaining why I had misjudged certain experiences, where I had gaps in my logic of the experience, and why the experts saw ways to convince the young man to hand over the skateboard voluntarily.

Expert John Hattie has spent a lot of time researching the value of feedback. He believes that it's one of the most importance aspects of learning, and every night that his sons would come home from school, Hattie would pester them over dinner with a question along the lines of "What feedback did you receive about your learning today?"

For Hattie, effective feedback isn't just about gaining corrective information, although certainly that can help a lot. Instead, Hattie and other experts argue that feedback works best when it offers someone a new form of reasoning, when it changes how someone thinks about a topic. As Hattie writes, feedback "is most powerful when it addresses faulty interpretations."

In this argument, robust feedback is like a type of map. It helps people see how they will progress forward in their understanding. In his book *Visible Learning,* Hattie puts this idea well, and he argues that good feedback always includes some aspect of "feed forwarding," or giving people a sense of where they will go next with their learning.

This all brings us back to cognitive apprenticeships because the programs underscore this more dynamic approach. This was clear in ShadowBox, and as I worked through the program on the police officers with Klein, I developed a sense of how the law enforcement experts reasoned about the situation.

For example, what mattered most for the law enforcement professionals was the trust—or lack of trust—between the officers and the people in the town, and they thought that the officer should have done more to de-escalate the situation, for instance, by stepping back from the young man and giving him more personal space.

For his part, Klein calls these sorts of shifts in reasoning a type of mind-set change, but all in all, it's much the same idea. In the end, we learn to change our thinking. We learn to reason more effectively, and at least in the case of police officers, you want to know why it's bad practice to point your finger at people if you want them to trust you.

The Nature of Struggle—and Repetition

If developing a skill begins with feedback, then we're bound to struggle. People will inevitably flounder. After all, feedback is about discovering what you're doing wrong.

Admittedly, this is not a popular view, certainly not of learning, and just about everyone dreams of trouble-free ways to improve. We want learning to be simple and straightforward, like eating a bowl of cereal or taking out the trash. This desire is evident in just about every subject, whether it's automobile engineering or computer-generated cartography.

One recent headline-making example is an app called DragonBox. The approach supposedly "secretly teaches math" by having kids play an algebra game. *USA Today* declared the app to be "brilliant."

Forbes dubbed it "impressive." Tens of thousands of people have downloaded it.

As a learning tool, DragonBox does not seem to teach students all that much, though, and people who play the game don't do any better at solving algebraic equations, according to one recent study. Researcher Robert Goldstone recently examined the software, and he told me that the app didn't appear to provide any more grounding in algebra than "tuning guitars."

In the bluntest of terms, there's simply no such thing as effortless learning. To develop a skill, we're going to be uncomfortable, strained, often feeling a little embattled. Just about every major expert in the field of the learning sciences agrees on this point. Psychologist Daniel Willingham writes that students often struggle because thinking is difficult. Cognitive scientist Bob Bjork argues that mastery is about "desirable difficulties." Practice guru Anders Ericsson calls practice "hard work."

Even history's most powerful minds have argued this point. It was Aristotle—the star pupil of Socrates, the tutor of Alexander the Great—who once argued that "learning is no amusement but is accompanied with pain."

We've come across a couple of reasons why the learning process requires this sort of cognitive pain. Learning is a matter of mental doing, as we've seen. Plus, excellent learning doesn't have a comfort zone, as Janet Metcalfe argued. In this chapter, we've seen some of the awkward embarrassments of landing feedback.

But there's one more reason, and it turns out that the development of an area of expertise requires repetition. In order to hone an area of expertise, we need to engage that area of expertise multiple times, preferably in multiple ways. To a degree, this is obvious in athletic endeavors. No one learns an overhand serve in tennis on their first try. People don't gain pole-vaulting skills in an afternoon.

But it also turns out to be true for any sort of knowledge. Psychologist Graham Nuthall pioneered a version of this idea some years ago, and as part of his research, Nuthall showed that people needed to engage with an idea at least three times before they actually learned it.

No matter what the material—math, geography, obscure civics lessons—people needed to experience the material a few times before they could gain any sort of takeaway. "If the information was incomplete or not experienced on three different occasions, then the student did not learn the concept," Nuthall argued.

Yet even three times might not be enough. In fact, three times might be the minimum, and in many cases, we have to come across skills and knowledge again and again and again. Expertise needs to become a kind of habit. Foreign languages give us a good way to understand this idea: If you want to become excellent in Russian, you need to have a rich Russian vocabulary, one that's highly practiced and seamlessly fluent. If you want to say, "Can I have a coffee?" in a café in Moscow, the word for coffee—"кофе"—needs to jump to the edge of your mind without hesitation.

This is true for just about every area of complex mastery. To develop a skill, people need to be fluent in the essentials. If you want to become a lawyer, you can't wonder what the word "plaintiff" means. Political scientists don't spend a lot of time thinking about the difference between a bill and a law. Expert filmmakers don't have to look up the word "gaffer."

Practically speaking, this means that if you want to hone your golf skills, take tens of thousands of golf putts. Want to become an expert in tango? Be prepared to put on your dancing shoes every day for a few years. Want to get better at Russian? Practice your Russian vocabulary repeatedly and "actively seek out new words," says Ericsson.

This sort of practice for fluency isn't mindless, as Ericsson stresses. We have to forever be looking to getting better. In other words, the comfort zone of learning always needs to be shifting, getting a little harder, always moving upwards, ensuring that each learning session is a struggle.

In recent years, researchers have debated a ten-year rule when it comes to expertise. Others like Malcolm Gladwell describe a ten-thousand-hour mark. But really, we should shrug. Ten years—or ten thousand hours—there's nothing revolutionary in the idea that expertise requires a massive investment in time and effort. Even in the Middle Ages, apprentices would often work for an expert for a decade before going off on their own.

Indeed, for experts, this idea is self-evident. Director Quentin Tarantino has watched so many films over the years that his friends paint him as obsessed, someone who watches movies all the time. So when a reporter once asked Tarantino about how he became an expert in film, the director laughed and threw up his hands, seemingly exasperated by the question, and said, "Well, when you kind of clear out everything in your life and focus on one thing, you better know a lot about it."

Let's look more closely at a type of development that requires a lot of struggle, something that experts call retrieval practice.

Bennett Schwartz is one of the nation's leading memory experts, and when I visited Schwartz in his office at Florida International University, he was standing at his desk. A soft sunlight crowded the room. Large windows framed the palm tree-lined quad outside.

Dressed in a short-sleeved shirt and slacks, Schwartz appeared to be quietly talking to himself, with hushed, mumbled words, and for a long moment, it seemed as if he was some sort of monk, living in another, more esoteric world.

"Hi?" I said tentatively.

Schwartz immediately turned around, putting the book away with an easy gesture.

It turned out that when I walked into the room, Schwartz was honing his Scrabble skills. He had a Scrabble tournament the next day, and he was practicing words from a book devoted to the game. "The director is allowing me to play against the good Scrabble players," Schwartz told me, laughing. "I have to make sure I know my words."

So how exactly does one of the nation's premier memory experts develop his Scrabble skills?

Well, Schwartz uses a type of self-quizzing: In order to hone his expertise, he's constantly interrogating himself to see if he can recall various words. So when Schwartz stops at a red light—or if he's just waiting in his office—he'll ask himself questions about what he's learned and what he wants to learn.

Known as retrieval practice, the approach fills the recent literature on memory, sometimes showing effects some 50 percent more than other forms of learning. In one well-known study, one group of subjects read a passage four times. A second group read the passage just one time, but then the same group practiced recalling the passage three times. When the researchers followed up with both groups a few days later, the group that had practiced recalling the passage learned significantly more. In other words, subjects who tried to recall the information instead of rereading it showed far more expertise.

Within the learning sciences, retrieval practice is sometimes referred as the testing effect since the practice is a matter of people asking themselves specific questions about what they just learned. But in many ways, the idea goes much deeper than quizzing, and what's important about retrieval practice is that people take steps to recall what they know. They ask themselves questions about their knowledge, making sure that it can be produced.

More concretely, retrieval practice isn't like a multiple-choice test, which has people chose from a few answers. It's more like writing a three-sentence essay in your head: You're recalling the idea and summarizing it in a way that makes sense. In this regard, we can think of retrieval practice as a type of mental doing: It's a way to actively create the webs of meaning that support what we know. As psychologist Bob Bjork told me, "The act of retrieving information from our memories is a powerful learning event."

A lot of the benefit of retrieval practice goes back to the nature of long-term memory. In her book *Mastermind,* science writer Maria Konnikova argues that long-term memory should be thought of as a type of attic. It's a storage space for our recollections, and in this analogy, our specific memories are often little more than cardboard boxes, a collection of remembrances, hanging loosely together by their connections.

Konnikova's idea emphasizes the loose web that holds our memories together, and if a box—or memory—sits for too long, it fades. Dust gathers.

Images degrade. The item eventually becomes gray, unrecognizable, without meaning.

Retrieval practice, then, help us ensure that we know what's in a memory box. It pushes us to foster associations—and make more durable forms of knowledge. When we reach into our memory and recall what's in the cardboard box, the recollection becomes longer lasting, more tightly woven into the neural ties that build understanding. As Schwartz argues, "retrieval practice also reminds us to keep track of where things are in memory—thus, they are more easily accessible when recently practiced."

Retrieval practice goes far beyond facts, and there are ways to use retrieval practice to hone conceptual understanding, too. One approach recommends that people first create a pile of cards that lists facts. Then people should build a second pile that asks things like "give a real life example" or "draw this concept." In this approach, learning is a matter of picking one card from the first pile and a card from the second pile, and then executing the task.

Retrieval practice doesn't have to be written down, either. When I was in college, I worked as a teaching assistant for a class that relied on a form of retrieval practice, and once a week, I would gather a group of students in a classroom and verbally ask them rapid-fire questions. The class was relatively short—just 45 minutes a week. But it was easy to see the effects of the free-recall type of practice, and the more the students retrieved their knowledge, the more they learned.

Schwartz has been doing the same thing for the students in his psychology classes, pushing them to ask themselves repeatedly about what they know. "For example, my students have to take a quiz every week," Schwartz told me, "and they would much prefer not to take a quiz every week. They don't like it. They complain. Every week, I get excuses about dead grandmothers." But the short exams ensure that students continually construct their memory boxes, and students end up posting higher grades on the final exams.

As for Schwartz, he did well at the Scrabble tournament, too. The director placed him in one of the highest divisions, and he went against some of the best players in the state of Florida. Using his technique of retrieval practice, Schwartz managed to notch wins in about a third of his games. As Schwartz joked in a follow-up email, "I didn't finish last, so I did okay."

We can see the benefits of struggle in our brain. Indeed, it appears that at a very basic neurological level, grappling with material in a dedicated way promotes a type of shifting of our neural circuits—and a richer form of expertise.

I learned a lot about this idea when I met up with Yuzheng Hu at a suburban coffee shop one afternoon. A researcher on brain plasticity at the National Institutes of Health, Hu has long been fascinated with how the brain develops over time.

Hu's story starts in rural China, where he grew up just a few hundred miles from the border with Vietnam. In his tiny village, running water was a luxury. Cars were rare. Few people had more than a high school education. "In my village, not much has changed since the Ching Dynasty," Hu told me.

Hu was one of the few who went to college, landing a spot at one of China's Ivy League schools, Zhejiang University, and he soon began researching something called white matter. A type of neural transmission cable, white matter helps distribute messages throughout the brain. It makes information flow more effectively, allowing electronic pulses to jump more easily from one neuron to the next. If the brain has a form of wiring, white matter serves as the copper, the substance that conducts the messages.

In one of his first studies, Hu and some colleagues decided to see if certain types of practice might boost white matter within the brain, and so they compared a group of young subjects who received a rigorous type of math training and those who didn't. The data suggested that the math approach built up the brain's transmission material, and under the bright scan of the MRI machine, certain white matter zones of the brain like the corpus callosum pulsed stronger in people who had studied the harder, more dedicated math skills.

Hu's study was built on a decade's worth of research that shows that there's very little fixed about the brain. Our brain systems are not like a piece of metal, something rigid in its fundamentals, hard and inflexible. The brain, instead, is something that can change, something that can adapt to its environment, more neural cloud than neural cement. If you master karate, for instance, there are clear, structural changes that happen to white matter structures within your brain. Similar changes happen when we learn to juggle—or learn to meditate.

This idea has a number of important implications for how we develop a skill. For one, there are far fewer neural set points than we generally believe. Our brains are not fixed at birth. Our mental abilities are not preprogrammed. For a long time, for instance, people believed in the notion of "critical periods," or the idea that we need to acquire certain skills at particular times in our life. But except for a few narrow abilities, we can acquire most skills at any time.

But what's new—and really most important—about this line of research is how exactly the brain builds new structures, and it seems that the brain creates white matter in an effort to deal with mental struggle. When there's a large gap between what we know and what we can do, the brain shifts its structures to address the issue. A group of German researchers recently put together a new way of understanding why this happens, and they argue that when "demand" overwhelms the brain's "supply," we build new neural structures.

When Hu and I met up, he argued that the brain responds to an opportunity to learn. When faced with rigor, it rises to the occasion. "This is your brain optimizing the way you perform that task," Hu told me. "If you practice something a lot, your brain will think, 'This is important,' and you will develop a strategy to better perform it."

In other words, the brain itself seems to understand the value of struggle, of learning as doing. On the evening that I met up with Hu at Starbucks, I gained the confidence to ask him about his right hand.

Honestly, it's hard to miss the deformity: Two of Hu's fingers are fused together. Hu told me that it was a birth defect. He had no idea if the abnormality had a name or a cause, and when I pressed him about it, Hu shrugged and sighed and told me that he rarely thinks about it.

Hu's nonchalance made sense. The disability didn't impact his abil-

True or false: Teaching others is an effective way to learn.

ity to work or drive or play with his son. But I also came to a slightly different takeaway, and it seemed to me that Hu's brain had already adapted. White matter had been built. Struggle had been overcome. Faced with a difficult hurdle, his brain had optimized itself.

This sort of neural optimization is crucial as we consider one more aspect of development, of struggling to acquire the basics of a skill or a bit of expertise: errors.

The Psychology of Errors

Learning researchers haven't always believed in the power of mistakes. Struggle wasn't always part of the learning process, and in more passive, more behaviorist models of learning, mistakes are exactly that: mistakes. They show that people are not learning properly. Blunders are a sign that someone is doing something wrong.

But it's now clear that understanding doesn't transfer immutably from one person's head to another. Our brain is not a simple storage device, a lockbox, or a warehouse that serves as some type of memory depot. Instead, we have to make sense of ideas, to grapple with expertise, and that means that errors are simply unavoidable.

This notion is pretty clear in something like retrieval practice. If you're constantly asking yourself questions, you're bound to have some misses. Someone like Bennett Schwartz, for instance, often gets something wrong as he practices for his Scrabble tournament.

Just as important, errors create meaning. They build understanding. For an example, consider this question: *What's the capital of Australia?* Unless you're from Australia, your first guess is probably Sydney. But that's not correct.

Second guess? Maybe Melbourne? Again, wrong.

Or perhaps Brisbane? Perth? Adelaide? All those answers are also off the mark.

The correct response, it turns out, is Canberra.

I know. Weird. If you're not from Australia, the answer of Canberra probably comes with a buzzing shock of surprise. A sort of *Wait, what, really? Canberra is the capital of Australia?*

But that feeling—that zinging moment—is learning. It's the signal of a shift in understanding. When we make a gaff, we search for meaning, and so we learn more effectively. This idea goes back to memories as a bunch of boxes that we discussed earlier. If there's an error—and it's a salient one—we put a red, Sharpie-made x on the memory box in our metal attic. Within our brains, we're telling ourselves: *Remember this idea. It's important.*

The problem here is undeniable, of course. No one likes mistakes. Errors are sharp and painful, humiliating and demoralizing. Even the smallest of gaffs—a misspoken word, a blundered errand—can haunt people for years. In this sense, mistakes make us rethink who we are; they're a threat to our being.

Not long ago, I met up with mathematician Jordan Ellenberg. By all accounts, he was a boy genius, and at least according to newspaper legend, Ellenberg was reading road signs at the age of three. By the age of seven, he could do high school-level math. He aced the math SAT, with the *Washington Post* dubbing him a "true genius" at seventeen. Today, Ellenberg is a professor of math at the University of Wisconsin, with a collection of well-regarded articles and books to his name.

Now, I haven't talked about talent much in this book for a pretty simple reason: Its role in learning is overblown, part hype, part excuse. Too often we conflate aptitude with everything else that matters like effort and dedication, practice and learning strategy. In the simplistic manner of a toddler, we want a single explanation for success, and so we cling to the idea of raw ability.

What's more, we forget that learning itself shapes intelligence. The two factors are deeply intertwined. Over the past few decades, IQ scores have been steadily ticking upward, and many experts believe the cause is schooling. "I always think of IQ tests as measures that combine both innate ability and learning," economist Ludger Woessmann told me.

Finally, a small but growing body of research suggest that how we learn can be more important than smarts. We've come across this idea already in this book, and robust learning methods have been shown to be one of the best predictors of academics success, with skills like metacognition being just as important as raw intelligence.

There are, of course, the occasional Jordan Ellenbergs—people who are clearly gifted, outliers on the intelligence bell curve. But there's a catch. Even geniuses need to struggle. In order to develop a skill, they will spend hours making mistakes, confused and bewildered.

When Ellenberg was a child, he was skeptical of this hard-edged aspect of learning, and he thought that errors meant that someone lacked intelligence. He believed the term "hardworking" was cruel, if not rudely derogatory. Like having red hair or being short, genius was something someone had or didn't have, and all in all, Ellenberg enjoyed being dubbed a prodigy. For him, talent was a type of gift, something that made learning almost effortless, his special power.

When I sat down with Ellenberg in a coffee shop, it was clear that he now believed something very different about the nature of building a skill. After spending years working at the highest level of math, he realized that learning demands mistakes. Errors are necessary for expertise. Doubtful blunders are eternal. "You have to have an incredible tolerance for failure," he told me. "You'll spend 95 percent of the time completely confused."

It felt good when I heard Ellenberg make this argument about the nature of mastery. He might be the smartest person that I've ever met in person. He's certainly the smartest person that I've ever shared a slice of pie with, and in the end, we have to realize that mistakes happen. All. The. Time. Learning or not learning, people are going to goof. Even the best learners—and the most talented mathematicians like Ellenberg—have slips and blunders.

But more than that, errors are at the essence of thought. They're at the core of developing any sort of idea. To learn, to develop any sort of expertise, there are going to be mistakes because that's what understanding requires. In her book *Being Wrong,* writer Kathryn

Schulz argues that banning errors is like banning skepticism—it robs of us a deeper form of reason. Mistakes, she writes, are an assured part of engaged thinking: Errors, she argues, are at the very core of being human.

If errors—and struggle—are an inevitable part of learning, we need to be prepared for them. While this notion is new to learning, it's been at the center of sports for centuries, and just about every coach—from pee-wees to the pros—will give throaty speeches on the value of emotional perseverance, about the need for mental toughness.

Football coach Jim Harbaugh is famous for these sorts of growling speeches. Likewise, the late women's basketball coach Pat Summitt. These inspirational talks generally hit the same themes. Delivered in a loud, smoky voice, with the players huddled around the locker room, the coach will ask something like: "Will you give it your all? Will you remain strong? Will you bounce back from losses, from hardship, and inevitable errors?"

Coach Herb Brooks gave perhaps the most well known locker room speech in 1980. At the time, the men's Olympic hockey team was a bunch of college students, most of them barely out of their teens. In contrast, the Russian team had a bench of superstars who had been dominating the sport for years.

Before their Olympic game, Brooks gathered the American players and underscored a type of emotional resilience. The Soviets might score goals, the Russians might even be the better team, he acknowledged. But Brooks pushed the Americans to believe in themselves. "You were meant to be here at this moment," Brooks told the players. "You were meant to be here at this game."

The young men were unquestionably inspired, and while the Soviets slashed a puck into the American net early in the game, the United States came back, eventually beating the powerhouse Soviet team 4 to 3. It was known as the Miracle on Ice.

Although the notion of mental toughness has sparked quite a few athletic victories, the idea has only recently influenced the practice of learning. In many ways, it all goes back to a single study, the marshmallow test. For many, the study needs no introduction, and Walter Mischel's ingenious experiment—first conducted in 1968—is among the most well-known experiments of the twentieth century.

Like most brilliant experiments, the study itself was pretty simple: Mischel invited a toddler into a room. The child could either immediately eat a small treat like a marshmallow, or the child could wait and eventually land two treats. Many of us are familiar with the results: Some gobbled up the sweet-tasting treat—they did not delay gratification. Others waited it out, being patient and controlled enough to land a second treat.

This sort of emotional kryptonite, a resilience against short-term decisions, made a lifetime of difference: Mischel found that the four-year-olds' ability to deal with their desire and emotions paid off in all sorts of ways. In fact, the kids who could delay grabbing for the marshmallow did better in school later, were more confident, and had an easier time dealing with stressful moments.

While Mischel's work sparked an academic blooming, it's done far too little to change the way that society operates, especially when it comes to dealing with mistakes. Many schools continue to protect their children from anything that smacks of failure. Helicopter parents reward all actions equally, throwing "good jobs" at their children for nonaccomplishments like going down a playground slide.

While the science of perseverance is young, it's clear that people need ways to deal with the emotional side of errors and setbacks, of losses and disappointments. We need a type of resilience. In this regard, the process of learning is often the process of emotional control.

This practice often starts with knowledge, and Yale University professor Marc Brackett argues that people have far more resilience if they identify their feelings. Whether it's a fierce argument with a friend—or just wanting a marshmallow—Brackett recommends labels. So we should tell ourselves: *My buddy is making me angry* or *I would really love that marshmallow.*

Once we know our emotions, we can take steps to manage them. After people tag a certain feeling, they can begin to think that feeling

POP QUIZ #10

A group of students wants to improve their long division skills. What is the best way for them to practice long division?

A. Do one long session of practicing division problems.

B. Do the same division problem over and over again.

C. Do some division problems, some multiplication problems, and then some addition problems before they go back to practicing division again.

D. There's no need to practice division problems over and over again. Just learn about the deeper underlying concepts.

through. Often this type of emotional coping requires a type of pep talk—we need to speak to ourselves, offering ourselves support after a defeat or difficulty.

A number of recent studies shed light on this process, and it helps if we speak to ourselves with authority. If someone wants that marshmallow, they should tell themselves: *You might like the one marshmallow right now, but two marshmallows will be even better.* Indeed, research shows that the second person "you" is more effective than using the first-person "I" in self-talk. The reason? The second person is more definitive, and so people are more likely to listen to the voice in their head.

Community plays a role, too. Fordham University's Joshua Brown has been researching social and emotional programs for years, and he argues that a lot of emotional resilience comes to down to a sense of social connection, a feeling of group-ish togetherness. One of the reasons that resisting a marshmallow was so hard for the children in the seminal Mischel study, for instance, was that the kids were alone in a room without any friends, without anyone to offer support.

For his part, Mischel argues for the shifting of thoughts. To boost emotional management, to be more resilient, people should reframe difficult activities in a different light. If someone is trying to lose weight, for instance, then a marshmallow should be seen as "poison" rather than a "treat," according to Mischel, because it makes the marshmallow itself seem far less tempting.

Similarly, Mischel advocates for "if-then" plans. So instead of thinking, *Maybe I'll study later,* people should think, *If I study now, then I can go out later.* Mischel argues that clear rules make it simpler for people to manage their emotions because there's less emotion to manage. Instead of feeling or even thinking, people are relying on a type of habit, and that takes less emotional energy. As Mischel argues, the goal is "taking the effort out of effortful control."

For all the discussion of different approaches to dealing with emotions, we still haven't really discussed with one of the most important underlying questions of this part of the learning process: Do we actually believe that setbacks are really good for us?

Better yet, think back to the last time that you failed at something: Maybe you goofed in a memo to your boss or perhaps you said something stupid to a friend.

After the error, did you think to yourself: *Great. Let me think about how I can be better?* Or did you think to yourself: *Shoot, I've always been bad at that.*

Psychologist Carol Dweck has been studying these different responses for decades, and in a series of studies, Dweck has shown that some of us are secret essentialists, members of what might be called Camp Nature. In this approach, people believe that nature—biology, genes, DNA—are the key determinants of success. People, then, are either smart or dumb, strong or weak, good or bad, and when we fail at something, we think: *Shoot, I've always been bad at that.*

In contrast, Dweck argues there are people who might be called nurturers. For them, any skill—surfing, math—can be developed. It's a thing that we can sharpen. With practice and development, anything can be achieved. These sorts of people are optimistic, of course. But more than that, they see the world as a place where people can grow and change. In short, Camp Improvement believes in progress, and when nurturers experience failure, they wonder: *Great. Let me think about how I can better?*

While Dweck's work has been around for a while—and might be just as popular as Mischel's work—recent research shows that these views have a tremendous impact on how people approach learning, particularly any sort of learning that requires challenge.

People in Camp Improvement, for instance, are far more likely to engage in mental doing, and studies show that they are more likely to self-quiz. The same goes with parents who are in Camp Improvement: They spend more time doing academic work with their children. In a way, people in Camp Improvement are simply more likely to believe in effort.

When I interviewed Dweck recently, she argued that our attitudes toward errors are often deeply social, and just a few words from a mentor or leader or parent are enough to spark a shift from Camp Nature to Camp Improvement.

Indeed, in one early study, some researchers praised kids for their performance with just the words: *You're so smart.* Others praised kids for their effort with just the words: *You're so hard working,* and even that small difference was enough to make an impact.

More recently, Dweck has found that actions have a far deeper impact than words when it comes to these sorts of Camp Nature and Camp Improvement attitudes. For instance, Dweck and a colleague showed not long ago that parents' beliefs didn't always transfer to their kids. More specifically, if a parent praised a kid's effort, that wasn't always enough to promote a Team Improvement approach in the child.

What mattered more was how parents actually reacted when a child experienced failure. Did the parents discuss the failure as a lack of ability like someone in Camp Nature might? Or did the parents discuss the mistakes in terms of a learning opportunity like someone in Camp Improvement might? If parents took the second approach, their kids were far more likely to be in Camp Improvement. Put differently, if parents actively showed that failure provided growth, kids were far more likely to also believe in the idea.

For individuals, some of the solutions revolve, again, around what we tell ourselves, and Dweck recommends changing your inner dia-

POP QUIZ #11

What is the best way to learn from some text?

A. Read and reread the text.
B. Explain key ideas to yourself while reading.
C. Underline key concepts.
D. Use a highlighter.

logue. Tell yourself not to worry about mistakes, to focus on improvement, to view gaffs and errors as chances to gain a skill or bit of knowledge. After a mistake, for instance, ask yourself, "What can I learn from this? How can I improve?" Dweck recommends.

For others like expert Angela Duckworth, the solutions are similar but a little different. A psychologist at the University of Pennsylvania, Duckworth recommends that people condition themselves to expect difficulty as they gain a skill. So if you make mistakes or struggle, think to yourself, as Duckworth does, "This is normal."

In this regard, Sian Beilock goes even further, stressing that people do more to push themselves, to make sure that they put themselves in more situations where they might make mistakes. "Don't be helpless," she argues. For someone who fears public speaking, that means doing more speaking in front of an audience. For someone who believes that he's not a math person, try to do more math, even if it's just calculating the tip at the restaurant.

This doesn't mean that people shouldn't mindlessly praise practice or effort. Mistakes aren't inherently good. Neither is resilience, and Dweck argues that people should specifically connect praise and outcomes when they're offering kudos. So tell people: "Do you see how your practice paid off?" or "Great job working hard at that and look at your great progress."

What might matter most, then, is a belief in development. To learn from mistakes, to develop in a focused way, there has to be full Camp Improvement buy-in. As Herb Brooks, the coach of the American Olympic hockey team that beat the Soviets, once argued, "Success is won by those who believe in winning and then prepare for that moment. Many want to win, but how many prepare? That is the big difference."

When it came to basketball, I've long held a secret membership in Camp Nature. Despite locker room speeches—and working in the field of education for years—I would often slip into an essentialist attitude while playing the game, the powerful voice of the nature doctrine playing in my mind.

I would miss a short jumper and think, *I've never been a good shooter.* I'd take foul shots and wonder, *Will I air-ball this?* It happened in pickup games, too: Someone would slip past me, and the notion—*always slow*—would flit across my mind.

Like a lot of beliefs, these attitudes have a bitter history, dating back to December 1991. I was a junior in high school at the time, a scrawny kid, barely six feet tall, and I landed on the varsity basketball team, largely to fill out the team's metal bench.

Back then, our high school's rival was Pleasantville, which had a powerhouse center named Otis Hill. At six feet, eight inches and some two hundred pounds, Hill would eventually lead Syracuse to the NCAA championships and play basketball professionally in Poland.

By our high school's low basketball standards, Hill was the second coming of Michael Jordan. He could dunk without a running start: one stride—and rim rocker. In contrast, most of our team's squad could barely touch the rim as high school seniors. I certainly couldn't.

Then came the game. It was a Friday night. We played Pleasantville in their gym with row upon row of fans holding drums and cowbells and airhorns. Within the early minutes, our guard Greg Conway came out on a wildfire streak. Three-pointers, running jumpers, twisting drives. He finished with almost 40 points.

At the same time, our defense smothered Hill, and the Pleasantville star center became so frustrated that he nearly got into a brawl at halftime. Then, in the fourth quarter, we took the lead, with a score of 55 to 54. The crowd was furious. We were a tiny high school riding the lightning bolt of luck. They had a forward who had a genuine chance to dominate in the NBA.

Then, with some 12 seconds to go, our coach, Ed Sands, called me into the game. To be clear, I had probably not played more than ten minutes all season. But one of our team's players fouled out, and now suddenly I was standing on the court, the crowd stretched into the ceiling, the game on the line, our team leading by a single point.

Just about every child dreams of leading a team to victory, making the big throw, the great kick, the huge run that wins the game with just a few seconds on the clock, and I remember thrumming with nervousness as I stood on the hardwood, flattening out my shorts.

Sands told me to play defense against Pleasantville's point guard. *Just keep him from driving at the basket,* Sands told me. *Don't let him dribble past you. Keep him in front of you.*

The guard brought up the ball. The noise of the fans—screaming, chanting, a constant drumming—seemed to envelop the court. I can't say I remember exactly what happened. But scrambling at the top of the key, I played the guard tight. I wanted to swipe the ball, to make the steal. Sand's advice, in other words, slipped me by.

The guard seemed to know as much—and in a flash, he sprinted past me for the layup. Pleasantville was now up by one point, 56 to 54. The seconds ticked away. The game was over. We had lost.

As I recall it, Sands was so angry that he refused to shake my hand, and years later, when we met up for lunch, he remembered the final moments of the game like it was the previous year's NBA finals.

"You were all hyped up, not focusing," Sands told me. "I'm like, 'Give him room, give him room.' But he beats you off the dribble and boom, layup, buzzer, game."

"I remember you wouldn't even talk to me after the loss," I said.

"It could be, absolutely," Sands said, laughing. "Probably this would have been the biggest win in the history of your high school, and you fucked up the whole thing."

The Pleasantville game was not the reason that I stopped playing basketball in my twenties. But at same time, the experience nudged me into Camp Nature when it came to sports. It made me think that I didn't have athletic talent, that I was too slow and uncoordinated. It gave me a label, a box, a classification for my basketball skills: *fucked up the whole thing.*

The point here isn't to relive certain moments of high school. The point is that labels are a type of essentialism. Notions like *fucked up the whole thing* hinge on a Camp Nature attitude, and as Dweck herself argues, essentialism is a form of typecasting.

Another way to think about this idea is that people have different aims for learning. We can aim for mastery, and so we learn in order to improve ourselves, to get better, to hone our skills. In this approach, we're less focused on labels and more interested in improving.

Alternatively, we can be focused on performance, and so we want to reach a certain level of achievement. We need to prove to others that we can do it. When people are really focused on outcomes, they always want to be the winners. They're the ultimate in Camp Nature: They want to show that they won the genetic draw, that they'll win the big game.

There's a continuum, of course. Mastery and performance are not binary sorts of things. The context, the task, the person—all make a difference. The problem is that even a few steps into a more performance-focused approach is dangerous. It makes a task seem like a threat. With a performance approach, all is good if we succeed at the task. Then we think that we're smart or strong or tough. But if we fail with a performance approach, there's no going back—we think that we're dumb or weak or fragile.

It gets worse, though, and a focus on performance makes us more vulnerable to other dangerous attitudes. We are more likely to get pulled in by labels. Take Joshua Aronson, who used to worry that people would see him as part of psychology's old boy network. To explain, Joshua's father, Elliot Aronson, is one of the world's most well regarded psychologists. At Harvard and later at the University of Texas, Elliot helped developed the notion of cognitive dissonance, or the idea that people experience discomfort if they do something in conflict with their ideals.

With this type of pedigree, Joshua was nervous when he arrived at graduate school at Stanford to study psychology. Joshua felt like he was an "affirmative action case," as if the school had accepted Joshua only because his father was a famous academic. Early on, a graduate student told Joshua: *We are honored that you're here,* and the comment sparked a mix of anger and fear. "It was like, 'Welcome, you are under the spotlight,'" Joshua told me.

Over time, Joshua overcame what he jokingly calls his "daddy issues." In other words, Joshua became more focused on gaining mastery than proving himself. But the experience shaped his research interests. During graduate school and later at New York University, Joshua began studying the labels that people use as they're learning, showing that the designations often shape performance.

More exactly, people often live up to the labels that they give themselves. Briefly remind people that Christians don't score well on science problems, for instance, and the people who are Christian will do much worse on science problems. Likewise, women will give a better speech if there are images of successful women in the room.

If people have performance goals, these labels have a lot more power. With a focus on outcomes, we get pulled into damaging narratives, thinking, *I'm always bad. I always fail. Woman always bomb big speeches. Kids of famous professors always get a free pass.*

These sorts of anxious thoughts can be the death knell of any effort to improve. Like a mental computer virus, the thoughts will corrupt short-term memory. In contrast, people with mastery goals have a much easier time shrugging off these sorts of narratives. With a goal of improvement, they don't need to prove their skills to others—and so they're more focused on the task.

I spoke to experts like Joshua Aronson and Carol Dweck long before I began my own dedicated basketball training. But without question, their view of learning shaped my approach.

I joined Camp Improvement, for one, and I would focus my mental energy a lot more on the process of shooting. I tried to see events as a way to improve. So if I missed a jumper, I'd ask myself questions: Were my feet square to the basket? Had I really used my legs? Did I follow through with my hand?

I took a similar approach to errors. If someone dribbled past me, I'd try to view the gaff as a challenge: How did they do it? How could I stop the drive the next time?

At the same time, I tried to keep myself clear of labels. I didn't want to get pulled into narratives. They seemed like the black holes of Camp Nature, and when I threw air balls, for instance, I'd be sure to remind myself that even professionals sometimes miss the rim all together.

Over time, I began to incorporate other, better forms of practice. The skills of learning filtered more into my development, and I did a lot more to monitor my performance. Sometimes I'd video myself while I was honing certain shooting skills so I could figure out better ways to improve my shooting accuracy. I also watched tape of myself playing defense (and realized that I didn't get down low enough to move quickly.)

Practicing on a court near my house, I also used another form of monitoring, noting what percentages of shots that I would make from certain places around the court so I could better track my progress. So I'd note five for ten from the corner, six for ten from the top of the key.

Taking a tip from memory expert and Scrabble player Bennett Schwartz, I also broke up my practice so that it was more quiz-like, more like a type of retrieval practice. So instead of hitting the court once a week, I'd visit a court almost every day to work on my skills. It didn't matter if it was raining or cold. It didn't matter if it was only for fifteen minutes. It didn't matter if I had to jump over a short chain-link fence or if it was the day after Christmas—I would get out and practice.

There were other important strategies, too. I also aimed to make certain skills more automatic, and I'd repeat my foul shot with the exact same movements: two dribbles, a pause, deep knees, and then a high arc.

Above all, I aimed to take a mastery focus. My goals were focused on my own progress: Learn how to rebound better. Try to make a basket every game. Defend better in the post. To be more exact, I improved my self-talk, and if I had a particularly bad night, I would remind myself: *It's just a game.*

Eventually, it all started to come together, puzzle pieces forming a pattern. I remember a Wednesday night when my shots started going in, the sweet sound of a snapping net. I hit one from the corner. I nailed one from the top of the key.

By then my teammates know something had changed. On that night, one teammate asked me barefaced, "Man, you been practicing or something?"

The next morning, I got a text from a different friend: "I heard you were a baller last night."

All in all, I didn't have much to say. I knew that I had practiced. I knew that I had believed. I knew that I had developed.

Chapter 4

EXTEND

IN 1936, THE painter Jackson Pollock signed up for a workshop in New York City. Pollock was twenty-three at the time, with handsome looks and a rebel swagger. In his mind, he was a subversive cowboy with a stubby paintbrush, and he'd roam the streets of Manhattan wearing a cowboy hat and boots, often drinking and brawling, breaking windows and insulting strangers.

The painting workshop was held by Mexican artist David Alfaro Siqueiros. A muralist and dedicated Socialist, Siqueiros was even more of a flag-waving rebel than Pollock. Between stints in art school, Siqueiros fought with a Marxist group. Later the Mexican muralist even tried to gun down Soviet exile Leon Trotsky with a machine gun.

The aim of the Siqueiros workshop was to help young artists like Pollock experiment with paint as a type of medium, to repudiate what Siqueiros saw as the dominance of the easel. In his classes, Siqueiros argued that brushes were little more than awkward sticks. As for the narrow confines of wooden frames, Siqueiros didn't think much of them at all. Art wasn't pretty—it was real—and in his studio, Siqueiros would wear overalls splattered with paint, sprawling himself across the floor while lecturing his students.

"A painter should work the way that a worker works," Siqueiros argued, and throughout the yearlong workshop, the Mexican artist encouraged students like Pollock to experiment with different painting methods. Sometimes Siqueiros would have the students drizzle paint over the canvas like children. Or the young artists would be encouraged to pour oils straight onto the cloth. Sand or dust or dirt on the canvas might help, too, giving more grit and depth. Siqueiros called art a type of "controlled accident."

Like a set of squabbling brothers, Pollock and Siqueiros would disagree. Before Siqueiros left New York City the following year, for instance, the two sparred at a party, hands wrapped around each other's throats. But the workshop experience undoubtedly influenced Pollock. His work on a Siqueiros float was a "grand thing," Pollock once wrote. Siqueiros respected Pollock, too, and the Mexican artist sent a letter to Pollock shortly after the workshop was shuttered. "Be patient," Siqueiros advised. "Our workshop will open again."

Siqueiros's workshop did open again—at least within the recesses of Pollock's mind—and Pollock expanded on the drip-and-pour approach to painting pioneered by Siqueiros. Driven and dedicated, Pollock returned to the artistic skill that he gained in the workshop again and again. Drip art by drip art, Pollock built upon what he knew, and for a short time, Pollock made drip-style dishes. Then, for a bit, Pollock painted drip style in the corners of his canvases.

Together with art critic Clement Greenberg, Pollock began to study other artists who experimented with the drip-style approach like Janet Sobel. Later, Pollock examined the works of Picasso and the Surrealists who often splattered paint. As an artist, Pollock came to see drip painting as a way of expressing emotion, and when *Time* once called Pollock's work "chaotic," the artist wrote a short letter in response: "NO CHAOS DAMN IT."

In the popular mind, part of the conventional wisdom, Pollock's drip paintings seemed to have fallen from the clouds, a visitation from postmodern angels. This was, in fact, how Pollock's fame began, with a fourpage photo spread in *Life,* which described him as a singular creative genius, the "shining new phenomenon of American art." The magazine even provided a James Dean–like photo of Pollock standing against a wall, cigarette dangling from his mouth, the young Brando of the art world.

The world loves a good born-to-genius story—and the Pollock cult continues. Pollock's most recent major biography declared him "the quintessential tortured genius," while the last major sale of one of his canvases notched a record $10 million, a price tag similar to that of a professional sports team.

But the Pollock-as-rebel-genius story overlooks the truth of the matter—that Pollock relied on a method of learning. He expanded on an artistic theme, developing an area of mastery by extending what he knew. "Pollock was not the only painter to experiment with the all-over drip technique," art critic Roberta Smith once argued in the *New York Times*. "But only Pollock pursued its possibilities, doggedly and methodically circling the technique."

In the previous chapter, we looked at how we develop skills—or how people can take a very focused approach to practice. But to become an expert, we also need to expand an area of mastery. Learning—especially richer forms of learning—is a type of knowledge extension, a matter of expanding on an area of expertise, and at this stage of the learning process, we need to deepen our understanding.

This is the nature of long-term memory, and the power of this approach goes back to the notion of learning as a series of connected roads. In this metaphor, we retain a lot more when we extend a street or alley and lay out new routes and hubs. In the words of cognitive scientists, we're building on our prior knowledge and creating a deeper, more networked sort of insight.

For a more concrete example of this idea, take summarizing, or the act of putting an idea into our own words. The learning activity pushes us to ask ourselves a series of questions: What's important? How can we rephrase this idea? These queries are important. Because by summarizing the most valuable idea, we're extending our grasp of that particular idea, we're making it meaningful, and the practice shows clear and positive effects on outcomes.

Most of us know what this sort of learning looks like: It's another form of learning as mental doing. Recall, for instance, a time when you read an article in a magazine and then detailed its argument for a friend? That's a form of learning expansion, and you're more likely to have gained from that article as a result.

For another illustration of extending knowledge, imagine you recently wrote an email detailing your thoughts on a documentary that you saw on Netflix. Again, you flushed out the idea—and engaged in a

POP QUIZ #12

Before reading this section, predict what it will discuss.

A. Personality quizzes
B. The value of knowledge
C. The importance of riffs
D. Learning styles

more direct form of sense making—and studies show that you'll have a richer sense of the Netflix movie and its themes.

Before we go any further, let's be honest. Learners are not experts, who push a field forward, who invent new ideas or fields. Most of us are not going to develop radical new forms of art like Pollock. But all of us learn better when we flesh out a skill, when we extend an area of expertise.

Pollock undoubtedly felt this way about painting. He always continued to extend what he knew, and even during his drip-canvas phase, Pollock's work grew more complex. He continued to expand on the central theme. It was a physicist named Richard Taylor who first discovered this aspect of Pollock's works. The Australian scientist began studying Pollock's drip paintings some years ago and found that the canvases contained a type of fractal geometry, with a set of interwoven, nonrepeating patterns much like crystals or snowflakes.

Even more surprising, Taylor found that the fractals in Pollock's paintings grew more dense over time. At the start of Pollock's drip phase, the fractal complexity of his work was actually pretty low. But over time, Pollock delved deeper into the approach, and the fractals grew more profound, each painting containing a more elaborate design than the next, a more sophisticated level of chaos. "This is what art theoreticians call the hand of the artist," Taylor once told a reporter. Or think of it as one of the true markers of expertise.

A different way to grapple with the idea of expanding an area of expertise is to consider the making of the jazz album *Kind of Blue*. You've almost certainly heard the Miles Davis masterwork. It's a stalwart in coffee shops around the country, the background to endless study sessions, the bestselling album in jazz history.

The album has a moody, almost celestial energy. The musicians loop and soar among a set of evocative melodies, with caterwauling solos and freewheeling piano riffs. With a throaty feel that came to define the genre of jazz, *Kind of Blue* manages to provide Beethoven-like complexity with a haunting Nina Simone sound.

Kind of Blue is more than a jazz album, though. It's also perhaps the most important master class in the history of jazz, a pinnacle of musical learning, and Miles Davis asked the group of musicians who produced the album to learn an entirely new approach to music. In the past, jazz bands played around chords so soloists would end their riffs within a number of harmonies.

But at the *Kind of Blue* session, Davis aimed to teach the group how to use scales—or modes—which would give the players a different way to engage melodies. "This distinction may seem slight, but its implications were enormous," writes jazz critic Fred Kaplan. The musicians could now "link chords, scales, and melodies in almost unlimited combinations."

A devotee of improvisation, Davis didn't give the musicians any preparation for the new approach. He did not schedule any trial runs or practice sessions, no studio meetings or trainings. Indeed, Davis provided the group of musicians with only a few short melodies before they met up in the spring of 1959. "Play in [the] sound of these scales" were the only words on the top of the sheet music.

The musicians in the room were all experts, and Davis wanted them to learn the new approach through a riff. He pushed them to expand, to flesh out the approach, exploring—and applying—the new technique in a very direct way. As Davis later wrote in his biography, "When you're creating your own shit, man, even the sky ain't the limit."

Miles Davis's musical intervention worked, and each of the men who left the studio on that morning soon began using the modal style. Within months, Bill Evans began playing modal jazz. So did saxophonist Cannonball Adderley. John Coltrane later built his career on the modal approach, using it to create his blockbuster albums *Giant Steps* and *A Love Supreme*.

As a learning method, playing riffs is a way to extend an area of expertise, and it promotes mastery because it pushes people to dive deep into an area of mastery. Playing riffs helps us get at the essence of a bit of knowledge, to build cognitive links and connections. Plus, it's hard to be passive if you're improvising. To paraphrase Davis, it's a matter of "creating your own shit."

In this regard, extending an area of knowledge is a lot like being able to explain an area of knowledge, and studies show that people gain a lot more when they ask themselves explanatory questions as they learn. Specifically: Can I describe the idea? Can I clarify the skill? Can I put it into my own words?

When we describe ideas to ourselves, we typically come away with a much richer understanding of a topic. Some years ago, for instance, cognitive psychologist Brian Ross enrolled in a computer science class at the University of Illinois. It had been at decade since Ross had taken any sort of class—forget anything technology related—and with his beard and balding dome, Ross stood out. Easily a decade older than anyone else in the classroom, Ross was—for all the other students in the class—just *That Guy.*

To help him through the class, Ross relied on a technique known as self-explaining. The practice is much like it sounds, and when Ross would read texts for the class, he would describe ideas to himself. So after each paragraph, after each sentence, Ross would ask himself, *What did I just read? How does that fit together? Have I come across this idea before?*

If Ross did not understand something, he would look it up online. He would also try to build associations, to see if he could explain the idea to himself relying on different words or concepts. "A lot of what you're doing in self-explanation is trying to make connections," Ross told me. "Oh, I see, this works because this leads to that and that leads to that."

By the end of the course, Ross could not program computers as well as the other students. He simply didn't have enough background knowledge. But Ross was able to answer questions that the other students couldn't answer—and in many ways, he had a more connected sense of the field. "I sometimes had the advantage," Ross told me. "I was focused on the bigger picture."

Another way to extend knowledge is to ask the question: Why? Now, when we know a topic, why questions are not that hard. If I asked you a why question about the town that you grew up in, the answer would come pretty easily, I imagine. If you asked me why my parents decided to move to Westchester, New York, I'd explain that my mother and father wanted to live in a leafy suburban area with good schools and quiet streets.

It's when we don't know something that why questions become more difficult—and create a way to develop an idea. To illustrate the practice, let's examine a query like: "Why are there waves?" No doubt, some of us can forge through a basic answer, at least when a five-year-old is posing the question. Maybe something like: "Well, waves have to do with the wind. When wind blows across the top of the water, it creates ripples of water."

But then comes the inevitable follow-up, "Why does the wind blow across the top of the water?" or "Why does the wind lift the water?" or "Why are there waves when there's no wind?" Then we draw a blank. Or at least I do, and so I start searching for some sort of answer, spinning through the Internet, reading up on how energy moves through water, and in the end, I gain a lot more.

Just as important, why questions help us think about our thinking. They push us to understand what we know, encouraging a more nuanced understanding of a topic. Why questions can be particularly helpful while people are reading, and to get more out of a bit of text, people should frequently ask themselves why queries. Why does the author make this claim? Why should I believe the author? Why would this matter?

It's clear that trumpeter Miles Davis loved why questions. As a musician, he continually extended what he knew, and over the years, he managed to reinvent jazz at least three different times. In his own painterly way, artist Jackson Pollock wasn't that different. He created a riff on what he had learned in Siqueiros's workshop. His drip works were a clear extension of what he had learned years earlier. Put more directly,

Pollock asked the question: Why not make a painting entirely out of drips and splashes?

Arguments are another form of learning expansion. They're a different way to riff on an idea, to extend a concept. Not long ago, I watched teenager Keoni Scott-Reid provide his opening statement in a debate tournament. Scott-Reid had been assigned to argue against mass surveillance programs, and standing in the front of the room, he spoke in rat-tat-tat bursts like a teenage version of a cattle auctioneer.

With a focused oratorical grace, Scott-Reid pointed out that mass surveillance programs were a form of "social control." He argued that mass surveillance programs operated on a slippery moral slope, quoting Benjamin Franklin: "It is much easier to suppress a first desire than to satisfy those that follow." With his notes in hand, Scott-Reid concluded his speech after several minutes—and several lines of argument—noting that surveillance ultimately sparks lawlessness, degrading social order. "Aggressive policing," he said, is "perpetuating the criminality that it's advocating to stop."

Much like a cross-examination in a courtroom, Scott-Reid's opponent peppered him with questions, and they sparred over whether or not the judicial system currently holds law enforcement in check. At one point, Scott-Reid sharply questioned his adversary. "Prove it," he said in a loud voice. "Show me your evidence."

At the end, the judge gave the round to Scott-Reid. His logic was tighter. He had better examples, and as the judge pointed out, Scott-Reid had expertly questioned his opponent's rhetoric, one of his big strengths as a debater. "I know you like to get a rise out of people," the judge told him.

In many ways, argumentation is just another example of learning expansion, a different way of riffing on an area of knowledge. When we marshal evidence to support a point, we improve our knowledge of that field, and argumentation works in the same way that riffs work. It makes people flesh out connections within a field. It boosts expertise by pushing people to think through an area of mastery.

But argumentation also adds another wrinkle to how we can extend an area of expertise because the practice forces us to engage with reasoning. It pushes us to grapple with logic. This idea is at the center of learning, as cognitive scientist Lauren Resnick points out. To gain expertise, Resnick argues, people need to be "doing interpretive work."

In this sense, inferences help promote understanding. When people develop judgments, they're building connections. We're grappling with how things fit together and thus improving upon what we know. This explains why a little confusion can help learning: It makes us think our way out of a problem.

Other research supports this approach. Give some young students classes in reasoning skills, for instance, and they'll typically land better grades in their reading and math courses. Or take Scott-Reid again. Before he joined the debate program, he landed mainly Ds and Fs in school. A year later, he posted mainly As and Bs.

The issue, of course, is that we often engage in weak reasoning. Psychologist Richard Nisbett gives a wonderful example of this idea, and he argues that most hiring decisions are based on little more than a hunch.

As Nisbett points out, managers often give a lot of weight to the in-person interview. But studies in all sorts of fields—nonprofits, military, academia—show that in-person interviews do very little to predict job success. Instead, what's far more important when it comes to someone's doing well in a position is the hard data—things like references, previous experiences, and a writing test.

The issue is that the interview "feels right," according to Nisbett. For most of us, the experience of interviewing someone is emotionally vivid, a powerful experience, and so we judge people on their ability to be charming for twenty minutes rather than on their résumé, which typically holds years' worth of actual evidence.

The same thing is true in learning. Weak evidence has its sway. It makes intuitive sense that the explanation for the seasons is all about the Earth's distance from the sun (it's not). There's a natural inclination to solve this problem—$\frac{1}{2} \times \frac{1}{4}$—by simply multiplying the denominators (that's incorrect). In foreign affairs, it's easy to believe that business interests always explain economic policies (they don't).

When we examine the evidence, we're not always going to come to the right conclusion. That's a job for experts, after all. But we learn a lot by carefully weighing different pieces of proof. The examination of logic provides its own type of mastery. As Scott-Reid told me, "What I learned was to extend your argument."

The Need for Application

The process of extending an area of expertise has its roots in perhaps the oldest form of learning—imitation. Many animals learn in this way. One monkey will spot another monkey opening a nut with rock, and so the first monkey will copy the behavior and start to pop open nuts with a stone.

As an approach to learning, imitation works because it's concrete. There's nothing vague or abstract. It's a simple matter of, well, monkey see, monkey do. This idea holds lessons for the rest of us. When we make learning more concrete, it's easier to understand, and when it comes to the learning process, we can apply what we know in order to better comprehend what we want to know.

Many years ago, for instance, I visited Jackson Pollock's art studio with a childhood friend. The studio sat behind the Long Island home that Pollock shared with his wife, Lee Krasner. An old converted barn, the studio was square and vaulted, almost like a small European chapel.

Inside, the studio hadn't changed much from the day Pollock died in a car crash. The floor of the studio was still thick with flecks of paint, like some sort of expressionistic carpet. Behind Plexiglas stood some of Pollock's cans of paint, complete with old, thin brushes thick with coloring.

Over the years, conservators have tied some of the paint splatters on the studio's floor with specific canvases. The cobalt-colored footprints? That's from the time that Pollock was making *Blue Poles,* which now hangs in the Australian National Gallery. The dots of red in the corner? That's from *Convergence,* now in the Albright-Knox Art Gallery. In order to stride across the studio floor, the museums asks visitors to pull on some styrofoam slippers to protect the paint-filled surface.

I had seen some of Pollock's art before, almost certainly in a book of some sort, discussed in some confusing art world speak, and it took stepping into the studio to grasp the raw energy of the canvases, to get a full sense of the rebellious beauty of his drip-style approach.

The studio often provokes this sort of reaction, and people have stepped into the space and started to curse and swear. A docent once called it a "holy place." My friend Dan Belasco attended the museum with me on that day, and he was similarly inspired, eventually becoming a professional art curator.

An expert in abstract expressionism, Belasco today often pulls together shows on some of Pollock's colleagues, crediting our visit to Pollock's studio as one of the reasons that he went into the field: It "was a more direct and personal experience of the man than a hagiographic museum exhibition," he told me. "Seeing the studio really made a visceral impression."

Our brain struggles with abstractions. We like things to be tangible. When things are direct and material, they're easier to understand. It's one thing to read about how Pollock created some of the most seminal works of the twentieth century in an old Long Island barn. But it's a very different, concrete thing to step into an old barn and spot Pollock's blue footprints running across the wood floor as if he had left the room the previous morning.

This urge for the tangible shapes just about anything that we think about. It alters just about everything that we hear or see or believe. Recall any sort of anecdote, as an example, because the narrative is a lot more memorable if it includes concrete details. Take this sentence:

The bear was big and large with very substantial paws.

And compare that sentence with this one:

The bear was the size of a Mini Cooper with baseball mitt-like paws.

Both of these sentences are talking about the same bear. They're both generally the same length. But the second sentence—the one with the more distinct features—is far more evocative. Because of the way that our brain works, a Mini Cooper–size bear with "mitt-like paws" seems a lot scarier than a "big" one.

When it comes to learning, this is important. Because making something concrete is a powerful way of extending what we know. By building something that we can smell, touch, or see, we're making it easier to understand. There are a number of reasons for this. The brain is a distinctly visual organ, for one. Even if you're not an aspiring Pollock, your visual circuits are your most powerful circuits.

Take, for instance, mental abacus, the math practice that we came across in the first chapter. One of the reasons that the approach to math is so effective is that it offers a visual way to engage with the subject. By seeing the beads and rods, people have an easier time executing the math.

Likewise, we can learn a lot by drawing. When we use pen and paper to draw something, we have a richer understanding, as psychologist Rich Mayer has found. So, for instance, if you're reading about plate tectonics, you'll gain more from the text if you draw images of the earth's mantle and crust. This goes for memory, too, and you're more likely to remember a Mini Cooper–size bear, if you illustrate an image of the bear.

Another example of the power of our visual ways is what stand-up comedian Bob Harris calls "sticky images." So when Harris wants to remember something, he'll create a visual picture. When Harris hoped to recall some of the names of E. M. Forster's novels, for instance, he imagined himself in a room, looking out the window to see "a giant, throbbing thirty-foot-wide buttocks." While the image is a bit unnerving, it also burned in Harris's mind the titles of the two books: *Room with a View* and *Howard's End*.

The power of concreteness goes deeper than the visual, though, and the other thing to remember is that learning is a whole body affair. Our emotions, our feelings, even our sense of touch all help to support what we know. In a very literal sense, learning is a form of doing, and people will learn more if they physically engage with a topic or skill. Or just consider that some forms of finger dexterity anticipate future math skills better than someone's IQ.

We can take advantage of this aspect of learning, and performing concepts can have beneficial impacts. If people read a text and then

POP QUIZ #13

What's a one-sentence summary of the previous chapter?

A. The author redeems himself after losing a high school basketball game.

B. The author argues that learning requires a lot of feedback and struggle.

C. The author believes basketball is key to learning.

D. The author is planning to join the NBA.

act it out, they learn a lot more than people who just read the text, as Mayer argues. In much the same way, people can improve their expertise at higher rates if they use some sort of simulation or role-play; it helps us get a concrete sense of the skill. This idea also explains why mental simulations can build self-efficacy, as we saw with the slalom skier in Chapter 2: By imagining his performance, he got better at his performance.

In a roundabout way, the museum devoted to the Pollock studio had discovered this aspect of the learning process on its own, and a few years before I visited, the staff began inviting people to make their own drip-style paintings, using brushes, sticks, and the occasional turkey baster to create their own version of Pollock's *No. 5*.

Some years ago, two fathers brought their kids to the event, recalls Harrison. The men were "Wall Street types," she says. They wore shorts and had their baseball caps on backward. Eventually, the two fathers decided to get down on their knees and help their children fling paint over a bit of butcher-block paper. "I'm channeling my inner Jackson Pollock," one of them declared, spilling the paint over the canvas, and no doubt, he was channeling his inner Pollock in a very concrete way.

Even from the outside, it's clear that High Tech High is a very different sort of school. It's located near the airport in San Diego, so planes often thunder overhead. Sunburned drifters loiter in nearby parks. There are some Marine barracks nearby, so divers occasionally surface out of an ocean inlet in front of the school, their heads poking from the water like large dark buoys.

Inside, High Tech High is part auto-body shop, part artist studio, with a sprinkle of Southern California cool. Inside the foyer, there's an old cigarette dispenser that's been converted into a so-called Art to Go device, where for $5, visitors can buy small canvases—little portraits, small landscapes—as a way to support the school. Farther down the hallways, futuristic contraptions huddle in corners, while artistic murals hang from the ceiling.

The brainchild of founder Larry Rosenstock, High Tech High is all about students applying their knowledge, having people create projects that demonstrate what they've learned. There is little homework at the school, at least of the traditional worksheet or problem sets kind. No textbooks, either. Binders are online portfolios. An informal motto at the school is "You can play video games at High Tech High, but only if you make them."

While there is a curriculum at High Tech High, students typically develop projects on their own. In a 10th grade chemistry class, a group of students once launched a small soap company, netting more than $10,000 in sales. In a middle school class, students have created their own kites in order to learn about the physics of lift. A group of 6th graders once designed an exhibit on fossils for the San Diego Natural History Museum.

We've already come across a few explanations of why a school like High Tech High can post such success: When we apply our learning, it helps us find gaps in our understanding. If you're working on the design-a-kite project, for instance, it's clear if the kite doesn't work: It simply won't fly. Relevance also provides motivation, as we've seen, and at High Tech High, I never saw any groups of bored teenagers loitering the halls.

But there's something that we have not considered. Because when we expand our learning—when we apply our knowledge—it becomes more integrated. The expertise becomes part of a richer system of knowledge. Applying our knowledge pushes people to understand topics as part of a whole. When students learn how to build a kite, they study physics, math, and engineering in an integrated way. When someone learns how to make—and sell—soap, he or she grapples with issues of chemistry, business, and marketing.

We can all take a page from the High Tech High playbook and work to apply our knowledge. Practically speaking, take data analytics. One way to flesh out our understanding of the practice would be to analyze some stats from a baseball game. In this approach, we'd see how analytics is a mix of science (we're making predictions) and craft (there're lots of rules of thumb).

Building engineering isn't any different. If you want to learn how to become a better builder, work on the creation of a new house: It makes it easy to see how plumbing, electrical, and engineering all work together. Same with any aspiring filmmaker: Start making films, even with your smartphone. By executing short films, you'll gain a much better sense of how a movie works as a system of visual narration, a mix of graphic and auditory, of exposition and action.

This isn't an argument for endless hands-on projects. Without conceptual understanding and fluency in the basics, they don't do much good. High Tech High remains a good example here, too. The school goes too far in many ways, and without a robust background knowledge, some graduates struggle in college, complaining that they don't know how to learn from textbooks.

But as we develop an expertise, mastery is something that we need to apply. Learning is a car that we need to take for a spin. People are often reluctant to execute what they know. It's the ghost of Albert Bandura's idea of self-efficacy from Chapter 2: We are often too worried that we're not going to succeed. But once we have a basic understanding—and some thoughtful practice—we need to apply our expertise in some clear and dedicated way.

This idea also explains why computer simulations can have such a positive effect on learning. They allow people to practice their skills on a model of a real situation or experience, to use their knowledge in a more systemic way.

I first learned the value of computer-based learning simulations some years ago when an email came across my virtual desk: "Be in the

POP QUIZ #14

True or false: Learning requires mistakes.

boardroom in 10 minutes." It was a missive from a senior vice president in the company named Alan Young. A huge fire had been sparked in the firm's call center, Young's email explained, and the company's CEO was out on his boat, so there was no way to contact him. To solve the crisis, the board has given senior staff emergency powers.

What do you do?

While it felt a bit like the start of a bad TV movie, this was a scenario in a computer-based simulation called vLeader. The technology allows people to apply their skills in a real-world setting without the high stakes. Other simulations give people the opportunity to learn how to become a better firefighter or improve their social worker skills.

Simulations work because they're a way to apply our knowledge. They help people model ideas and concepts in more integrated ways—and the evidence is pretty clear that they help people learn. A group of researchers once compared an online learning class with focused simulations and other more active forms of learning to a traditional online learning program and found the more engaged approach helped provide outcomes that were some six times higher.

The researchers titled the paper, "Learning Is Not a Spectator Sport," which in many ways summarizes the point: In order to fully gain a skill, we have to actually participate in that skill.

There's another way to apply what we know—teach someone else. Some years ago, for instance, David Goodstein had a question about quantum statistics. A physicist and vice provost at Caltech, Goodstein wanted to know more about how quantum physics might predict the behavior of a specific type of subatom.

So Goodstein visited Richard Feynman. One of the nation's most well-known scientists, Feynman had helped create the atomic bomb and developed new models of photons and eventually won a Nobel

Prize. "Explain to me, so that I can understand it, why spin one-half particles obey Fermi-Dirac statistics," Goodstein asked Feynman.

After hearing Goodstein's question, Feynman paused and then told Goodstein that the best way to explain the notion would be to develop a class for some undergrads on the topic. "I'll prepare a freshman lecture on it," Feynman declared to Goodstein.

Feynman then took some time to dwell on the issue. But eventually he became stuck. This aspect of quantum physics seemed oddly out of reach. So Feynman sheepishly returned to Goodstein. "You know, I couldn't do it. I couldn't reduce it to the freshman level," Feynman explained. "That means we really don't understand it."

It might seem odd—even ironic—that teaching others is a good way to gain insights into a topic. Yet there's a deep body of research on the idea. Whether we instruct a class of thousands—or just try and explain something to a small class of freshmen—we gain a better sense of an area of expertise by teaching it.

Researchers call it the Protégé Effect, and it's really a form of knowledge application: By providing a lesson on a topic, we're giving our own twist on an idea. We're articulating what's important about the topic, putting it into our own words, and thus improving our expertise.

As a learning method, teaching others also requires a form of meta-cognition. To explain something, we have to think about the thinking of the person that we're instructing. Put differently, when people educate someone else, they're asking themselves a series of important questions: What's the best way to explain this idea? How will they understand this notion? What is the most important takeaway?

These questions promote learning for the instructor because they force the person to turn the problem around in his or her head. People have to engage with the material in a more meaningful way, and it turns out that we don't actually have to do any teaching to gain the benefits of this approach.

In one recent study by psychologist John Nestojko, for instance, subjects who believed that they were going to teach learned more than a group of subjects who thought they were going to be tested on a topic. According to Nestojko, the benefit boiled down to the fact that subjects who thought they were going to provide instruction processed the material in a richer way, even if they didn't actually end up providing any training.

The other important thing about teaching as a form of learning is that instruction is social. It's an emotional activity. When we teach, we think about value and meaning, about passion and enjoyment. After all, no one wants to have their students slumped in their chairs like they're waiting in line at the DMV, and so we think about how to make the material more engaging, how the ideas and skills might relate to the audience.

People simply work harder if they know that they're going to teach someone else. The social aspect of teaching others makes us more willing to put forth effort. Moreover, teaching is iterative. A face goes blank? Present the idea again. Eye roll? Take a moment to engage emotionally. The student stumbles on a bit of prior knowledge? Review that fact again. In this regard, the Protégé Effect is strongest when people are watching the learning in action.

Teaching as learning has been a driver of many of the successful programs that we've already come across. When I visited the University of Washington's pioneering freshman biology classes that we saw in Chapter 1, I observed lots of teaching as learning, and students frequently worked in small groups. Same with the Success for All model, which we came across in Chapter 2. Cooperative forms of learning are central to the reform approach.

Over the years, some individuals have developed this approach, too. David Rönnqvist, for instance, is a computer graphics developer in Sweden, and some years ago, he began visiting Web sites like Stack Overflow that allow people to post and respond to questions. To help Rönnqvist extend his skills, he would sometimes spend more than an hour each day on Stack Overflow, answering queries. The site was his browser's home page, and he loaded up the site every morning, sometimes writing long, thousand-word answers.

As an animator, Rönnqvist would typically answer animation-related questions, and over time, he found that he developed a lot of new techniques and perspectives by answering questions on the site.

Another developer once posted a question about repeating an animation. It was an approach that Rönnqvist wasn't familiar with, and so he learned more about the technique and now uses the practice frequently in his own work.

"I would learn a lot by answering questions," Rönnqvist told me from his home in Stockholm. "I would push myself to answer questions that were a little harder than before" in order to gain more skills. Eventually, Rönnqvist even used one of his longer Stack Overflow posts as a way to land a job at a Swedish tech firm. His write-up on the Web site showed that Rönnqvist knew the material and could explain it to others in a thoughtful way.

Physicist Richard Feynman had come around to the notion of teaching as a form of learning well before David Goodstein appeared in his office to ask about subatoms. In the 1940s, Feynman had worked on developing the first nuclear bomb at the Los Alamos Lab. This was long before Feynman had become famous, and back then, Feynman was a quantum nobody, one of the most junior staffers at the lab. It was everyone else who was well known, and the lab brimmed with a Who's Who of physics fame from Robert Oppenheimer to Enrico Fermi.

Still, famed physicist Niels Bohr would often meet with Feynman privately in a small meeting room. At the time, Feynman had no idea why the esteemed Bohr would care about his thoughts or why Bohr would schedule meetings between the two of them, usually early in the morning.

POP QUIZ #15

What is retrieval practice?

A. A game for dogs.

B. A type of self-quizzing.

C. A new exam format.

D. A better way to play tennis.

E. A sport invented in Australia.

But eventually, Feynman realized that Bohr intimidated almost all of the other physicists at the lab, and they would just defer to his theories. Feynman, however, would push back. He asked questions, and even at their first meeting, in front of a large group of fellow researchers, Feynman pointed out an error in Bohr's logic.

So, in the early morning meetings, before the other physicists came strutting into the conference rooms, Bohr would present new ideas to Feynman, while the junior scientist tried to ask pointed questions. Feynman would put out flaws or problems or confusions in Bohr's ideas. "This is no good," Feynman might say. "This may be possible if you did this."

Put differently, Feynman pushed to Bohr to teach—and thus to understand.

The Value of Uncertainty

In this chapter so far, we've come across a number of artists. Some of them are well-known like Jackson Pollock and Miles Davis. Others like Richard Feynman simply travel in creative fields. For still others, art is a hobby. The fractal scientist Richard Taylor is an amateur painter. Helen Harrison of the Pollock museum studied sculpture for years.

This isn't a bizarre stroke of chance. Expanding an area of knowledge requires a type of creativity. We need to feel at home with nuance and uncertainty, and in fact, research shows that people will learn more if they believe that an area of expertise is tentative, ambiguous, something that they can discover and explore.

All in all, we probably should have addressed this issue earlier. It's hard to expand any sort of skill without the expectation that you can expand it. If you believe learning is just a matter of collecting information, of developing steadfast procedures, there's no reason to flesh out mastery in deeper ways.

Plus, knowledge is uncertain by definition, and just about every area of expertise has tentative ideas, subtle nuances, fresh areas waiting for discovery. This idea is self-evident, at least for experts. If you're an authority in a field, ambiguity is a given. Expertise is always changing.

In science, top researchers are constantly building up new areas of knowledge—just look at the constant churn of journal headlines. In literature, every week, it seems, another analysis of the Great American Novel hits the already overladen bookshelves.

But even the most basic math problems are really not that different. They can exhibit mind-stretching complexity, offering all sorts of room for ambiguity. Consider adding 75 to 962. At first glance, it's remarkably basic. But consider that there are—literally—more than a thousand different ways to solve the question, none of them any more correct than any of the others.

This approach is more than a way to mastery. It's an actual goal, as physics educator Andrew Elby told me. After all, we learn areas of expertise as a way to grapple with the world, to understand complexity, to shift our patterns of thought. This is true for well-known experts—and raw beginners. "Learning is about reasoning and explanation, not just right answers," Elby told me.

More than that, this idea also reflects the world that we live in, and the Knowledge Economy has become the Thinking Economy. In other words, we need more subtle forms of knowledge in order to succeed, and even academic areas that might seem rote just aren't that rote anymore.

Take the military. There was a time not a long ago when the armed services were all about learning the rules, following orders, and executing commands. The United States won World War II in exactly this manner: Five-star generals ordered massive amounts of men onto the shores of Belgium to battle their way to Berlin.

But the military is changing because the world is changing, and the United States is never going to win a war in the same way that it won World War II. The days of fixed battles, of set marches are over. As one military science professor explained, "What we're trying to get away from is the 'right answer' type of training."

At least within the field of learning, no one seems to take this idea more seriously than psychologist Mark Runco. More any other learning expert that I interviewed, Runco tries to avoid "right answer" approaches to expertise. When I reached Runco at his office at the

University of Georgia, he told me that he never drives the same way to work, always commuting on a different set of roads.

To embrace uncertainty and promote new ways of thinking, Runco also shaves differently each day. Sometimes Runco uses his left hand, sometimes he uses his right. He always starts at a different point on his face. Runco even tries to tie his shoes in a new way every day. "That's actually gotten kind of difficult," Runco told me. "There's a finite number of ways to tie your shoes, I think."

Runco argues that this approach makes him more open-minded. It ensures that he's mindful of small differences. Plus, Runco argues, people often need a little prodding to be more nuanced. In studies in Runco's lab, for instance, people will engage in a lot more open-ended forms of learning if they've been told to engage in open-ended forms of learning. "In many cases, 'only think of original ideas' is all you have to say to people," Runco said.

Part of the benefit of Runco's approach is that it pushes people to question their beliefs. In Runco's case, for instance, he doesn't assume that highways get him to work any faster. He doesn't assume that shaving with his right hand is any better than shaving with his left, even though he's right-handed. These sorts of variations have helped Runco learn some new streets in his neighborhood. He's also become a bit more ambidextrous—and much better at tying knots. "Creativity is a type of learning," he told me.

Admittedly, Runco might go too far. There are right answers, certainly when it comes to driving somewhere in the fastest time possible. But the core lesson is an important one: Effective learning requires uncertainty. We need to see ambiguity. Expertise rests on shifting how we think about a skill or bit of knowledge.

This is why changing perspectives can be such a powerful learning tool. Because when we consider other points of view, we acquire a more subtle form of understanding. So, if someone is learning about the fall of the Soviet Union, they would gain a lot by looking at the issue from different perspectives. How did Soviet leader Mikhail Gorbachev understand what happened? What about President George H. W. Bush? If you lived in Moscow, would you take to the streets to support the fall of the regime?

POP QUIZ #16

True or false: Intelligence is fixed at birth.

Self-questioning can also help us find subtlety, and we can learn more if we ask ourselves: Why do people believe this idea? Why might they be wrong? What's a different explanation?

Psychologist Keith Sawyer has a helpful way to think about this approach. Specifically, Sawyer argues that people should "stretch" and "squeeze" issues to uncover more nuance. When we stretch a problem, we make it more abstract—and thus potentially easier to solve. Or people can squeeze an issue and make it more concrete, which often gives different insights.

If we're having a hard time with sailing, for instance, we can stretch the practice and ask: Why exactly does the wind make a sailboat move? How does tacking actually work? Or we could squeeze the issue and make it more concrete as a way to learn more: How do I use the rudder in windy conditions? How do I slow down a fast-moving boat?

As Sawyer argues, thoughtful questions are often the biggest drivers of more subtle forms of learning. They create new ways to frame problems, and just about every major invention basically answers a new question, according to Sawyer. The query "How can I put a yearbook online?" sparked Facebook. The reason that Sal Khan created the online tutoring program, the Khan Academy, was to answer the question: How can I help my cousin Nadia get better at math?

Ask yourself: How can I extend what I know?

One easy way to introduce more nuance and complexity into learning is social diversity. The people who surround us have a deep influence on how we think, and inevitably, people from different backgrounds promote more complex forms of expertise.

For an example, recall the story of the Dutch tulip crash, perhaps the world's first economic bubble. According to historians, the tulip economy began just as the Netherlands started to become wealthy in the early seventeenth century. Because of overseas trade, many Dutch merchants grew rich, a sudden rash of immense wealth, and tulips became a symbol of money, the McMansions of their time.

The prices for bulbs began to climb, and in many ways, the story becomes familiar to anyone who follows the news: The traders made riskier and riskier bets on tulips. Contracts grew more complicated and byzantine. People began trading bulbs that they didn't know anything about, while quick profits soared with markups of 100 percent or more.

But then the tulip bulb market bombed. At one point, bulbs were trading for more than the cost of a fancy Amsterdam home. Yet within a matter of weeks, the same small brown, earthy bulb was worth close to nothing, barely enough to trade for a slice of bread. It became known as *Tulpenwoerde,* or tulip mania.

By modern standards, the tulip bubble wasn't all that much of a bubble. But the crisis shines a light on one of the causes of economic crashes: too little social diversity. Because as researcher Maurits van der Veen recently argued, many of the Dutch traders knew each other socially in some way. The men all shared churches and families. They had similar jobs and backgrounds. The group of traders formed a set of "dense social networks," van der Veen writes in his paper on the crash. They "all knew one another as fellow aficionados."

These social connections influenced the traders, and they had "an inflated sense of the expertise of their peers," according to van der Veen. Indeed, for van der Veen, the "dense, localized social network made the bubble possible" through a type of peer pressure. Or think of the tulip bubble as a type of economic groupthink.

What's important to keep in mind is that a trade is essentially an argument. By purchasing something in a market, we're saying that the item is undervalued. That's why trades are often called bets or hedges, and for the most part, markets work because groups have a certain intelligence. When we average the opinions of a large body of people, they're generally more accurate than the opinions of the individuals.

Lots has been written about this idea in wonderful books like James Surowiecki's *The Wisdom of Crowds.* Ask a lot of people to solve a problem, and generally you're going to get a better solution. Put a difficult issue in front of a group, and the answer will be better developed and reasoned. This is true even within large companies, and more social diversity leads to higher productivity.

For us, the first takeaway is that diverse groups promote richer forms of thinking. When we're with people who are different than us, we are more likely to engage in complex thought. Sheen Levine at the University of Texas at Dallas has studied how people of varying ethnicities think in groups and found that differences in ethnic backgrounds make people do more to consider the evidence.

Levine believes that people become more critical of their own thinking when they're surrounded by people who are not like them, and he has shown as much in experiments that approximate a stock market. "In the presence of people who look different than us, we put less trust in the reasonableness of the actions of people," Levine told me. "So people tend to think for themselves rather than mimic others."

In Levine's work, ethnic diversity promotes critical thinking by making people more skeptical. It pushes people to ask more questions. In his own life, Levine takes this idea pretty seriously. When Levine makes any decision—buying a car, taking a new job—he tries to consult with friends from different backgrounds. For research projects, he tries to create as diverse a team as possible, and for one of his stock market studies, he made sure that his colleagues differed in age, gender, religion, ethnicity, and professional background. "Diversity makes you brighter," he told me.

When it comes to learning, there's more going on here. Diversity does more than promote doubt. We also develop expertise from the perspective of others. Maybe the best way of understanding this idea is to imagine a group of people who generally have similar backgrounds. Let's call them the Geeks. Then imagine what I might call the Lunch Room. It contains some geeks, but also some jocks, goths, and airheads.

According to experiments done by scholar Scott Page, the Lunch Room will typically beat out the Geeks when it comes to problem solving. While the Geeks might be bright, they're limited by their intellectual toolbox. They can't think differently about a solution. They are stuck with a Geek way of thinking. In contrast, the people in the Lunch

Room benefit from diversity, and so they're better able to solve problems. They gain a more intricate form of expertise. "Novel perspectives on problems do not come from the ether," Page writes. "We often construct them from other perspectives."

The bottom-up nature of technology can make a difference here. It can help create the communication that fosters this sort of learning, to help build links across different groups. In a way, this is simply one of the inherent benefits of the Internet. It's made the cost of connecting with vastly different people basically zero.

Not long ago, for instance, Melissa Schaser enrolled in a Bible class at Vanderbilt University. As part of the course, Schaser—an aspiring pastor—had to build her own Wikipedia entry, which other students would comment on. She also reviewed the work of other students and provided feedback. "Thorough explication of the text!" she noted on one entry.

The online exchange of views helped Schaser develop her understanding. It pushed her to think more deeply about the way that the Bible is woven into the modern world. One student, for instance, detailed the role of salt in the Bible. He discussed different types of salt—and described the various ways that the Bible talks about the mineral in different rituals. "I would have never thought about salt in the Bible," Schaser told me.

Today, Schaser is a pastor in Nashville, and due in part to the divinity school class, she'll often weave everyday culture references into her pastoral work. In one recent article, for instance, she made use of a recent commercial rolled out by the office company Staples. "Once you're in tune to it, you see biblical metaphors everywhere," she told me. "It's a very human text."

There's an important qualification here. Online or off, we don't actually enjoy diversity. It's socially uncomfortable to engage with people who are different from us. For many of us, engaging people who don't our views or background produces social anxiety. As one academic paper concluded simply, "diversity contributes to increased conflict."

This explains why people tend to spend time with people similar to them. They want the comfort of people who look and act like them.

POP QUIZ #17

True or false: Learners shouldn't set goals.

When I spoke to Levine, he pointed out that when he asks students in his classes to form groups, they often partner up with their peers. The black male students pair up with the other black students. The white women gather in clusters. "They frequently select those who are superficially similar to them," he told me.

Surprisingly, this happens *after* Levine has explained the powerful benefits of diversity. They "disregard the advice to feel the emotional benefits of ethnic homogeneity," Levine says. The solution? Levine assigns groups to ensure more diverse perspectives. "The students are not happy with this, but it makes them more willing to challenge each other," he says, and thus, they learn a lot more.

In a way, I've been arguing that richer forms of learning require a type of skepticism. To gain expertise, to expand on what we know, there has to be doubt. We need to question—and even rebel.

As a case study, then, Jackson Pollock remains valuable. His learning was fueled by a type of dissent, and when Pollock first arrived in New York, many believed that he was a glaringly awful painter. One high school friend said, "That fellow couldn't draw!" Another colleague declared that Pollock "didn't have what it takes."

Still, Pollock worked on his technique. Dedicated, almost obsessed, Pollock practiced, clocking hours upon hours in his studio. Eventually, he collected a few ardent supporters. Painter Thomas Benton admired Pollock's sense of unorthodoxy. Art critic Clement Greenberg championed Pollock as an uncommon talent. It helped that collector Peggy Guggenheim would occasionally snatch up a painting or two.

Pollock admitted that he never wanted to master every technical flourish. He wasn't a modern-day Vermeer. Yet Pollock had a fight that he wanted to fight, a rebellion that he aimed to lead. It wasn't that Pollock always believed in himself. Ravaged by mental health problems, he died in an alcohol-soaked car accident. Rather, with some ambition—and a lot of rebellion—Pollock believed that he had something to say and that he was going to say it.

Most of us aren't like this—and generally, people like certainty. Like an old winter coat, certainty provides a sense of comfort. It's simpler to learn a set of facts. Procedures come pretty easily to us. *Just tell us the answer*, we will say.

This affinity for assurance is baked into our brain, and our thoughts generally tend to swirl around the same ideas. We anchor ourselves to whatever seems accepted. As an example, let's imagine that I spin a wheel numbered 1 to 100. The number 10 pops up. Then I ask you something like "What percent of Beatles albums won a Grammy?" Your answer is likely going to hover around 25 percent, according a study by psychologist Daniel Kahneman.

But then I spin the wheel again. This time a higher number pops up—the number 65. Then I ask you a different but similar type of question, "What percent of dogs are black?" Research by Kahneman shows that your answer is now likely to hover around 55.

For experts like Kahneman, what's happening here is pretty clear: The first number that I would say—the 10 or the 65—has a grounding effect. The figure, it seems, to provide a type of certainty, anchoring our thoughts. So when we think about the number 10, we think about lower numbers, and when we think about the number 65, we think about higher numbers.

For many of us, distrust is what changes this equation. A streak of rebelliousness makes us more curious—and creative—and at this stage in the learning process, people should have a rooted willingness to consider different ideas, to seek out competing theories.

When it comes to individuals, much of the take-home advice is things we've discussed: Ask lots of why questions in order to make connections. Make sure to apply what you know so you have a keen sense of the material and its complexity. Try and teach mastery to others so you really know what you know. Also don't hesitate to argue a point—you'll learn a lot more by developing your reasoning.

As is true of so many ideas in education, it's easy to go too far, and

I'm not saying that every question has multiple answers. The answer to 75 plus 962 will always equal 1,037. Nor can we easily develop these sort of thinking skills outside of a specific domain. In other words, the Knowledge Effect still rules.

But we have to acknowledge that learning runs on difficult questions. It requires an insurrectionist attitude. This approach ran strong in Pollock, and as art historian Deborah Solomon argues, the artist eventually rebelled against every mentor that he ever had, from Thomas Benton to Clement Greenberg.

As a learner, it turns out, Richard Feynman was no different. He sometimes would fake his knowledge of Italian, simply making up words, especially when drivers tried to cut him off riding his bike. "You have to have absolute confidence," Feynman advised.

The best tip, though, might come from Miles Davis, who once wrote: "The thing to judge in any jazz artist is, does the man project and does he have ideas." When it comes to learning, we should have similar estimations—and try to extend what we know. To paraphrase Davis, then, the thing to judge in any learner is, does he or she expand and have new ideas.

Chapter 5

RELATE

ALBERT EINSTEIN WOULD often engage in thought experiments. Perhaps the earliest one dates back to Einstein's teens. It was around 1895, and Einstein was living in Switzerland. He was a young man with a slim, handsome face and a thick head of hair. Enrolled in a local high school, Einstein took physics and chemistry classes and often spent his evenings deep in his textbooks.

As part of his thought experiment, Einstein imagined a light beam moving through space like a wave, with regular crests and dips, much like a wave moving through the ocean. Then Einstein imagined himself speeding alongside the beam of light. In his mind, Einstein would be moving at the same speed as the beam of light, traveling at the exact same rate. If that happened—if Einstein was right next to the beam—he realized that the wave of light would appear stationary, like it was not moving at all.

For a different example of Einstein's realization, imagine for a moment you're driving your car at exactly sixty miles per hour. If you look over at another car, the second car would seem like it's motionless. Since the second car is going the exact same speed as your car, it would appear to be stationary like a tree or rock.

Immediately, Einstein realized that something did not add up. The speed of light was supposed to be a constant. But in his mind, Einstein could imagine a scenario in which the speed of light didn't seem to move, at least to the person who was moving next to the beam of light. These

POP QUIZ #18

True or false: Highlighters are a good learning tool.

two things should not be true at the same time, and it produced "all sorts of nervous conflicts," Einstein later wrote.

As a learning exercise, thought experiments date back to the ancient Greeks, and generally, they are a way of thinking an idea though. They're something that pushes people to understand how a skill or bit of expertise comes together as a system, and in this chapter, we're going to look more closely at how we can learn by looking for relationships within a field of expertise.

Understanding a topic's underlying connections is often the hardest part of the learning process, yet in the end, it's also why we learn. It's how we create mastery. In fact, Einstein credited his thought experiment as the trigger of his theory of special relativity. As Einstein later wrote, "One sees in this paradox the germ of the special relativity theory is already contained."

Some of the early research on systems thinking occurred around the same time that Einstein published his theory of relativity. The study took place at the University of Chicago, and as part of the project, psychologist Charles Judd had two groups of subjects fire darts at a target submerged under water.

The first group of subjects simply practiced the procedure, repeatedly firing darts at the underwater target some four inches away. The second group executed the same procedure, but they also learned about the notion of refraction, or the way that light shifts when it's under water.

Then Judd moved the underwater target to a spot twelve inches away, and while both groups did equally well at hitting the target at four inches, only the second group could hit the target with any accuracy at twelve inches.

The students who understood the relationship between light and water, it seemed, were better able to hit the target in a different setting.

They could use their learning in a new context. Because their knowledge was part of a richer system of thought, their knowledge was more flexible.

Cognitive scientist Lindsey Richland has written a lot about this idea in recent years, and in a landmark paper, she argued that to build concepts, to solve problems, to engage in any sort of critical thought, people need to grapple with patterns within an area of expertise.

Richland developed this idea after spending years hunting through a wide body of academic fields—from math to history—and showing that mastery is ultimately defined by a sense of how knowledge structures connect to each other. "The underpinnings of the ability to do higher-order thinking really comes down to reasoning about relationships," Richland told me when I visited her at the University of Chicago.

Experts engage in this type of systems thinking a lot. In their fields, dedicated specialists understand how things come together, and so they can look past chaos and complexity and uncover the essence of an idea. Pablo Picasso is famous for once having sketched a bull using just seven lines. Great lawyers like Thurgood Marshall have similar skills and can easily find the key argument in a jumble of legal details. For another illustration, just think of the purified elegance of a pop song by the Beatles: The band made the musically complicated seem perfectly uncomplicated.

What's more, Richland showed that if people relate what they know, they develop sharper reasoning skills. So, for instance, if someone learns more about relationships and systems within math, they have deeper math reasoning skills. If someone finds out more about the way that historical details couple to each other, they have a richer historical understanding. "Effective learning comes down to thinking about relationships," Richland argues.

As an example, take learning about the ocean. Richland argues that some people might dwell on a stand-alone fact like the temperature of the water or the volume of the ocean. But to develop reasoning skills, to create a systems understanding, people should examine questions like: What happens to the ocean if the level of salt goes up? What's the difference between oceans and lakes? How do reefs impact ocean currents?

These sorts of questions do a lot to push people to develop their thinking about a field—and fully understand an idea or topic or skill. "You don't just want to be memorizing a whole bunch of stuff," Richland told me. "To learn effectively, people should be finding causes, finding analogues, finding differences."

Richland developed her theory based on academic fields like physics and math, and after speaking with her, I was intrigued. So I thought I'd see if her argument extended to something a little less scholarly and signed up for a class on, yes, wine. There are, of course, a number of ways for people to hone their viniculture skills. Someone could globe-trot though vineyards or attend workshop or even just sample a lot of wine.

But given Richland's work, I slipped into a class on how to match wines with foods. I wanted to know: Would thinking about relationships give me richer insights, a better way to polish my knowledge?

Wine expert Amanda Weaver-Page taught the class on a rainy Friday night. Dressed in an all-white chef's outfit, Weaver-Page started the class by explaining some wine basics. She spoke about issues of acidity, detailing the idea of tannins, which give red wines their sharp flavor. Texture was crucial, too. "Think of a light-bodied wine as comparable to skim milk," Weaver-Page said. "And a full-bodied wine is more like whole milk."

Weaver-Page argued that the matching of a wine was about complements. The food, in other words, should support the wine, while the wine supports the food—a type of nourishment ying-yang. That's why lighter wines often go so well with lighter meals like fruit, while heavy red wines support something like a grilled rib eye: "Pair a light-bodied wine with something texturally heavy like steak, and it's going to overwhelm the wine."

At first, I was generously skeptical of some of Weaver-Page's points. Like people talking about high-end art or fancy cars, there's a hefty dose of exhibitionism that comes with wine talk. But then came the first pairing. A goat cheese salad was matched with a Spanish Albariño wine, and the relationships between the two were clear, giving me an insight into the nature of wine that I had never experienced before. The wine's essence—soft and lime-like—seemed beyond question.

POP QUIZ #19

A young child solves a basic math problem, writing "3 + 3 = 6." The child's parents want to see if the child also understands the underlying addition principle. What should they *not* ask?

A. Do you know another way of adding two numbers so that they equal the number 6?

B. Can you elaborate on your answer?

C. Why is that the correct answer?

D. Is your answer correct?

Then came the next wine—an Australian Shiraz. Weaver-Page paired it with grilled lamb with mint pesto, and again: The wine's flavor was crystalline—rich, almost lewd, like something from a medieval carnival. When I posed Richland's theory to Weaver-Page, she nodded in agreement. "Pairings give people a good introduction to the way that wine works," she told me.

In fact, Weaver-Page had a similar experience during her early years of culinary school. An instructor had given her a tannin-filled wine, which made her lips pucker like a grade school kiss. Then the instructor gave her a bite of cheddar. "The fat smoothed out the tannins. It tasted totally different," she said.

When I left the class some two hours later, there were still gaps in my knowledge. Weaver-Page had put a lot of thought into the pairings, and if I had picked up a bottle of plonk and matched it up with some McDonald's fries, I would have had a very different experience. But I could also say with certainty that my thinking about wine had changed. I had a glimpse of what it was like to think like a wine expert, to see the world of wine in a more systemic way.

Perhaps one of the most important things about looking for relationships within an area of expertise is that it provides insights into a field's deeper structure. I learned this aspect of the learning process myself in an awkward sort of way when I met up with psychologist Rob Goldstone.

A professor at Indiana University, Bloomington, Goldstone is tall and bald with a wry smile. We met up at a coffee shop in downtown Washington.

"You seem like a smart guy," Goldstone said after we'd been talking for a bit. "Can I put you on the spot?"

"Sure," I said, nervously fingering my notepad.

Goldstone then presented me with a version of the following problem:

An aging king plans to divide his kingdom among his daughters. Each country within the kingdom will be assigned to one of his daughters. (It is possible for multiple countries to be assigned to the same daughter.) In how many different ways can the countries be assigned, if there are five countries and seven daughters?

After Goldstone finished, I wrote down some of the key points, noting the five countries and seven daughters. Then I started to draw the provinces. Would a representation of the situation help me figure out the answer?

"Does it have something to do with factorials? That somehow seems familiar?" I said.

Goldstone scratched his neck. "You're getting closer."

I kept working at the problem.

"Can I give you a hint?" Goldstone said. "If the king gives Germany to one daughter, he can still give France to the same daughter."

I nodded but still struggled, and eventually Goldstone just explained the answer: "If there are seven options, or daughters, for each of the five things, or kingdoms, that need to be assigned to an option, there would be $7 \times 7 \times 7 \times 7 \times 7$ or 7^5 possibilities," he explained.

Goldstone explained that the problem hinged on a math concept known as sampling with replacement. The topic was typically taught in middle school and could be boiled down to formula: "The number of options raised to the power of the number of selections."

So why did I get the answer wrong? To answer that question, it's important to first understand the nature of problems. Psychologists like

Goldstone describe problems as having both surface and deep features. Surface features are typically the concrete or superficial elements. In the king problem, for instance, the surface features were the lands and the children and the age of the king.

The deep features tend to be concepts or skills, and in the king problem, the deep features were "the notion of sampling with replacement, the concept of an option, and the concept of a selection event," according to Goldstone. In my case, I couldn't see the deep feature. The superficial elements distracted me.

As we sat next to the coffee shop window, Goldstone argued that people often get distracted by the shallow details of a problem. He calls it "the greatest cognitive difficulty." Take a look at this problem for another example:

> *A homeowner is going to repaint several rooms in her house. She chooses one color of paint for the living room, one for the dining room, one for the family room, and so on. (It is possible for multiple rooms to be painted the same color or for a color never to be used.) In how many different ways can she paint the rooms, if there are 8 rooms and 3 colors?*

The problem also comes from Goldstone's study. But unless you've had some experience in sampling with replacement, it's not immediately clear that the problem is also getting at the same issue of sampling with replacement. In other words, it's hard to grasp that the problem has different superficial features but gets at the same deeper features. "To see this connection you need to see the role that daughters and colors play in their respective scenarios—they are alternatives," Goldstone argues.

So how do people see the deep feature in a problem or area of expertise? Well, one of the easiest ways goes back to the notion of systems, of relationships, and it often pays to mix up our learning. When people see multiple examples with different surface details, they're far more likely to understand the underlying system.

Goldstone has seen this in his lab: If people come across a variety of different sampling with replacement problems with different surface features, they're far more likely to understand the core idea. They get a much richer sense of the deeper system.

A library of research provides further support for the value of mixing up our learning. In one study from the 1990s, some young women learned to fire off foul shots. Some practiced only foul shots. Others took more of a jumbled, mixed-up approach—they practiced foul shots as well as eight- and fifteen-footers. The results were remarkable: The jumbled-shot group performed much better, with a deeper sense of the underlying skill.

The same is true in more academic fields, from memory tests to problem-solving skills: By mixing up practice, by interweaving different examples, people have a better sense of the underlying relationships. They get a keener sense of the system with outcomes sometimes as much as 40 percent higher.

There are some pretty clear practical applications of this research, and people should vary their practice—and avoid repetition. "The ultimate crime is practicing the same thing multiple times in a row. Avoid it like the plague," psychologist Nate Kornell told me. Instead, "practice for a long chunk of time but don't repeat anything."

For example, let's take someone who wants to learn more about American history, and they're supposed to read two articles about the Revolutionary War, two articles about the Civil War, and two articles about the Cold War. The research makes clear that the person would have deeper insights by mixing up the texts: So first a Revolutionary War article, then a Civil War article, and then a Cold War article, and then repeating the process. Why? Because mixing the articles helps people identify links across the different topic areas.

Granted, people will do this on their own. In skiing, for instance, someone might try to gain experience in different environments— twisty mountains, mogul-filled hills—along with different snow conditions, from powder to icy. In woodworking, people will try different tools and practice on various sorts of wood, oak, pine, or fir.

But people don't typically vary their practice—or examples— nearly enough. To spot deep connections, we need a lot of examples. In Goldstone's experiment, for instance, people really learned the deeper structure only after doing a half-dozen problems.

More important, we need to mix up those instances in a very direct way. The contrasts between the examples need to be immediate—and explicit. In the skiing example, for instance, it's not enough to ski a powdery slope one year and an icy hill the next year. The benefits of a more jumbled form of learning come from having the experience directly after each other. So, then, find an icy hill to shoot down right after skiing the powdery one.

The other thing to keep in mind here is that relationships can be slippery. It's often hard to find systems, to see the deeper structure. Psychologist Brian Ross recommends, for instance, that people be explicit about the deep structure they've identified. In his research, Ross has found that people solve problems a lot more easily if they write the name of the concept—or deep structure—next to the issue.

So if someone comes across a question like this:

A skateboarder enters a curved ramp moving pretty quickly, flying along at about a speed of 6.5 miles per second. Then the skateboarder leaves the ramp in a jump, slowing down slightly to 4 miles per second. The skateboarder and the skateboard have a combined mass of 55 kilograms. What's the height of the ramp?

The person should be clear about the principle and write down the concept alongside of it. In this case, something along the lines of: *The total mechanical energy is the same in the first and final state.* Similarly, I should write down *sampling with replacement* if I come across another problem featuring a monarch with seven daughters and five lands.

There's another way to find relationships within a field of expertise, and that's speculating. As a tool for understanding, as an aspect of the learning process, conjecture is a pretty old practice. It's certainly as old as the Bible, and the Good Book is littered with different types of hypotheticals.

"What if there are fifty righteous people in the city?" Abraham asks before the destruction of the city of Gomorrah. Later in the Old Testament, Moses asks God, "What if people don't believe me?" Jesus of Nazareth also frequently relied on the rhetorical device. "What if you see the Son of Man ascend to where he was before?" he once asked his disciples.

At least in this regard, the Bible isn't prophetic. The Quran also relies on all sorts of hypotheticals. So do the Analects of Confucius. For ancient writers—and most modern ones—the purpose of speculative queries is to push us to consider how ideas come together as a whole. Hypotheticals make us grapple with systems.

Consider, for instance, the question: *What would happen if you could not talk for the rest of your life?* There's not a simple yes or no answer to the query, and if you spend any time thinking about your answer, you'd think about systems, noodling over how you communicate with friends, how you network with colleagues, how you ultimately engage with any person that you meet.

Speculation forces a type of reasoning, a manner of thinking. Recall, for another example, Einstein's thought experiment that we discussed at the beginning of this chapter. In many ways, the exercise was little more than a set of hypotheticals: What if Einstein was moving at the speed of light? What if light appeared to be not moving at all?

Einstein continued to use hypotheticals through his career, using much the same approach to discover the theory of general relativity. In that instance, Einstein asked himself: What if someone was falling from a roof? What if the person falling had a toolbox that fell next to them? Later, Einstein called this bit of conjecture "his happiest thought" in large part because it unleashed a wave of new understanding.

There are more recent examples, too. Apple cofounder Steve Jobs understood the value of the approach, and he would ask speculative questions when he wanted to grapple fully with an idea. When Jobs returned to Apple as CEO in the late 1990s, for instance, he wanted to get a better handle on the company. So he pulled in managers, peppering them with queries like "If money were no object, what would you do?" and "If you had to cut half of your products, how would you do it?"

We can do this ourselves. If you're working on a tough problem, ask yourself "what if" questions. What if we had more time? What if we had more people? What if we had more resources? The answers are often pro-vocative and shed light on how a problem comes together as a system.

Interestingly, the power of this sort of hypothetical thinking goes back to our childhood, or back to someone about as different as Steve Jobs as possible: your average toddler. If you spend much time with kids, you know that it doesn't take much for them to engage in pretend play. Most children can clock hours playing school or they'll convince themselves that they're Superman, leaping off a couch, arms outstretched, screaming: *To the rescue!*

What's important here is that pretend play is a type of hypothetical. When kids engage in imagination games like pretending to be a caped crusader, they're engaging in speculation. And for researchers like Allison Gopnick, this activity goes a long way to developing robust thinking skills. "Pretend play, in particular, is related to a very specific but very important type of learning and reasoning—namely the kind of counterfactual reasoning that is intimately involved with causal knowledge and learning," writes Gopnick and a colleague.

As adults, we can't pretend to be Superman, at least not at work. But there are other ways to develop systems thinking in an area, to find an understanding of the relationships that matter.

One approach is the scientific process. Most people probably remember the basics—it's a strategy of understanding the world through a process of experimentation. The steps are as follows:

1. Look at the evidence.
2. Develop a theory.
3. Test the theory.
4. Come to a conclusion.

What's interesting is that the scientific process isn't all that different than a "what if" question. It's a speculative process that relies on data, and both methods require people to think in a more related way, to develop a more systemic form of expertise.

What's more, the scientific method of "theorize, test, repeat" can be applied in just about any discipline, helping people understand everything from photography to Shakespeare plays. Think of the approach as a matter of learning through dedicated problem solving. People propose different hypothesis, develop theories, and then reason their way to a conclusion.

So if people want to know more interior design, they might ask themselves: How would I design a bathroom if my client was wealthy and loved gold? How would I design a bathroom if my client was young and disabled? How would I design a bathroom with a nautical motif?

Take any bit of literature, as another example. People can gain a lot by discussing the implications of hypotheticals. Want to better understand *Romeo and Juliet*? Then consider what would have happened if the young lovers had not died. Would the Capulets and Montagues have continued their feud? Would the lovers have gotten married?

Perhaps the most convincing example of the power of this approach might come from illustrator Steve Brodner. In all likelihood, you know Brodner's work. His sketches run regularly in magazines like the *New Yorker* and *Rolling Stone*. Brodner has a trademark swirl-infused, burlesque style that's half cartoon, half H. L. Mencken. He is often hailed as one of the nation's most successful illustrators.

For decades, Brodner has been teaching an illustration class, using the scientific method to help people understand illustration. In Brodner's class, the theorize, test, repeat approach starts before students actually even illustrate a bit of text. He recommends that people write a one-sentence summary of their drawing before they even put charcoal pen to paper. This is the "theory" of the illustration. "Students need to ask themselves, 'What is it that I want to say about this?'" Brodner told me.

Then, as people begin to sketch, there's a "test" phase, and Brodner will have students try to refine their illustration. He wants people to experiment with different angles, with various frames, with unusual compositions. For Brodner, illustrators should be constantly asking themselves questions: *What if this feature came forward? What if that detail moved back?*

While Brodner advocates a type of focused experimentation, he will also offer a lot of how-to advice. He'll discuss the value of foregrounds or show examples of old Norman Rockwell sketches. He also spins his own theories on illustration, arguing how everything needs to come together in a sketch. Brodner called this idea his "unified theory" of

POP QUIZ #20

What's the most effective approach to learning something new from some text?

A. Circle key points in the text.

B. Reread relevant portions in the text.

C. Take an informal quiz based on the material in the text.

D. Highlight the crucial ideas in the text.

composition: "If you move one thing in an illustration, then it affects everything else," he told me.

The success of Brodner's approach can be measured by his graduates. Many are now professional illustrators themselves. More than that, there's Brodner himself, and he learned illustration in this way. As a kid, he would study his favorite illustrations looking for patterns, hunting for models, trying to understand how other artists put together sketches and illustrations, asking himself, *What if I took their approach? How would my sketch turn out? What would be different?*

It was learning by experiment.

When it comes to the relating phase of learning, dedicated experimentation is a powerful way to understand the system that underlies an area of expertise, so let's examine one more example—hacking.

Now, this is different than hacking as a crime. It's hacking as a learning method, a matter of using the scientific process to develop a skill. When programmers want to learn more about a bit of code or a specific program, they'll often just start to tinker. As programmer Eric Raymond argues, the hacking credo is to "make, test, debug, and document your change."

At least in tech circles, hacking has become a pretty popular approach, and there are now hacker-thons and hacker classrooms and hacker conferences. Many hacker spaces are little more than old garages. But some are pretty formal; I once visited a hacker space that felt a lot like a high-end children's museum.

Like so much in learning, process is key. Honing a skill often requires a type of awareness, and without much background knowledge and dedicated support, hacking is like unguided, unplanned learning: People don't gain much at all. Without deep knowledge along with a good amount of prior practice, people will become lost in the details. Cognitive load is overwhelmed, and outcomes are pretty low.

But rooted in content—and thoughtful guidance—hacking can hone skills. It's a practical version of a thought experiment. It's a way of applying the scientific method to a slice of mastery—and making relationships within a body of knowledge more clear.

To better understand the approach, take Facebook, which recently developed a hacking program for its new engineers. The goal of the six-week program is to get people tinkering with the company's software as soon as possible, and within a day or two of the start of the course, engineers start polishing the social network's software.

The new hires are encouraged to find bugs, to build new apps, to develop better software. Everyone works on live code, and if something goes wrong, the entire social network can go offline, a crash of updates and friend requests. This happened during one boot camp—a new employee brought down the service for millions. Today, the story is heralded within the company as an example of how much Facebook supports learning through focused experimentation.

To be clear, boot camp doesn't teach people how to gain the general skill of programming. Most of the boot campers arrive with significant software experience. Instead, it's a matter of polishing programming skills on Facebook's specific code—and learning the ways in which the company approaches problems.

"I would describe [boot camp] as a way for us to educate our engineers not only on how we code and how we do our systems, but also how to think culturally about how to attack challenges," Facebook's Joel Seligstein once told a reporter.

Facebook founder Mark Zuckerberg has pushed other ways to integrate hacking into the company's culture. The firm now has a "testing

POP QUIZ #21

To which of the following should you tailor your learning?

A. Learning styles (visual, auditory, etc.)
B. Previous knowledge
C. Interests
D. Ability
E. Right and left brain dominance

framework" that allows employees to experiment with the company's code without bringing down the social network. A few times a year, there's a hackathon at the company. One of the company's mottoes, Zuckerberg argues, is "move fast and break things," and for people who have some background skills, it's a valuable way to understand the underlying system in an area of expertise.

There's another way to learn a system within an area of expertise: visually.

In many ways, this was the lasting contribution of John Venn. A professor at Cambridge during the late nineteenth century, Venn was fastidious, fond of detailed lists and rigorous designs. An amateur engineer, Venn created one of the first machines that could "pitch" a cricket ball and might be the only philosopher to strike out members of the Australian national cricket team.

Venn was fascinated by the intricacies of logic, which often revolves around syllogisms. The classic syllogism is, of course, this one:

All men are mortal.
Socrates is a man.
Thus, Socrates is mortal.

In a book published in 1881, Venn added an important twist to the syllogism, arguing for a visual approach. So instead of using text to describe a bit of logic, Venn proposed using circles. People needed "visual aids," Venn argued, and for the previous syllogism, the diagram would look like this:

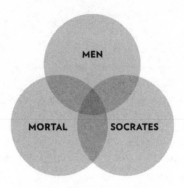

When it comes to learning, Venn's diagrams underscore an important point: People gain a lot by seeing a visual representation of a system of mastery. When we engage with some graphical form of relational expertise, we often develop important insights.

Concept maps are a helpful example. A cousin of the Venn diagram, a concept map provides a graphical way to grapple with a bit of knowledge. To get a sense of how concept maps work—and how they promote a systems understanding—let's go back to John Venn himself.

So first read this short biography of the British philosopher.

Born on August 4, 1834, John Venn is best remembered for inventing the Venn diagram. Early in his career, Venn helped popularize George Boole's work on logic, which became the basis for computer programming. A University of Cambridge lecturer, Venn also developed a theory of probability—called the frequency theory. Today, just about every statistician relies on the approach. Venn died on April 4, 1923, and in 2014, tech firm Google posted a version of a Venn diagram on the company's home page to honor the British philosopher.

Then take a look at the same material represented in a concept map, as follows:

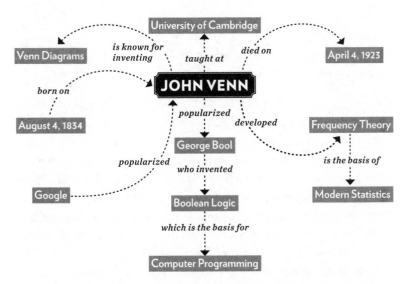

Compare the two approaches to understanding Venn's biography, and it's clear that the concept map helps people better understand relationships. The concept map suggests, for instance, that the fields of logic and computer programming have similar historical roots. The concept map also makes it easy to see that Venn was not a one-hit academic wonder. His writings also helped pioneer the field of computer science.

In the biographical text, however, these links are less clear. The linear nature of the text makes it hard to see these sorts of interwoven relationships. Certainly, I barely noticed them when I read the encyclopedia text for the first time.

Researcher Ken Kiewra has been studying different types of concept maps for years, and he argues that one of the main benefits of graphic organizers is that they show deeper associations within an area of knowledge. "Graphics organizers help people put the pieces together," Kierwa told me.

In his own life, Kierwa uses the learning tools all the time. At work, he uses graphic organizers for any sort of writing or research project. At home, Kiewra often relies on them to make important decisions, and he recently hauled out a version of a concept map to help his son sort out some decisions about college. "Things will just pop out," he told me.

When it comes to graphical representations like concept maps,

True or false: Young students learn more if they "trace" a math
problem with their finger.

technology can help a lot. The technical devices that cause information
overload can often help us map our way out of that overload.

The *Atlantic*'s James Fallows provides useful advice on this point.
One of the nation's most well-respected journalists, Fallows often
reviews information management software, and he has long sworn by a
concept-mapping software known as Tinderbox. The tool helps organize files in a way that draws links across fields and topics, and Fallows
describes it simply as a "software-for-thinking" program.

Similarly, writer Steven Johnson is a proponent of a concept mapping tool called DEVONthink. He argues that the software offers "con-
nective power," and it helps him spot relationships that he would not
have uncovered otherwise. When Johnson uses DEVONthink, "larger
idea takes shape in my head, built upon the trail of associations the
machine has assembled for me."

For my part, I've become a devotee of the writing software known as
Scrivener. For me, it's software for writing because it takes more of a
concept-mapping approach, offering a virtual corkboard and a more
networked management system. Not surprisingly, both Fallows and
Johnson also rely on Scrivener, and at least like Fallows, I tend to use
the software only for large projects like books. In other words, there has
to be a lot of text to make the software worthwhile.

This last point is important. Because if we have lots of data, we need
robust tools to sort our way through that data. If we have a lot of trees, we're
going to need some device to uncover the connecting forest. This is why we
need to learn relationships, too. They're ultimately what help us learn.

The Value of Analogy

In this chapter, we've been pretty focused on relationships, studying
ways to improve learning by looking for deeper systems. We've examined

ways to improve learning by mixing up our practice and glimpsed the
ways that activities like hacking can provide a type of understanding.

This is all important. But we're missing something. More specifically, we're missing a way to understand how exactly skills and knowledge relate to each other, and it's that idea that brings us to analogies, or
the way that we learn through comparison. Put differently, relational
thinking has a driver, and that driver is analogical thought.

Granted, analogies can seem like an esoteric thing. They often
spark memories of IQ tests (*Nest is to bird, as doghouse is to* _____) or
bizarre turns of phrase like the term "the pecking order." But analogies
are at the heart of understanding relationships, of grappling with systems of thought, and they can help us solve a new or enduring issue.

As an example, let's consider Tom and Ray Magliozzi. For years, the
two brothers had a radio show on WBUR in Boston in which they talked
about car repair. Called *Car Talk,* the show typically featured the two
brothers jawing like two teens in the back of math class—cracking bad
jokes, teasing each other, throwing out double or even triple entendres.

"Don't drive like my brother," Tom would say.

"No, don't drive like *my* brother," Ray would say.

In between the slapstick humor and goofy jokes, the brothers
would solve car problems. One day, for instance, a woman named
Mary Gordon Spence phoned the Magliozzis. From her home in
Texas, Spence explained that every time that she tapped on the brakes
of her Mazda Tribute, there'd be a loud squeak. It's "a high-pitched,
one-note sound," Spence told the brothers.

The brothers listened and then declared: *There's a problem with the
power brakes' vacuum booster.*

This is impressive. To review the facts again: The brothers had never
seen Spence's car. They didn't know if Spence's Mazda was leaking oil
or had an old timing belt or if there was rust in the radiator. But still, the
Magliozzis managed to solve the problem.

So what happened? What, mental trick did the brothers use to crack
the problem?

Well, a lot of the answer goes back to analogy. Since the brothers
couldn't physically evaluate the Mazda, they made a comparison in

their mind. They thought about other experiences in which they had a squeaky brake issue with a Mazda or comparable car. In the simplest of terms, the brothers thought of a parallel.

To anyone who listened carefully to the show, this approach was a constant. When the Magliozzis helped a woman with rust on her old Subaru, they talked about rust on their old cars. When someone called in from Africa, the brothers discussed their own visits to Africa. And when a man's electric winch died, the Magliozzis began describing a similar problem that they had come across, declaring "everything you say fits."

To a degree, analogies can seem like just another type of relational thinking. But when it comes to learning, the approach goes deeper than that. At the heart of an analogy is a comparison. More exactly, analogies make us find similarities and differences. They help us understand things that are new or different, which makes them very powerful learning tools, as we will see.

To get a better sense of how analogies help people learn, let's consider this well-studied problem: Imagine, for a moment, that you're a doctor, and a patient comes in one morning with a deadly tumor in her stomach. There's no way to operate—the patient will suffer too much blood loss. Luckily, one of your colleagues recently created a tumor-killing ray— let's call it the Vapor 3000—and with just one long blast, the tumor will be gone.

There's a crucial hitch, though. If you fire the tumor-killing rays at full blast, everything around the stomach—intestines, liver, colon—will also become vaporized. In other words, you can't shoot one huge blast to solve the problem. But then again, if you fire a weak blast from the Vapor 3000, nothing happens to the tumor. Just one low-power shot just isn't enough.

So what do you do?

Over the past forty years, psychologist Keith Holyoak has presented this problem to hundreds of different people. The riddle has come to define his career, in fact, and the answer rests on a concept known as convergence. Specifically, the best solution is to fire short blasts of rays from the Vapor 3000 at the tumor from various angles.

There are a number of ways to help people arrive at this answer, and people with a background in engineering have an easier time. It's the Knowledge Effect all over again. Not surprisingly, advice helps a lot, too, and if someone like Holyoak gives someone a tip, they're much likely to find the answer.

But what Holyoak has shown over the decades is that analogies provide one of the best ways to help people learn. Giving people a likeness of the answer dramatically improves their ability to crack the riddle. Holyoak first demonstrated this fact some four decades ago using the tumor problem—and evidence for his argument has grown far more robust over time.

Most recently, Holyoak showed some subjects an animation that depicts an analogous solution to the tumor problem. Imagine multiple cannons in a circle firing on a castle, and after seeing the video, people were far more likely to provide the right solution. "The continuous representation forced people to think more in terms of the analogue," Holyoak told me when I reached him in his office at UCLA.

Part of the benefit of analogies is that they help us understand new concepts and ideas. They give people a way to understand something that they're not particularly familiar with, and people can use analogies to get their heads around something new in the same way that we can use Latin to understand Italian or use Spanish to grapple with Portuguese.

Companies know this, and many start-ups will use Uber as an analog, a way to help them explain a new product or service. The company Blue Apron has presented itself as the Uber for high-end cooking. The dry-cleaning company DRYV has been described as Uber but for dry cleaning. There's also now an Uber for haircuts and for shuttling kids around.

Marketing efforts are often similar. The insurance firm State Farm has relied on the jingle: *Like a good neighbor, State Farm is there*. Politicians do this all the time, too, and policymakers sold the notion of a "three strikes" crime law based on a baseball analogy, as writer John Pollack argued in his wonderful book *Shortcut*.

You can also think of analogy as the rightful mother of invention. It's a way for us to create unexpected links, and it turns out that the history of creativity is littered with analogical twists. Johannes Gutenberg invented the printing press after seeing a wine press. The Wright brothers studied birds in order to build the world's first airplane. Twitter is half text messaging, half social media.

In this regard, analogies serve as a bridge between two ideas or concepts. Most people are familiar with *Romeo and Juliet,* for instance, and so an analogy makes it easier to explain the musical *West Side Story*: Just think of a 1950s version of *Romeo and Juliet* set in New York City.

Another example is the C. S. Lewis novel *The Lion, the Witch and the Wardrobe.* One easy way to explain the plot is to reference the Bible, and the book is a fantasy-novel version of the New Testament. The film *Thelma and Louise*? Actress Susan Sarandon starred in the 1980s blockbuster, and she describes it well: It's a "cowboy movie with women instead of guys."

As a way to promote understanding, analogies require some attention. Holyoak recommends, for instance, that people rely on a source analogy that they know well. The idiom "it cuts like a knife," for instance, works as an idiom because people are pretty familiar with knives.

When using an analogy to understand something, people should also be sure to outline the exact similarities between the two things or ideas. In the tumor problem, example, people solve the problem more easily if the analogues are presented next to each other, if not side by side, according to Holyoak.

Granted, analogies don't always work. Sometimes there's not much of a similarity. It's hard to make a robust link between, say, the president of the United States and a set of car keys, or a goldfish and Mount Kilimanjaro.

Yet even weak analogies have their own sort of power, and some comedians like Steven Wright built their careers out of toying with analogies. "It's a small world, but I wouldn't want to paint it," Wright once said.

Jerry Seinfeld wasn't all that different. "I was the best man at the wedding," he once remarked. "If I'm the best man, why is she marrying him?"

POP QUIZ #23

True or false: Learning should be spaced out over time.

Same for the Magliozzi brothers, and not long after the first call from Mary Gordon Spence about the Mazda, the two brothers reached out again to her again. The brothers wanted to make they sure that they provided Spence with the correct answer to her car problem.

"So was it the vacuum brake booster?" one of the brothers asked.

"You know, I would not have called y'all," Spence said, "unless you were going to tell the truth, and you were right on. So right on."

Spence did have one complaint, though. Without the noise from the brakes, she couldn't tap out songs anymore like *Jingle Bells*. "I get so bored down now driving down the street."

The brothers laughed, and then they thought of an analogy, a new twist on the problem.

"I'm going to suggest that you take up the harmonica."

As a learning tool, analogies work because they make us ask a specific set of questions: How are these things similar? What makes them different? How are they comparable?

In other words, analogies help us understand categories. They make us think about groups and what constitutes a group. When people say that apples and oranges are both fruits, for instance, they're relying on a type of analogical thinking. They're matching up the attributes of apples and oranges—both have seeds, come from trees, have a type of flesh—to declare them to be fruits.

Another example is dogs. While a furry malamute and a five-pound pug look almost nothing alike, we have no problem calling them both dogs because we understand the analogue that connects them. We understand that both animals have certain things in common—they are social mammals with noses, tails, legs, and sharp teeth.

We've come across the value of similarities and differences before when we discussed Rob Goldstone's work, and one of the reasons that people should mix up their learning is that it pushes people to think in commonalties. Specifically, we get a better sense of the category of fruit if we come across various fruits. Likewise, we better understand the category of dog if we come across various dogs.

Analogies can help, and they can sharpen the distinction between different ideas or things. They provide a compare-and-contrast approach to learning. Take the radio show *Car Talk* again. At first glance, the show might seem pretty revolutionary, at least for NPR, given the goofy jokes and practical subject matter. But make a comparison, and *Car Talk* was a pretty normal outgrowth of NPR's programming history. Before *Car Talk*, for instance, there was Garrison Keillor's *Prairie Home Companion,* which was also part vaudeville, part social commentary.

Another example is Einstein, whom we discussed at the start of this chapter. We can learn a lot by comparing him with other great physicists. By seeing similarities and differences, people get a keener sense of the deep features of a fact or concept. Relative to other top physicists, for instance, Einstein was much less of a dedicated mathematician. Einstein's contemporary Paul Dirac had equations named after him. But Einstein, not so much. Einstein was also much more interested in social justice issues than many of his peers—and much more of a risk taker.

Still doubtful of the value of compare and contrast? Take a study that occurred some years ago at a business training session when a group of managers and aspiring managers all piled into a room. As is true of so many business training seminars, there was a training packet with some sample cases, and the group was supposed to read the cases.

The managers were going to learn about contingent contracts, which are generally pretty helpful in negotiations. When a contract is conditional on certain actions or outcomes, both parties typically have more flexibility. But for all sorts of reasons, people tend not to use contingent contracts in actual negotiations. People are not aware of them—or they just don't understand them. This training aimed to address that issue, and all of the individuals had to read the training packet before they began to role-play their negotiation.

A few psychologists oversaw the training, and they slipped one small tweak into the session. One half of the consultants would just "describe" the case studies. The other half had to "think about the similarities" of the cases.

It wasn't much of a difference, only a few words, really. But the use of the more analogical prompt had a dramatic effect. It pushed a compare-and-contrast approach, and the second group was almost twice as likely to use contingent contracts. They also understood the underlying idea a lot better.

Dedre Gentner was one of the psychologists who worked on the negotiation training study, and I met up with her recently in the hallway of a drab conference hotel. We were both getting coffee.

When I indicated an interest in analogies, Gentner pointed at me excitedly. "If we see the same thing over and over, that's a good way to get started. But if you don't see more dissimilar things, basically, you'd better stay in same village your whole life."

"But analogies are hard," I countered.

Gentner nodded. "But analogies are what allow you to take knowledge on the road."

There's one final thing to keep in mind about analogies when it comes to learning: They can help us engage in a deeper form of reasoning.

It was Dartmouth College professor Pamela Crossley who helped me understand this idea. In her classes, Crossley likes to assign books and articles that are wrong. She'll hand out articles that brim with wild ideas and absurd concepts. Students in her class will watch documentaries that argue that the planet Venus once nearly slammed into Earth, or they'll have to read journal articles that argue that the early Egyptians were behind much of the success of ancient Greece.

This can all seem a little absurd. Certainly, it felt that way to me when I enrolled in Crossley's class some years ago. I was in my early twenties, a senior in college, and as part of the class, Crossley assigned a book called *Holy Blood, Holy Grail.* Written in the 1980s, the book argues that the descendants of Jesus aimed to control Europe through a network of secretive groups including a modern-day version of the Knights Templar.

But we couldn't simply dismiss the book as a freak conspiracy theory, and as part of the class, Crossley pushed us to figure out what the book got right—and wrong. In other words, she wanted people to reason their way through the book's claims, and it turned out that some aspects of the book were, in fact, accurate. The Knights Templar did exist—and the king of France eventually outlawed the group, burning its leaders at the stake.

But we also had to show what the book got wrong, and *Holy Blood, Holy Grail* brimmed with tenuous logic. In the book, the authors argued, for instance, that if Jesus and Mary Magdalene knew each other, then, ergo, they had children. But there's no evidence that suggests that the two individuals were married. Moreover, there's not a shred of support—really nothing at all—for the notion that the descendants of Jesus and Mary are still alive today, forget planning to take over the world.

For me, Crossley's approach to teaching—and learning—was wildly different. In my previous courses, things were right or wrong, true or false. But in Crossley's view, the world wasn't quite like that. Nor was learning, and students had to build explanations. She wanted us to study how we inferred our way to an answer, to compare lines of thinking, to engage in analogical thought. "Reasoning is the course. It's about looking at the methods of reasoning as an object of study," Crossley told me recently.

In many ways, the seeds of this book were planted in Crossley's class. The course sparked a fascination with how people gain effective thinking skills. But more important, the class underscores one of the final benefit of analogies, and it turns out that analogies are the driver of reason. By being at the center of any sort of concept, comparisons foster logic. As cognitive scientist Douglas Hofstadter argues, analogy serves as the "fuel and fire of thinking."

We can get better at this sort of reasoning, and analogical thought can help us learn about the nature of errors. Take overgeneralization, or making sweeping conclusions based on little evidence. Overgeneralization is a common mistake, basically a case of taking an analogy too far. If you don't drive a certain road because you once had an accident there, that's an overgeneralization—and a weak analogy.

POP QUIZ #24

A parent praises a student for solving a math problem. Which praise will be the most effective in motivating the student to work through difficult problems in the future?

A. You must be really smart.
B. You must have worked really hard.
C. You've got a brain for math.
D. Math must come easy to you.

Similarly, we need to consider assumptions. We will often ask leading questions or reason from a weak premise. Lots of ideas—and analogies—suffer from this problem. People argue, for instance, that since it's cold outside, global warming is a myth. The weak assumption here is that ambient temperature is a good judge of global warming.

And then there's the weighing of facts. This was one of the main problems with the book *Holy Blood, Holy Grail*—and really most conspiracy theories. In *Holy Blood, Holy Grail*, for instance, the authors argue that since Jesus and Mary Magdalene knew each other, they must have gotten married and had children.

But that argument conflates two very different activities—acquaintance and marriage—and when it comes to developing conclusions, to creating robust analogies, we need to be careful not to give some things too much weight.

Like just about everything in learning, the Knowledge Effect plays a role, and as researcher Dan Willingham and many others have argued, it's very hard to teach these sorts of reasoning skills outside of a topic area. In learning, content comes before connections. But in the end, if we don't learn thinking skills within a topic, we haven't really learned.

The Skill of Problem Solving

We've been talking a lot in this book about the ways that problem solving can help us learn. In the previous chapter, we discussed schools like

High Tech High, where students use problems to learn math and science. In this chapter, we've been looking at the scientific process as a way to hone our skill and examined Steve Brodner's illustration class—and Facebook's hackathon boot camp.

Yet there's something important that we have not addressed. It's an idea that goes back to taking a more connected approach to learning, to relating what we know—that's the actual skill of problem solving.

This is important for two reasons. First, problem solving itself matters, and we often learn skills to resolve issues. Second, we're better at solving problems if we have a relational form of expertise. Understanding systems helps people use their knowledge in different contexts—and ultimately problem solving boils down to a type of analogical reasoning.

Gurpreet Dhaliwal provides a case study of this idea. An emergency medicine doctor, Dhaliwal has been dubbed a "superstar" of medical problem solving. Academic journals often call on him to model his diagnostic thinking skills. He teaches the practice of clinical reasoning at one of the nation's most esteemed medical schools.

I met up with Dhaliwal not long ago in the corner of a hotel lobby, and he has a remarkable mental Rolodex of illnesses. From his decades of practice, Dhaliwal knows the classic signs of Sjögren's syndrome—a sawdust-dry mouth. If someone has a knife-like pain in their side, Dhaliwal will look for common illnesses—appendicitis, kidney stones—but he'll also consider a more obscure illness like a loss of blood to the kidney.

Still, knowledge isn't enough for the simple reason that symptoms don't always match up with an illness. Textbook cases, it seems, are found only in textbooks. Dizziness, for instance, can be the signal of something serious—or might be the symptom of a lack of sleep. The same with fatigue or chest pain. They might be signs of a pressing heart issue—or the result of nail-biting stress. "What is tricky is to figure out what's signal and what's noise," Dhaliwal told me.

Context plays a big role. So does the history of the patient. When it comes to adults, a complaint about back pain is probably nothing serious. But in children, back pain could be the sign of a deadly illness like cancer. For another example: If someone owns a pet parrot and comes into the ER, the list of potential diagnoses is very different because the birds often transmit lung diseases.

What's central, then, is matching the symptoms with a diagnosis, creating a link between the disease and the symptoms of the disease. This is perhaps the most important skill in medicine, Dhaliwal argues, and the practice boils down to a hunt for a connection, a recognition of patterns. "Diagnosis is often a matching exercise," he argues.

To get a better sense of how this works, I once watched Dhaliwal solve a perplexing case, trying to diagnose the case of an older man who was hacking up blood. It was at a medical conference, with Dhaliwal standing at a dais at the front of a room. Another doctor, Joseph Coffman, provided the specifics.

Basically, a man came into the ER one day—let's call him Andreas—and he could not breathe very well. Andreas also had a slight fever and had recently shed a lot of weight.

At the start of the diagnosis process, in the early steps of the approach, Dhaliwal recommends developing a one-sentence description of the problem. "It's like a good Google search," he said. "You want a relevant and concise summary," and in this case, it was *sixty-eight-year-old man with hemoptysis, or coughing up blood.*

Dhaliwal also aims to make a few tentative generalizations early in the process to help guide his thinking. In the case of Andreas, Dhaliwal thought that maybe the man had a lung infection? Or maybe an autoimmune problem?

There wasn't enough data to offer any sort of reliable conclusion, though, and really Dhaliwal was just gathering information. Then came images from a chest X-ray, the results from an HIV test, and as each bit of evidence rolled in, Dhaliwal talked about various scenarios, assembling the data in different ways to see if it might fit different potential theories of the case. "To diagnose, we are sometimes trying to unify, and sometimes trying to split, to slice," he said.

Dhaliwal's eyes flashed, for instance, when it became apparent that Andreas had visited Ghana. It meant that Andreas could potentially

POP QUIZ #25

True or false: To really learn a subject, you need to know the facts in that subject.

have an uncommon disease like Ebola. Dhaliwal then discovered that Andreas had worked in factories that dealt in fertilizer and lead batteries. Again, Dhaliwal's mind accelerated through different scenarios. The factory detail meant that Andreas was exposed to noxious chemicals, and for a while, it seemed that a toxic substance like lead might be at the root of Andreas's illness.

Dhaliwal had a few strong pieces of evidence that supported the lead poisoning theory, including some odd-looking red blood cells that came up on a lab test. But Dhaliwal wasn't comfortable with the depth of the proof. It seemed insufficient, given all the symptoms. "I'm like an attorney presenting in a court of law," Dhaliwal told me. "I want evidence."

As the case progressed—and Andreas got sicker—Dhaliwal came across a new detail: There was a growth in the heart. This shifted the potential diagnosis in a different direction. It knocked out the toxic chemical angle because lead poisoning doesn't spark growths on the heart.

Eventually, sometime later, Dhaliwal uncovered a robust pattern, an effective analogue between Andreas's symptoms and Dhaliwal's knowledge of illnesses, and Dhaliwal settled on a cardiac angiosarcoma, or heart cancer. It explained the red blood count, the mass in the heart, the hawking up of blood. "Diagnosing often comes down the ability to pull things together," he argued.

Then, finally, there was an autopsy of the heart, and Dhaliwal's diagnosis was proven correct. A dozen other doctors flocked to him after the event with follow-up questions. "You don't think about he had hemoglobin in the lung?" one doctor asked.

After some minutes, the crowd faded, and then Dhaliwal thought how to get to the airport. Would he take an Uber? Or should he grab a cab? It was another issue to solve, and he decided on an Uber. It was likely to be cheaper and equally comfortable—it was the solution that best matched the problem.

Much like learning itself, problem solving is a process, a method, an approach. It was George Pólya who first put forth this idea. A Hungarian mathematician, Pólya was one of those important but obscure Europeans from the early part of the last century. With his twinkly eyes and heavy glasses, Pólya had the look of an eccentric academic. He had the personality of one, too, and a university once kicked Pólya out for hitting another student.

As a young mathematician, Pólya revolutionized the field of probability with a series of groundbreaking papers. Numerical theory became another expertise, and Pólya established one of the field's organizing theories. Over the years, Pólya also developed important papers about polynomials and combinatorics. Eventually, he had some five different theorems named after him, and many consider Pólya to be one of the greatest mathematicians of the twentieth century.

In his late sixties, while teaching at Stanford University, Pólya turned his focus to the methods of problem solving. He wanted to map out "the motives and procedures of the solution" to any sort of problem, and eventually Pólya detailed a systemic approach with four distinct phases:

> **The first phase** was "understanding." In this phase, people should look to find the core idea or nature of the problem. "You have to understand the problem," Pólya argued. "What is the unknown? What are the data?"
> **The second phase** was "devising a plan," in which people mapped out how they'd address the problem. "Find the connection between the data and the unknown," Pólya counseled.
> **The third phase** of problem solving was "carrying out the plan." This was a matter of doing—and vetting: "Can you prove that it is correct?"
> **The final phase** was "looking back," or learning from the solutions: By "reexamining the result and the path that led to it, [people] could consolidate their knowledge and develop their ability to solve problems."

Pólya's approach was pioneering. No one had studied the issue of problem solving before, at least in any sort of dedicated way. Not the

Greeks, not the Romans, not early philosophers like Hobbes or Confucius, and almost a half a dozen publishers simply rejected Pólya's out-of-left-field manuscript, penning letters along the lines of *thanks but no thanks.*

Titled *How to Solve It*, the book eventually found a publisher, selling more than a million copies, and Pólya's technique soon filtered into fields far beyond math. In fields like medicine, the process has become just about universal. Gurpreet Dhaliwal, for instance, more or less followed Pólya's method on the day that he diagnosed Andreas with heart cancer.

Dhaliwal's "Google search term" analogy, for instance, is much like Pólya's phase two. And much like Pólya's phase three, Dhaliwal recommends that doctors read up on an illness to double-check details. "It's like visiting the Wikipedia page," Dhaliwal told me. "You want to refresh your knowledge."

In areas like engineering, Pólya's strategy evolved into something known as design thinking, and the approach has more of a social sciences bent. Stanford professor Bernard Roth specializes in design thinking, and when it comes to problem solving, he argues that people should put themselves in the role of the person who has the problem and ask themselves: "What would it do if I solved this problem?"

These approaches to problem solving provide surprising benefits. A health writer for the *New York Times*, Tara Parker-Pope is generally pretty jaded, taking a harsh eye to the latest medical trends. In her work, Parker-Pope has debunked various fads and bits of accepted pop science wisdom, showing, for instance, that some marriages will benefit from arguments.

But when Parker-Pope decided to apply design thinking to her own weight problem, she saw clear impact. As part of the problem-solving process, Parker-Pope first aimed to understand the issue (Pólya's phase one). Eventually, she came to the conclusion that social connections—along with sleep and diet issues—were to blame. "Weight loss was really not my problem," Parker-Pope argued. "Instead, I needed to focus on my friendships, boosting my energy, and getting better sleep."

Parker-Pope targeted these specific issues and then planned out her solutions (Pólya's phases two and three). She ate less wheat-based products, which had led to an afternoon "carb crash." She focused on getting more sleep. Friends also became a priority, and Parker-Pope managed to slough off some 25 pounds. Eventually, she also wrote an article reflecting on her experience for the paper (Polya's phase four).

When it comes to problem solving, there are other important techniques. Studies suggest that people who ask themselves questions are more effective at problem solving than people who don't. For instance, ask yourself: Is there enough evidence? What's the counterargument? Likewise, we need to reason about our reasoning. Have we fallen for any weak logic? Are we susceptible to any bias?

Prioritization is important, too, and in many fields like medicine or car repair, some problems are more pressing than others. If someone is trying to solve an issue during a military battle, the first thing to do is to check on their own safety. This also explains why flight attendants tell fliers to put their own oxygen mask on first in the case of an emergency: It's hard to help others if we can't breathe ourselves.

When I reached out to Stanford psychologist Dan Schwartz, he argued that people also need to recognize when approaches are failing—and try something new. Good problem solvers know when something isn't working out and will try a different strategy. "We have to self-generate feedback," Schwartz argued.

Successful problem solving also relies on many of the things that we've already seen in this book, and people need to set goals and develop plans. They need to be engaged and develop background knowledge and then takes steps to execute those plans. People also should stress-test different ideas, looking for relationships and analogies, and use planners like concept maps to come up with patterns and systems.

For his part, Pólya also recommended the value of reviewing, of looking back, of reconsidering solutions. This idea is at the heart of Pólya's phase four, and it's the issue that we will turn to next in this book.

Chapter 6

RETHINK

DANIEL KAHNEMAN IS one of the most important psychologists of our time. Because of his pioneering research on the biases of the human mind, Kahneman won the Nobel Prize a few years ago. Together with his colleague Amos Tversky, Kahneman basically created the field of behavioral economics. If you've read a book like *Predictably Irrational* or *Nudge* or even *Moneyball,* they all depend in some way on Kahneman's work.

A few years ago, a reporter from the *Guardian* newspaper interviewed Kahneman. They were sitting in a London hotel, tucked in a side room of the hotel lobby. In his eighties, Kahneman was muted, his voice barely louder than a murmur. The reporter must have asked him something along the lines of *how can humans become better thinkers?*

"What would I eliminate if I had a magic wand?" Kahneman asked rhetorically. "Overconfidence."

The simplicity of Kahneman's comment belies its importance, and all of us suffer from overconfidence. We think we know a lot more than we do, and just about everyone thinks that they're smarter, prettier, and more skilled than average. In work settings, we think we're more productive than the typical person sitting next to us. At parties, we think we're more charming than the usual people in the room.

This sort of overconfidence can trip up just about anyone. In politics, exhibit A might be the "Mission Accomplished" banner that hung on a battleship during a war in Iraq that was far from over. In business circles, only brimming self-confidence can explain the implosion that

POP QUIZ #26

True or false: Students are good evaluators of educator quality.

was the AOL–Time Warner merger—or the collapse of Lehman Brothers in the housing crisis. In sports, there's boxer Lennox Lewis. After winning the heavyweight championship, Lewis got knocked out by a guy who basically came in off the street.

Overconfidence goes a long way to preventing effective learning. When people are overconfident, they don't study. They don't practice. They don't ask themselves questions. Overconfidence is particularly harmful to engaging in more challenging forms of learning. If we think we know something, we're simply not going to take the hard steps of relating ideas or extending what we know.

The issue is more than a matter of monitoring or even metacognition. We also simply don't do enough to deliberate, to reflect, to make sure that we have internalized what we've learned. And it's this idea that brings us to the last stage of the learning process: the ways in which we need to rethink what we know.

Do you know how a toilet bowl works? I'm going to assume so. You use the toilet every day. Most of us do, and at one point or another, you've probably opened up the cistern that sits behind the bowl, maybe to check the stopper? Or jiggle the handle?

So then answer this question: From 1 to 10, rate how well you understand the functioning of a toilet bowl?

1. **Not at all.** I have no idea how a toilet works.
5. **Medium.** I have a basic understanding of the workings of a toilet.
10. **Expert.** I have even installed a few toilets.

I'm going to guess you'd give yourself probably a 5 or 6—you're a little better than average but no handyman.

At first glance, psychologist Art Markman was pretty sure he knew how a toilet worked, too. Markman spent a lot of time tinkering with toilets when he was a kid, as he describes in his wonderful book *Smart Thinking*. Markman's parents would often yell at him to stop fiddling with the plumbing. All in all, Markman would have most likely rated himself at least a 5 or a 6 when it came to having an understanding of how a toilet works.

But then, one day, Markman began asking himself some questions about toilets. How did the water flow out of the toilet? What was that bump at the bottom of the outside of the bowl? Did he even know how the water flowed into the bowl? It was then that Markman realized that his explanation of the toilet didn't do much. He didn't actually have a systemic understanding of how the device actually worked.

Markman's understanding of the toilet was a sleight of mind. He thought that he understood. He believed that he could explain. But in reality, Markman couldn't describe how the device actually came together or make any real sense out of it. He certainly couldn't take a toilet apart and put it back together again.

The problem wasn't time. Like the rest of us, Markman has had plenty of hours to contemplate plumbing technology. He doesn't lack talent, either, and he was once the executive director of the Cognitive Science Society. But in the end, Markman simply overestimated his ability. "For all of the time I spent watching the water leave the toilet tank," Markman writes, "I don't know the mechanism that carries the water from the tank to the bowl and distributes it."

This brings us to a type of learning catch-22: The more we know, the more we think we know. In this sense, a little bit of knowledge is more than figuratively dangerous. It actually confuses us. Psychologists have studied this idea for decades, and they've come up with all sorts of snappy names—the expert blind spot, the fluency heuristic, the illusion of explanatory depth.

All of these fancy names boil down to the same essential idea: We often think we know more than we do. We overestimate our skills. We don't realize how much we don't know. So you might rank yourself as a 6 on your knowledge of toilets. But all in all, you're probably a 4.

This brings us to the first lesson of rethinking what you know: Be humble. I've seen the need for this humility in my own research, and as part of a survey, I once asked people to estimate how good they were at identifying great instructional practices. If people had a good sense of their skills, there should have been an equal distribution: 50 percent below, 50 percent above. But there wasn't, and almost 90 percent of people said that they were at least average at identifying great teaching.

Admittedly, this sort of brashness has its benefits. Without some overconfidence, no one would write a book or publish a study. Confidence can also give a type of motivation. College students who exaggerated their GPA in interviews, for instance, later showed more improvement in their grades than students who were more honest. As one of the researchers on the study explained to me, the exaggerators had "higher goals for achievement."

It's also just embarrassing to give the I've-got-no-idea shrug, and I am chagrined to admit the occasions that I've been overconfident. Over the years, I've lost money to street hustlers—and shown up for a flight on the wrong day. Some years ago, I gave a presentation to the California State Legislature that was so off message that one of the legislators half-joked that he wanted to challenge me to a fistfight.

One driver of overconfidence in learning is familiarity. If an idea or fact comes easily to us—or we've just come across it a lot—people are far more likely to think that we know something about it, even if we don't. This explains why people are overconfident about toilets—they're around them all the time. This also explains why people are overconfident in their ability identify great teachers—they've seen a lot of instruction.

We overestimate our ability in other ways. For example, if something looks simple or common, then it seems a lot easier to learn. If people read an article with large images, they're more likely to think that they will understand the content. If someone watches a professor enthrall a class, they'll believe that they will learn more from that professor, even if they don't.

When I reached Art Markman at his office of the University of Texas, Austin, he gave another example: TED Talks. The iPad of the lecture circuit, TED Talks are highly polished speeches on everything from juggling to morality. There's lots of storytelling and dramatic moments, bright klieg lights and sharp camera angles. Many of the videos have been viewed more than ten million times.

But for Markman, TED Talks can do more harm than good when it comes to learning. "My problem isn't with the talks," Markman told me. "It's the way we consume them. We hear this fluently presented topic for 15 minutes, and then we move on to the next thing." Put differently, TED Talks might seem like a learning experience. There's an expert lecturing on a well-lit stage, after all. But because the material is so easily learned, it's also easily forgotten.

Alone, this might not be a big deal. So what if a TED Talk takes a highly polished approach to a topic? Who cares if the videos are slickly produced? Ironically, however, this sort of polish can keep us from learning. Some psychologists call it the "double curse" of learning: If you don't know if you're right, then you don't know if you're wrong, and not surprisingly, people study less if something seems easy. They put in less effort if something appears simple and easy-to-know.

There is, then, a second very important driver of overconfidence in learning, and that's past performance. Prior experience often shapes our learning judgments. If we always ace our chemistry tests, we're much less likely to study for a chemistry test, even if the next exam might be far more difficult than the previous ones. If we are constantly developing PowerPoint presentations, we're going to do less preparing for a presentation, even if the upcoming meeting is much different than earlier ones.

The military calls this Victory Disease. If generals win a lot of battles, they become big-headed. They believe too much in their ability. Custer's Last Stand is the classic example. Before the Battle of the Little Bighorn in the summer of 1876, Lt. Col. George Armstrong Custer had shot up the ranks of the Army. He played heroic roles in major Civil War battles like Gettysburg. When Robert E. Lee surrendered at the courthouse in Appomattox, Custer was in the room, just a few steps behind Ulysses S. Grant.

It seems that the experience made Custer believe that he could

POP QUIZ #27

True or false: Right-brained people learn differently from left-brained people.

never lose, and despite all sorts of evidence and endlessly clear signs, Custer dramatically underestimated how many Native American warriors he would encounter in the Battle of the Little Bighorn. He never thought that the group of Sioux would plan to cut off any route of escape—and ignored suggestions that Sitting Bull might have a fighting force five times larger than his group of tired soldiers.

So Custer didn't plan ahead or develop a contingency strategy or even give particularly specific orders. More than a thousand Native Americans would eventually kill Custer and his 200 soldiers, yet, according to legend, Custer's last words were "Hurrah, boys, we've got 'em!"

The need to rethink our learning goes deeper than issues of overconfidence. People also often don't pay attention. In this sense, we need to review our learning because we're often more robot than human, more droid than deliberate. The issue is not that we misjudge something; it's that we don't even judge in the first place.

When I was a kid, for instance, a picture of the Virgin Mary hung right outside of my bedroom door. The picture was a reproduction of a medieval canvas, an elegant painting of Mary embracing baby Jesus, a glimmering white shawl hanging over her head. A small wood frame enclosed the painting, and I probably passed the artwork a half-dozen times each day.

What happened next is a bit of family lore, one of those stories that has been told so many times that it's a mix of memory and cautionary fable. The narrative starts with my mother rushing into the kitchen one day. She demanded to know who had scrawled a mustache on the Virgin Mary, making the mother of Jesus look like Groucho Marx.

Who has done such a thing? she demanded to know. *Who has van-*

dalized the painting of the Virgin Mary? Who has put the black mustache on her?

At first my mother fingered my brother as the most likely offender. He was a teenager—and undoubtedly mischievous. Did he know anything about this? she said. Had he taken a marker to the painting? Did he know how serious this was?

My brother denied everything.

Then my sister came under fire. Had she drawn on Mary? Was this some sort of joke? my mother asked.

My sister also denied everything. She protested and declared innocence. Defacing the Virgin Mary? She'd never do such a thing.

I was young, maybe six or seven at the time—too young to be the likely culprit. Yet, according to some versions of the story, I also received an interrogation. *Do you know anything about this? Did you put a mustache on the paintings?*

At some point, maybe at the time of the accusations—or later that day—my father gave a chuckle. Days earlier, maybe even weeks earlier, he had taken a marker and drawn the mustache on the painting. The image, my father argued, was underappreciated. Quietly elegant, a moment of poetic beauty, the artwork should play a bigger role in our lives, he argued. "The revenge of the mustache" is how my father later called the incident.

There's a pretty simple explanation for what happened, as Kahneman has shown, and it turns out that we all have two different types of thinking. There's our instinctive brain, which is automatic and fast. In contrast, there's our deliberative brain, which is slow and ponderous. More often than not, we rely on our instinctive brain, and generally, the approach serves us pretty well. It takes less time—and effort—and we'd rather not spend energy to take mental stock.

But this means that we often miss details. We will read a bit of text but not really understand it. We will watch someone teaching a skill, but we won't really learn it. Every day for weeks, we will pass the Virgin Mary with a large mustache and not even notice it.

Research on the instinctive brain is extensive—and often a little eerie. One study asked people if they knew the location of the closest fire extinguisher, and while many of the subjects had worked in the building for more than decade, only about quarter could indicate the location of the nearest fire extinguisher.

In another study, subjects ran past a brawl that had been set up by a group of psychologists. Yet only around 50 percent of the subjects noticed the fight. To repeat, two men were pummeling each other amid groans and screams on the side of the street, but only about half of the subjects spotted the incident. The researchers titled the paper "You Do Not Talk about Fight Club If You Do Not Notice Fight Club."

On one side, it might seem that we're simply lazy, and cognitively speaking, that's certainly true. We don't want to pay attention. It takes energy to really focus. But even when we do pay attention, our instinctive brain also plays a role. Even when we're trying to be deliberate, our instinctive brain jumps into action. Before we even have had a chance to really consider the facts, we often engage in a type of mental "I told you so."

In my own life, this happens a lot when I'm shopping. I'll want to buy a gas grill, for instance, and I'll drum up all sorts of evidence that the new grill will save me time and money. In order to convince myself to buy the item, I'll gather in my mind a long list of self-serving explanations: *I can't use my charcoal grill in the rain. I'll eat healthier with a new grill. It'll be easier to buy canisters of gas than to find charcoal. This one's on sale.* And then—click!—there's one in the mail, which now sits unused in my backyard.

No one is immune to these sorts of cognitive biases. Experts fall for them just as much as amateurs, masters can get snagged as much as apprentices. It doesn't matter if there's lots of money on the line—or how much smarts is in the room. Charles Darwin made predictions about genetics that never panned out. Thomas Edison thought that alternating current would never work at scale. And frankly, if you lived in my house growing up, you would also have missed the black mustache on the Virgin Mary. Next, we will take a look at what we can do about it.

The Need to Evaluate

On the morning of my fortieth birthday, soon after I had opened a few gifts, an email popped into my inbox: "Trying to reach Ulrich Boser

ASAP." It was a message from the Bill and Melinda Gates Foundation.
They wanted to set up a meeting between Bill Gates and me to discuss
education funding. Could I give the foundation a call as soon as possible?

At first I thought the email might be a hoax. It seemed like a goofy
trick that my brother might pull, a bit of fortieth birthday tomfoolery.
My wife thought the same thing when I told her about the missive, and
she fired off a glance at me that said: *Come on. Bill Gates does not want to
meet with you.*

The request was authentic, though, and some weeks later, I stepped
into a large conference room. Books lined the back walls. The conference table gleamed like a mirror. In the distance, a harbor, some boats,
a glimmering Yarrow Bay, and in the far corner, the world's richest man
chattered away with a colleague.

In the days before the meeting, the staff of the foundation and I had
pulled together a memo on funding and educational outcomes. The
document was some forty pages long and included eight different appen-
dices. The memo had been sent to Gates shortly before the meeting, and
just as the discussion began, with everyone sitting around the conference table, Gates asked a very detailed question about some of the figures that we had provided.

*So what's this issue with the expenditures differing between the appen-
dix and the text of the memo?* Gates asked.

It was an obscure issue, the footnote of a footnote, like considering
the weight of neutrinos on Mars or the name of the first American to
win a gold medal in shot put. At first I thought that maybe I misheard.
But after a moment, I spoke up, explaining the detail. In the appendix, I
said, we included total costs, which included capital expenditures. In
the body of the memo, we included current costs, which did not include
spending on buildings.

It helped that I had knew that Gates might ask this sort of question.
Before I flew out to Seattle, colleagues told me that Gates often started
off meetings with highly detailed queries—often revolving around a
very specific data point. "Gates wants to make sure he's playing volleyball with someone who can keep a ball up in the air," Harvard's Tom
Kane told me.

From a management perspective, one might argue that Gates has a good bullshit detector. He asked an obscure question because he wanted to see if the people in the meeting deeply understood the material. In cognitive science circles, people tend to be a little more polite than in management ones, and Gates was engaged in a form of evaluation: Were the experts in the room truly experts? How well did the individuals know the issue? Did the person in the meeting really understand the difference between capital and current expenditures?

I don't know for sure why Gates took this approach. But there's no question that people like Gates need to closely track the information that comes across their desk. First, there's the "yes, of course" approach to managing up—and people will often tell a boss whatever that boss wants to hear. Second, people will be overconfident—as we've seen—and individuals will think that they know something when they don't actually know anything at all.

When it comes to learning, Gates modeled something important: We need to review what we've learned. To avoid bias, to steer clear of overconfidence, to really master a field, we need to examine our thinking—and the thinking of those around us.

We've come across versions of this idea a few times in this book already, but in this phase of learning, the final phase, this sort of dedicated rethinking is central. When it comes to gaining a specific skill, we need to ask ourselves: Does anything seem confusing? What's unclear? How do I know what I know?

In her classes at Carnegie Mellon, Marsha Lovett will often give students one or two written questions after they finish a lecture. Lovett calls the questions "wrappers." As part of the activity, students ask themselves questions: *What did I learn? What was hard to understand? What seems unclear?*

For Lovett, a lot of the benefit of wrappers is that they focus a student's thinking on misunderstandings as well as "how the students could improve their learning," she says. Lovett often recommends that students focus on the areas that give them the most difficulty. By focusing on what Lovett calls the "muddiest point," students get more out of their learning. "It's about getting in that habit of mind of thinking: 'Okay. How well do I know this?'" Lovett told me. "'Where am I feeling confused?'"

Slight changes in context also make a difference. When we change the medium, it makes it easier for us to find issues. This explains why you should read emails out loud before hitting send: It makes it simpler to find gaffs and grammatical errors. This also helps us understand why printing out a memo and reviewing it on paper can help uncover typos. When we see something printed out—instead of on a screen—it provides a different perspective on the material, and mistakes become more apparent.

Perhaps the most important thing when it comes to this sort of review is attitude, and while I was working on this book, I realized that I had become complacent with my performance in some key aspects of my life. I would write documents or give talks but not really think about how I could improve. I would parent my kids and manage people without dwelling on how I could get better.

Blame my middle-aged ways—or a hectic work life—but I simply wasn't evaluating my own performance in any sort of systemic way, even in things that I cared a lot about, like parenting. I decided to push back against this bit of laziness. Nothing big. Just some postperformance evaluation.

Sometimes I felt flat-footed giving talks, for instance. I would mumble and stutter—my thoughts stumbling out of my mouth like a late-night drunk. So I would watch recordings of myself giving presentations and look for certain tics. I also once sat with a public speaking coach, and for a few hours, the coach advised me and a handful of colleagues on ways to improve.

Same with writing: I knew I could do better, and I tracked down a freelance editor so that I could get some dedicated criticism, to identify some weak spots in my sentences and paragraphs. In this regard, I also began to see therapy in a new light and regularly visited a counselor not far from my house who helped me focus on ways to improve my mindfulness, to better control my thoughts.

In all of these efforts, the goal was to evaluate my expertise a little more closely, reviewing my successes and failures. In other words, I gave tasks a bit more Monday-morning quarterbacking. This wasn't learning in any traditional sense—I didn't take classes. No lectures or exams, no videos or texts. I just tried to review my performance in a more dedicated way, and even that was enough to help me improve.

In the end, it's easy to forget that developing expertise often runs on a willed type of awareness. We all need to ask ourselves: How did I know? What do I know? Have I checked for what I know? Bill Gates himself once argued that "your most unhappy customers are your greatest source of learning," and within an economic context, that makes sense.

There's no reason to limit the sentiment, though, and I'd argue that often the most important driver of learning might actually be a simple willingness to review, to figure what you actually know, to make your unhappy errors your greatest source of learning.

When it comes to rethinking our learning, we need external checks. After all, people often fib to themselves. Like con artists, we believe our own lies, especially about learning, and most of us think that we know a lot more than we do. This is why we need outside reviews and external responses, pointed questions and dedicated feedback.

The Value of Educators plays a key role here. When it came to public speaking, for instance, it helped that an instructor gave me tips and feedback. My writing improved because I landed outside help and dedicated evaluation. For another example, recall my basketball trainer Dwane Samuels? He helped me understand what I did—and did not—understand about shooting jumpers.

Another source of powerful feedback are peers. Our colleagues can be deeply helpful in evaluating our expertise. In the Air Force, there's a common approach to making sure that people gain focused criticism, and after a training flight on an F-16 fighter, a team will gather with the pilot to discuss lessons learned. Other organizations have similar efforts. In political circles, group review sessions are known as postmortems. In hospitals, they're called debriefs.

In a way, we're talking again about the idea of feedback, and even people at the highest levels of their profession gain by knowing if they're right—or wrong. It takes a lot, for instance, to become an umpire in

Major League Baseball. Umpire Tom Hallion started his career more than thirty years ago and clocked years in the minor leagues before he finally got called up into the majors, where he is now known for dramatic, spinning strikeout calls.

Hallion's job is unquestionably difficult. A pitch thrown by a major leaguer easily hits speeds of 100 miles per hour, and there's almost no time at all for the umpire to make the decision—strike or ball. Errant throws have also smacked Hallion in his mask, while jeering and taunts are constant. Manager Don Mattingly once told Hallion to "wake the fuck up." (Hallion threw Mattingly out of the game for the comment.)

For his part, Hallion readily admits that he makes errors. Maybe he misses a strike or misjudges a wide curveball or doesn't see exactly how a pitch came over the plate. "We like to get every play right," Hallion once told a reporter during a postgame interview. But, "we're human beings and sometimes we get them wrong."

To help make umpires like Hallion a little less wrong, Major League Baseball rolled out a new technology some years ago that showed if an umpire called a strike correctly. Using sophisticated cameras and various motion tracking devices, the software showed if a ball was really a ball, basically helping the umpires evaluate their performance.

The effort resulted in better umpires, and the data suggested that umpires began calling strikes in a more consistent manner. What's more, the technology was particularly helpful to younger umpires, who used the software as part of their training. Indeed, many of the younger umpires now arrive at the Major Leagues with skills similar to someone highly experienced like Hallion.

The point is that even among specialists, people learn more if they closely track what they know and don't know. Like any sort of feedback, this sort of evaluation needs to be immediate. One benefit of the Major League Baseball data on strikeouts, for instance, is that it's processed almost immediately. As one umpire, Dusty Dellinger, explained after studying his strike-zone data: "I was able to quickly make adjustments based on having that information, which was huge to me."

Quizzing is yet another form of evaluation—it provides a way to know what you know. Experts in learning like psychologist Regan

Gurung remind students of this fact all the time, telling them: Test yourself, answer the questions in the back of the textbook, take practice exams, do as much quizzing as you can. The effects are immediate, according to Gurung. "The grades of the people taking the quizzes just shoots up," he told me.

To get a better, concrete sense of this type of test-based review, I once dropped into a physics classroom at the University of Maryland, College Park. A junior named Brandon Fish was sitting in one of the middle rows, and I sat near him in one of the narrow, blue plastic molded chairs.

Like most of the hundred or so students in the class, Fish had brought a clicker with him. The device looks like a small TV remote control, and it allows students like Fish to answer simple quiz questions via radio waves.

It was the first day after spring break, and the professor, Ben Dreyfus, began by asking a joke of a clicker question that was posted on the large screen at the front of the classroom: "How was spring break?"

Then, after some muted laughter, came four low-stakes questions. The queries revolved around how electric charges spread across capacitors. I drew a blank. There was no understanding for me to evaluate. But Fish fired off his answers by pressing a little black button.

This wasn't a stressful experience. Each question wasn't worth much—just a few points. Fish saw it as a way to track what he had learned. After the quiz was over, a chart appeared upon the screen. It showed the correct answers to the quiz questions as well as what percent of students got the items correct.

Overall, the results weren't good. It seemed that many students had forgotten the material over spring break, and on a few items, half the class gave the wrong response. In other words, Dreyfus helped the students evaluate their learning—and the students found that they hadn't retained a lot of material.

Dreyfus then basically spent the rest of the class reviewing the key ideas—and giving more clicker questions. When I spoke to Fish after the class, he told me that the quiz-focused approach was helpful. The

POP QUIZ #28

You're learning how to throw darts for the very first time. What practice will be the *most* effective?

A. Emphasizing the learning process (e.g., reflecting on performance, knowing how to hold the darts)

B. Focusing on the learning outcome (e.g., hitting the target, focusing on getting a bull's-eye)

C. Introducing the skill in various learning styles (e.g., visual, kinetic, etc.)

D. Discovering how to throw darts (just start throwing and see how it goes)

questions signaled what he needed to learn—and what he had mastered. "In this class, they really emphasize what's important. I find it a really effective way to teach kids," Fish told me. "It's more helpful to know what you don't know."

Fish and I talked for a little while longer. He told me about what he wanted to do after graduation—he wanted to "become a population researcher." I asked him if he had any issues with the quiz-based approach. "There can be awkward pauses, if people don't want to answer questions," he said.

It seemed, too, that Fish had internalized this type of evaluation. He understood the power of finding out what he hadn't fully learned, and by the end of our interview, Fish told me something that I thought that I'd never hear from a college student: "I like the quizzes."

We all forget. It might take a few days—or just a few minutes. But learning often leaves as soon as it arrives. When it comes to memories, the brain is a lot like a sieve. Many recollections will vanish after just a few moments. Still worse, even the details that do stay often disappear with time.

This happens in schools all the time, even after dedicated bouts of studying. Medical students, for instance, sometimes fail to remember more than 50 percent of what they've learned within a few months, according one study. So while an aspiring doctor might ace an anatomy test during her first year at Med U., she's likely to bomb the same exam less than a year later.

Granted, we want to believe that we will remember everything that we see or do or experience. It's painful to think that we won't remember key memories—a big graduation, a close friend, our first kiss. But when cognitive scientists study forgetting in the lab, they find that our memories seem to come with a type of timer. If the timer rings—and we have not re-engaged that memory again—the memory is forgotten. Researchers call it the forgetting curve.

While the research on memory and forgetting has been around for decades, it's generally lived in dusty research journals, obscure books written by bearded academics. At least until Roger Craig came along. Ever since Craig was a kid, he has loved playing games. Chess, Scrabble, poker, baseball—he's been devoted to them all. "I'm very competitive," Craig told me. "I like to win."

So in grad school, Craig decided to compete at *Jeopardy!* As a kid, Craig had watched the game a lot with his grandparents. In graduate school, some of his buddies had tried to get on the show, too. Craig also thought that he might have an edge after coming across a *Wired* magazine article that detailed the value of spacing learning out over time.

"All students have been warned not to cram," the *Wired* article argued. "But the efficiencies created by precise spacing are so large, and the improvement in performance so predictable, that from nearly the moment [a researcher] described the spacing effect, psychologists have been urging educators to use it to accelerate human progress."

Craig had a sense that the *Wired* article might provide an important advantage. When Craig would study for tests in college at Virginia Tech, he would often revisit ideas so that he wouldn't forget them. He even wrote a short computer program to help him space out his learning so that he would revisit ideas at regular intervals.

But the *Wired* magazine article promised a much deeper approach to spacing out learning, and Craig soon downloaded a bit of software called Anki. Using a highly developed algorithm, the software relied on the principles of spaced learning, and it would quiz people at the very edges of their memory. Or as the software's website argues, "Only practice the material that you're about to forget."

Armed with a database of past *Jeopardy!* questions, Craig started to hone his game-show skills, and he would review facts—details about presidents, names of old movies—that aligned with his rate of forgetting. So if Craig got a fact wrong, Anki would ask him about the fact again in a few minutes. If Craig landed the fact correct, then the question might not reappear again for a few days. If Craig landed the fact correct a second time, the fact would not appear again for a few months.

A more visual way to think about this approach is to consider a chart of the forgetting curve. It shows how long you remember something that you've just learned, and it suggests that after a few days—or even a few minutes—of learning something, you've probably forgotten it.

So if you meet someone at a party, and he says his name is Terry, that's the solid line. It shows that you're unlikely to remember Terry's name after a few days. If you remind yourself a few minutes later about his name, that's the dotted line. It suggests that reminding yourself a few minutes later helps memory, but it doesn't help by much: After a few weeks, you'll have forgotten Terry's name.

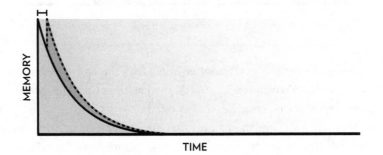

But you if review Terry's name again a few days after the party—*his name is Terry, his name is Terry*—then the dotted line shifts a bit farther down the graph, and now remembering looks more like this:

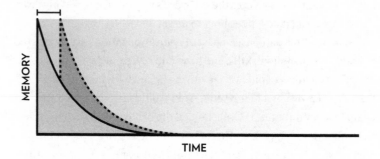

If you review Terry's name again some weeks later—*his name is Terry, his name is Terry*—the rate of forgetting now looks like more like this:

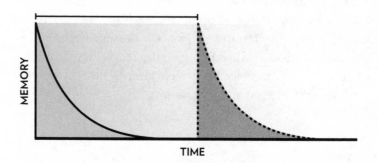

Again, the key thing is the dotted line. That's the sign of learning. That's the sign of remembrance. And that's what Roger Craig did with as many *Jeopardy!* answers as he possibly could.

Craig landed on the show for the first time in September 2010, and in a small room with Alex Trebek and his two competitors, Craig basically didn't miss a question. He destroyed his two competitors. He

POP QUIZ #29

True or false: When studying, students should alternate between learning things that they don't know and things that they've recently learned.

banged though *Jeopardy!* item after item, eventually setting a record for the most amount of money won in a single game, blowing away the record that Ken Jennings had set some years earlier.

When Craig got back to his Los Angeles hotel that night, he was almost more surprised than excited. He knew that he would do well at the game; the effect of spacing out practice was rooted in some very robust science. But Craig just did not think that he would do that well—he gave such a dominant performance that he thought, *Oh wow, maybe it worked too well.*

Craig had a hard time sleeping on that night. Would *Jeopardy!* invite him back? Would Trebek think that he had somehow cheated? Craig hadn't done anything wrong—he had simply relied on basic memory research to hone his skills. In the end, *Jeopardy!* did ask Craig to return, and he won a half-dozen more games during his first appearance and also eventually aced the Tournament of Champions, which pits the game's all-stars against each other.

Today, Craig lives in New York City. He works as a data scientist. He often uses Anki for work—and different games. As for spacing out learning, Craig argues that it's simply a better way to grapple with knowledge. It ensures that we don't forget. "Everybody that wants to succeed at a game is going to practice at the game," Craig once told an NPR reporter. "You can practice haphazardly, or you can practice efficiently. And that's what I did."

Roger Craig's call to end "haphazard learning" has not gone unanswered. At least a half-dozen software programs now promise to help people spread their learning out over days, weeks, months, or even years. SuperMemo is the grandfather of the field, perhaps the oldest program.

More recently, VocApp allows users to include pictures to their spaced learning. DuoLingo's approach focuses exclusively on foreign languages, allowing people to spread the learning of their Spanish language words out over time.

The spacing approach has spread to other fields, too. Some corporate training programs have tried to take a more distributed approach to learning. Verizon, for instance, will now send follow-up training material to an employee's computer to help keep their memories fresh. Some of Thomson Reuters's learning tools use the approach to keep strategies "top-of-mind."

Yet for the most part, learning remains concentrated. A spaced approach has not caught on, and in ways big and small, people still cram. Instead of spreading their practice out over time, people will try and learn everything in one afternoon, or they won't revisit important ideas or details. Most people, for instance, don't know the name of the last battle of the Revolutionary War? (Hint: It wasn't in Lexington.) Why? I'd argue that it's because they have not revisited the material.

For their part, schools often encourage cramming. With the exception of perhaps a "review" session at the start of the year, there's little revisiting of material. Cumulative tests—which encourage more spaced learning—are limited to the end of the semester. Many textbooks also fail to include dedicated review sessions, except for maybe a question or two at the close of each chapter.

Yet even the slightest amount of spacing can improve outcomes. When people take small steps to spread out their learning, they often see dramatic improvements. Without question, my favorite example of this idea comes from Nate Kornell. While Kornell was landing his post-doc at the University of California, Los Angeles, he noticed something curious about how the students approached their schoolwork.

As Kornell wandered the campus, he found that some of the undergrads would quiz themselves with a small pile of flashcards, using a half-dozen or so cards to test their understanding of a specific idea or detail. With just a few cards in each pile, the students would quickly flip through the small batches and then tuck the flashcards away, feeling like the material was well learned.

Other students on the campus who used flash cards took a very different approach. They would create a large pile of flash cards. In some instances, these stacks of cards were big—an inch or two thick—and so the students learned the material in a more distributed, spaced-out sort of way. More exactly, there'd be longer intervals of time between the revisiting of a flashcard, with students more likely to come across a card that they might have forgotten.

Kornell knew the students themselves didn't dwell much on the difference. But he thought that the size of the stacks might shift what's being learned. So he drew up a quick experiment. In the lab, one group of subjects would practice learning vocabulary words using a large pile of flash cards. Then Kornell had a second group, who learned the same material using four smaller piles of cards. All of the students needed to know the meaning of the words, and they were high-level words that they had not heard before, words like "effulgent" and "abrogate."

Another way to think about Kornell's experiment is to imagine that you're preparing for a talk. Maybe you're giving a presentation to a client—or perhaps you have a speech to give at some family event. The question is: Are you better off practicing the full speech once a day for five minutes over a four-day period (like the students with one large stack of flashcards)? Or should you split the speech into four smaller sections and focus on one section each day for five minutes (like the students with four smaller stacks of flashcards)?

For their part, the subjects in the study voted for the smaller piles. They wanted to batch their studying in order to concentrate their learning, and before the experiment began, just about all of the students indicated that they would learn more if they used four small heaps of cards. In other words, most people think that the best way to prepare for a speech is by splitting the talk into four short sections.

But Kornell found the exact opposite, and the results of more spacing—of distributing the practice—were dramatic. In the experiment, just about all of the students who practiced using one large stack of flashcards scored higher, even if the amount of time spent learning was the same. What's more, many of the students who studied with one large pile of cards learned about a third more.

For anyone who wants to learn anything, the takeaway is clear: Anything we can do to distribute our learning over time pays off, and people should space out the development of a skill. If you're practicing the violin, don't just rehearse a melody for a few hours; return to the melody periodically so that it stays burned in your memory.

Want to ace a high-stakes exam? Start early so the learning can be spread out over time, and re-quiz yourself every few weeks to ensure that you know the material. In my house, we've started doing less homework on weeknights and more on the weekends for the simple reason that it spaces out learning.

Today, Kornell is a professor at Williams College. He still often sees students quizzing themselves with small stacks of cards—and shakes his head every time that he sees it. "Spacing doesn't require any more time. No extra resources. You don't have to buy an iPad," he told me. "It's kind of like a gift—you learn a lot more and it's free."

The Need for Reflection

Rethinking our learning is not just a matter of evaluation. We also need to look for a deeper sense of understanding. We need to deliberate on knowledge and skills.

As a society, we're not inclined toward this sort of rumination. Our world places a lot of emphasis on action. Thinking is often a sign of weakness. People who spend a lot of time noodling over decisions can seem lazy. Former president George W. Bush called himself the decider in chief, not the deliberator in chief.

For another example, take soccer goalies. During a penalty shot, it typically pays for a goalkeeper to stay in the middle of the goal rather than diving for the posts. By a small but measurable margin, most penalty shots are aimed toward the center, and the goalies have a better chance at stopping the ball if they stay in the middle of the goal.

But generally soccer goalies dive to the left or right. Why? According to Giadia Di Stefano and her colleagues, "it looks and feels better to have missed the ball" by doing something rather than doing nothing. In

other words, the goalie wants to look purposeful and engaged and deci-
sive, and so they jump to the left or right, despite the fact that they're
actually less likely to prevent a goal.

For an education-related example, take something like changing an
answer on a test. Should you switch the answer? Or go with your raw
instincts? Talk to a few people, and most believe that the first answer on
a test is the best answer. In other words, generally people want to go
with their gut. Like the soccer goalie, they don't want to seem like
they're waffling or brooding or overly pensive. But a solid body of evidence suggests otherwise: Fixes to test items usually boost scores. By
thinking through an answer one more time, we generally improve our
performance.

It turns out that deliberation is a crucial part of learning. To understand any sort of skill or knowledge, we have to reflect on that skill or bit
of knowledge. This is different than simply checking on the details. It's
a matter of dwelling on the experience.

Experts do this all the time. "It's more important to think about what
you're doing than it is to do it," was the quote that *Car Talk*'s Ray
Magliozzi had hanging above his desk. Same with New England Patriots
coach Bill Belichick, who will spend hours mulling over previous games,
looking for missed opportunities, figuring out ways for his team to get
better, contemplating approaches to improvement.

The best example, though, might be guitarist Pat Metheny. In the
world of jazz guitar, Metheny is a superstar. He's landed some twenty
different Grammys, playing with everyone from B. B. King to David
Bowie. But Metheny continues to reflect on what he knows, setting
aside time to figure out ways that he can get better. After each show, he'll
write up half a dozen pages about the experience. The short essay
reflects on how he performed, detailing musical successes and failures,
describing what he thought worked—and didn't work.

It's no accident that Metheny writes down his reflections. As a
medium, writing slows our thoughts. It pushes deliberation, and one way
to improve learning is to use a diary. Think of it as a learning journal, in
which you write down everything that went well during class or practice.

The thoughts don't have to be profound. "In hockey class today, I discovered that I need to use my hips more." Or, "My acting instructor told me that I need to project my voice more." Yet even these sort of mundane scribblings can be enough to spark a richer form of learning.

Talking out loud can help a lot, too. It's another way to slow down the thinking process, and after an experience—or even during an experience—people can improve their learning if they talk to themselves in ways that promote reflection: "So what do I do next?" or "What am I solving for again?"

To find out more about the role of reflection in learning, I once met up with Susan Ambrose. A cognitive scientist, Ambrose wrote the important book *How Learning Works* and is now the senior vice provost of Northeastern University in Boston. We met up in Ambrose's office, which was tucked away among a burrow of well-appointed rooms in the college's central building.

Ambrose argued that people often simply assume that reflection happens. Put content in front of someone, and they'll transform that material into learning. "You see this in a lot of college courses," Ambrose argued. "Faculty love their subject, and so they give students as much material as possible."

That's not how learning works, though. People need time to think through a skill or bit of knowledge in some sort of focused way. As Ambrose told me, "The more knowledge that you get, the more you need to make those connections. But you need to be intentional about it."

At Northeastern, Ambrose has rolled out various initiatives to help students engage in more of this sort of reflection. In the school's internship program, for instance, students now regularly answer questions on what it's like working for a company or nonprofit. Kara Morgan was one of the students who participated in the college's revamped internship program, working for the Cambodian Center for Human Rights in Phnom Penh.

For Morgan, the experience of living in Cambodia was exhilarating.

A new country, a new language, a new job, and the writing assignment served a crucial purpose, encouraging Morgan to make sense of her experiences, to reflect on what she learned. "It made me consider what else I wanted to accomplish while I was there," she told me. "The essays forced me to take a step back and think," and in many ways, that was the point.

The type of reflection that I've been talking about usually requires a moment of calm. Maybe we're quietly writing an essay—or talking to ourselves as we're in the shower. But it usually takes a bit of cognitive quiet, a moment of silent introspection, for us to engage in any sort of focused deliberation.

There is, then, something of a contradiction in learning, and it turns out that we need to let go of our thinking in order to understand our thinking. When we step away from a problem, we often learn more about a problem. Read a software manual, for instance, and a good amount of the comprehension can come after you shut the pages. Get into a discussion with a colleague at work—and the best argument arrives while you're washing the dishes that evening.

Reflecting, then, does more than give us a chance to reconsider our learning. It also provides its own form of schooling. Sleep is a fascinating example of this idea, and it turns out that we sleep in order to make sense of our thoughts. When we take a nap, we're tidying up our knowledge.

Sleep shows some pretty remarkable outcomes. It works to make us better humans. More shut-eye equals bigger incomes, and another 60 minutes of sleep each night boosts salaries. Sleep also makes it easier to lose weight. Or take sports: People are much better sprinters—and have far better hand-eye coordination—after getting more sleep, according to one study of college athletes.

When it comes to learning, sleep plays a particularly important role. To put this research in perspective, I worked with my colleagues Catherine Brown and Perpetual Baffour, and we showed that if the nation's middle schools opened one hour later, test scores around the country would jump by almost a grade level. In other words, opening school later by 60 minutes would help a student go from producing 7th grade results to almost producing 8th grade results.

The need for cognitive quiet also helps explain why it's so difficult to gain skills when we're stressed or angry or lonely. When feelings surge through our brain, we can't engage. We can't deliberate. Sure, in some sort of dramatic high-stakes situations, we might be able to learn something basic like a phone number. But for us to gain any sort of understanding, there needs to be mental tranquility.

I got a very concrete sense of this idea when I met up with neuroscientist Mary Helen Immordino-Yang, who has done some important work on the emotional nature of learning. A professor at the University of Southern California, Immordino-Yang was in Washington for an event, and she asked me if I could pick her up from the airport for our interview.

It was a Thursday evening, and as we drove away from the terminal, Immordino-Yang's suitcase stashed in my trunk, I began to ask a few questions. But while Immordino-Yang provided nuanced explanations, I found myself struggling to understand. Because I was nervous about the traffic and the driving and the directions, my mind could not really engage with her remarks.

I merged onto the highway, half listening to her talk, recognizing words but not grappling with any sort of meaning. Immordino-Yang explained that "the brain's default mode is not just a kind of resting state. It's an active consolidation mechanism."

I anxiously wondered about the best way to drive to Immordino-Yang's hotel, navigating streets and stoplights, while Immordino-Yang continued. "Students need to have time and opportunities and skill and encouragement to be able to go inside and kind of internally reflect," she said. "Dynamic learning is a process of moving between thoughtful reflection and a kind of simulation in your head."

Immordino-Yang argued that people often don't take enough time to engage in reflection. Maybe the person is driving a car—or checking their email—but they're not fully engaged. They're distracted, and so they don't have the feeling of emotional composure, of mental quiet, that supports more meaningful forms of understanding. People, she argued, need to engage in "productive mind wandering."

Similar conclusions have been filling research papers in recent years, and it turns out that a serene walk in the woods can help people think through problems. If someone plays with some plastic bricks for a while, they do better on creativity tests. Daydreaming has also been shown to boost cognition. These sorts of reflective activities matter a lot for metacognition, too. We're much better at thinking about thinking when we've had some quiet moments, and even a short break can improve our metacognition skills.

Practically speaking, people should consider their emotional state as they learn. They need to ensure that they feel calm and focused, ready and centered. For someone like Immordino-Yang, feelings of serenity and deeper forms of learning run in lockstep, and without some sort of cognitive peace, there is no cognitive understanding.

Some organizations have taken up the banner for increased rumination. Technology is the target in some areas. A few universities have banned cell phones, while France has gone so far as to limit Wi-Fi in daycares. Other organizations have established "quiet" rooms, and in Baltimore, a marketing start-up named Groove created a library with a "no-talking" rule. Same with Google. While the company is famous for its open floor plan, the tech firm encourages employees to book a private office if they need really to focus.

After my talk with Immordino-Yang, I also experienced the benefits of this sort of relaxed contemplation. After I dropping the scientist off at her hotel, I began to drive home, and my mind started to drift. I began to think about her argument and how it might fit with everything else that I knew.

As the car purred along the streets, as I steered my Honda toward my house, I felt relaxed—and I was finally able to grapple with what she

POP QUIZ #30

True or false: Students should learn how to think about their thinking.

meant by the brain being a "platform in which we construct coherent understanding," that people need to "internally reflect in order to learn."

What does Immordino-Yang's research look like for someone who is trying to learn something? Julius Robinson knows—and he still remembers the activity known simply as "the fist." Robinson was in high school at the time, a freshman, wearing the school uniform—blue shirt, khaki pants—and in an empty classroom, Robinson stood across from a boy named Christian.

Robinson and Christian were friends, both talkative and outgoing, always eager to volunteer for things. At the front of the room stood a counselor with a program called Becoming a Man, or what everyone calls BAM.

"Christian, close your fist," the counselor said on that day, and so Christian balled up his hand.

Then the counselor turned to Robinson. "Now, can you open his fist?"

The first thought that rushed through Robinson's head was something along the lines of *Rip it open.*

So Robinson stepped forward and began to tug on Christian's hand, pulling and yanking. Christian laughed and kept his fist closed. The two men good-naturedly tussled for a bit, with Christian putting his hand higher in the air so Robinson couldn't reach it.

The grappling, the jerking and prying, continued for a few more moments. Then, the counselor stepped in and simply asked Christian, "Can you open your fist for me, please?"

So Christian opened his hand, extending his fingers, and Robinson thought to himself, *Ah, I got it. I should have asked him the question instead of wrestling him.*

As researchers like Sara Heller have pointed out, "the fist" activity sums up the purpose of the BAM program: By stopping and thinking, people are more likely to get what they want. In BAM, this activity is known more broadly as "slow thinking," and in many ways, it's a matter of putting Immordino-Yang's research into action. By learning to be more deliberate, by checking our emotions, by being more calm, people make better decisions—and learn a lot more.

This approach was new for Robinson. He grew up in one of the deadliest areas of Chicago. Robinson's brother and father had both been gang members—Gangster Disciples. In his South Side neighborhood, murders occurred about once a month. Just about every day, someone was assaulted. Two parts Wild West, one part war zone, it was a world that prized instinct and raw automaticity.

A BAM counselor, Peter Agostino led "the fist" activity with Robinson on that day, and Agostino soon became one of Robinson's mentors. He would meet with Robinson and the other BAM students each week, and they would talk about friends and families. They would discuss school and girlfriends. Agostino taught the students relaxation techniques like meditation and deep breathing. "The goal is to help the students to think more soundly and clearly," Agostino told me.

In his own life, Robinson started using the "slow thinking" tools all the time. If Robinson argued with his father, for instance, he would try and slow himself down. If he needed to get some schoolwork done, he'd count down using deep breaths: *One, inhale, exhale. Two, inhale, exhale.* When I spoke to Robinson, he had recently gotten into an argument with his brother and to avoid an escalation in the exchange: "I just sat down in front of the TV and did my breathing exercises," he told me.

Because of BAM's emotional management techniques, Robinson got better grades in school. He could concentrate more easily during stressful moments. Like every teen, Robinson had difficult moments, and in high school, he landed a suspension for ditching class. But eventually Robinson walked across the stage and got his high school diploma. He now has a job—and hopes to go to college.

Lab studies give additional support to this approach. A group of international researchers led by Giada Di Stefano once gave a group of subjects a brain teaser and then provided them with some training on it. Then the subjects had a choice: Did they want to practice the teaser more? Or did they want to reflect?

Overwhelmingly, the subjects in Di Stefano's study chose to practice

POP QUIZ #31

True or false: Rereading is a highly effective approach to learning.

more, but it turned out that the group that chose to "think and write" had much higher rates of learning. In other words, reflection had more impact than additional practice. "The bias for action," the researchers concluded, is "ultimately detrimental to our learning."

It doesn't take much to engage in more slow thinking. Before engaging in a learning task that takes a lot of concentration, people should work to push aside anxious thoughts. The BAM program gives some helpful advice, recommending that people simply count their breaths, much like Robinson did: *One, inhale, exhale. Two, inhale, exhale.*

Similarly, consider meditation. It can also help slow our thinking, and there's now a long and surprising list of meditation devotees. There's actor Clint Eastwood and Congressman Tim Ryan. In sports, Seattle Seahawks quarterback Russell Wilson has a "mental conditioning coach," while business leaders like Salesforce CEO Marc Benioff and music mogul Russell Simmons all swear by the practice.

Solitude is also helpful. By spending time alone, we dial down the speed of our thinking, and so we can contemplate different angles, improve our reasoning, or just think about our thinking. In much the same way, visualizations can help us improve outcomes, and we can engage in slower forms of thought by imagining how we might perform in a given situation.

Whatever the specific approach, time is crucial. To engage in more reflective thought, we need long uninterrupted moments to think or write or just deliberate, as Georgetown computer science professor Cal Newport argues. In order to write a business plan—or study for an important exam—people should swear off distractions. That means no Snapchat, no Facebook, for at least a few hours. "Deep work" is how Newport refers to the concept.

The approach of former Homeland Security secretary Janet Napolitano provides an example of "deep work," and she has gone so far as to swear off email. Without the technology, Napolitano argues that she's a lot more effective at work, and if Napolitano needs something from someone immediately, she'll pick up the phone. As Napolitano once explained to reporters, not using email "allows me to focus on where I need to focus." In other words, it allows Napolitano to think slowly.

There's an odd thing about rethinking our learning: It makes learning a type of endless process. If we're always reassessing what we know, we're never going to stop deliberating. We're never going to stop reflecting.

This idea turns out to be at the heart of the learning process—and increasingly the modern world. After all, expertise itself is constantly evolving. Skills have stopped being static. I'm in this ever-churning boat along with everyone else, and within days of this book being released, a study—or even a Tweet—will make some aspect outdated. A big research project will hit the wires. Some new data will be released, and then, despite all my efforts, a passage within these pages may seem more past than present.

There's some good news here, and technology can help us reconsider. Blogs might have done as much for reading and writing as the Gutenberg press, as Clive Thompson argues in his excellent book *Smarter Than You Think*. Sites like Wikipedia have pushed a powerful democratization of knowledge, while communication apps like Twitter have sparked public debates as fierce as those in ancient Rome. "Today's tools make it easier for us to find connections—between ideas, pictures, people, bits of news—that were previously invisible," Thompson argues.

I've touched on this theme a few times. Mind-mapping tools can help us think and see relationships. Computer simulations can help us practice and apply what we know. Some software programs like Anki can help slow our forgetting ways by spacing out our learning. Technology can even help us teach, or just recall David Rönnqvist, who would spend days on Stack Overflow, answering questions in an effort to learn new coding techniques.

Like every technology, learning applications have trade-offs. Connected devices don't generally foster sustained attention, for one. In classes with unfettered Internet access, students often post lower scores. Even the "mere presence" of a cell phone turns out to reduce the ability to concentrate. In other words, just seeing your iPhone on a table makes you less focused on a task.

At the same time, learning devices are prone to techno-sizzle, loaded up with unnecessary bells and distracting whistles. Psychologist Rich Mayer has done some powerful research in this area, and when it comes to technology-enhanced learning, less is often more. Indeed, a number of studies show that people post higher outcomes when they engage with simpler representations of an idea or skill.

For all the debate over technology, one thing will not change, and learning will always requires learning. No matter what the device, understanding relies on a dedicated search for significance. It's a focused hunt for meaning. A few years ago, writer Atul Gawande wrote a book called *The Checklist Manifesto*. He argued that when it came to sophisticated activities like medicine or engineering or piloting a plane, people needed checklists to help them reduce errors—and improve performance.

But it turns out that even checklists have clear limits. While the memory tool increases productivity, it's subject to very human foibles. When auto mechanics rely on checklists, for instance, they often ignore the bottom of the checklist, reviewing only the items at the top.

So if something like "check blinker lights" appears at the start of a checklist, a mechanic will give the blinker lights more attention than the things that appear at the bottom, like brake lines. This happens despite the fact that brake lines are clearly important than blinker lights.

Nobody denies the value of checklists—in some cases like car repair, they can grow revenue by 20 percent. But whether it's fixing a Honda or engineering a bridge, there's something more important: meaning. In this regard, we have to work to make sense of things, to focus our skills, to hone our abilities. After all, even the simplest memory-enhancing technology like a checklist can become a mindless crutch if we're not engaging in the activity in some meaningful way.

The debate over technology, then, underscores one last point: Look to learn. Be a sense maker. Always aim to develop—and reflect—on skills and knowledge. We see this drive in most successful individuals.

It's true in politics, and while most Americans read around five books a year, for instance, President Barack Obama cruised through more than twice that amount. It's true in sports, and after losing a big game in the 2016 NBA finals, LeBron James almost immediately began reviewing the tape of the game. "I'll figure out ways I can be better, starting as soon as I leave this podium," James said.

It's true in business, too. AT&T CEO Randall Stephenson recently told a reporter that if someone does not clock at least a half a dozen hours each week learning something new, they'll make themselves "obsolete." Stephenson sees constant learning as a minimum, like knowing how to type or knowing basic math. "There is a need to retool yourself, and you should not expect to stop."

EPILOGUE

THE STAKES RUN pretty high for airline pilots. When a captain of a 747 steers a plane into the sky, hundreds of lives hang in the balance. Up until recently, though, many pilots lacked a crucial bit of training—and the story of how pilots developed this expertise gives us a few final insights into the learning process.

Let's start, though, with flight Northwest 255. It was supposed to take off from Detroit's Wayne County Airport on the evening of August 16, 1987. The destination was Phoenix. In the cockpit were two experienced pilots, John Maus and David Dodds.

Each seat on the flight was filled. Almost 150 people were on board. College kids, newlyweds, a player for the Phoenix Suns. An engineer with a tight mustache and the nickname "Captain Crunch." A California teen who had a sweatshirt with her boyfriend's name emblazoned on it. Four-year-old Cecilia sat near her mother and brother.

As the plane pushed away from the gate, the two pilots were in a light mood. Jokes, a bit of singing, some humming.

The pilots went through the safety checklist. Brakes? Check. Pumps? Check. Circuit breakers? Check. During the procedure, there were distractions—a change in the runway, a debate over the plane's weight, some back and forth with the controller.

Eventually, Maus sped the plane down the runway. He mentioned the throttle. It "won't stay on," he said.

"Won't go on?" Dodds said.

"Okay, power's normal," Maus said. "TCI was unset."

The plane roared past a hundred miles per hour. Then the wheels lifted off. The plane was in the air, and it immediately became unsteady—shaky, wobbling, yawning. From the outside, it looked more like a kite than a 40-ton aircraft.

Inside the cockpit, the stall warning system began to ring. A wing slammed into a building, before the fuselage rocketed into the middle of a highway, becoming a skidding, metal inferno. Except for one small child, everyone on the plane died.

At first it appeared that an engine caught fire, a freak mechanical accident. Another whispered theory was that the runway was too short, and so the plane didn't gain enough speed. As in so many accidents, bad luck made a visit, and the plane's automatic lift warning system wasn't working properly at the time.

But in the end investigators determined that Maus and Dobbs had never set the flaps on the wings. A type of air rudder that hangs on the edge of the wings, the flaps provide lift, and without flaps, a large plane simply cannot fly.

Many experts were in disbelief over the discovery. Setting the flaps on a plane is like opening the garage door before backing out. It's obvious, and the two pilots had all sorts of opportunities to address the problem, including during the ten or so minutes that they had spent taxiing to the runway.

But even as the plane rolled and shook, Maus and Dodds didn't diagnose the issue. Even as the plane wobbled in the sky, the pilots seemed unaware. They couldn't even categorize the difficulty. One National Transportation Safety Board member later wrote that the crash was a matter of "blindness."

It was Mica Endsley who helped future pilots to see—and learn. She took the blindness that plagued the two Northwest pilots and turned it into a type of sight.

At the time of the Northwest accident, Endsley was living in Los

Angeles. She was studying for her PhD in systems engineering at the University of Southern California. The Detroit crash occurred late on a Sunday night, and Endsley would have heard about the incident on the news, with accounts like "Life or Death Turned on Twists of Fate" continuing in the papers for days.

In her graduate school work, Endsley had been thinking a lot about the causes of airline crashes, and Endsley believed that something called situational awareness—a type of ambient perception—might be the root cause of the issue. As a skill, situational awareness has a good amount of history, and at least since World War I, pilots have been debating the true nature of the skill and its role in flying.

At the time of the crash, situational awareness was still a vague concept, often understood as something innate, a roll of the DNA lottery. But Endsley was an engineer, not a pilot. She wanted data, not dramatic narratives. Starting in graduate school, she conducted a series of experiments on situational awareness, showing that situational awareness was something that people could hone over time. It was a type of expertise, something that could be mastered with focus, practice, and reflection.

Endsley found, for instance, that just about every pilot could misread a problem if they didn't have sufficient background knowledge. She also found that metaskills like awareness and metacognition were crucial, and pilots without these skills were more likely to make major mistakes. For the first time, she also demonstrated that situational awareness required planning and developing as well as a type of relational knowledge that allowed pilot to solve problems during stressful moments.

Endsley soon began taking her research to airlines and flight schools, helping them develop better training programs. Endsley encouraged pilots to ask themselves "what if" questions to help them develop a more systemic understanding of flying: What if this didn't work? What if this didn't happen? What if the engines stopped functioning?

Endsley also pushed for the direct application of the skill of situational awareness, of learning as mental doing, and she and her staff would often sit with pilots in a flight simulator, helping them develop a more concrete sense of how situational awareness works. At the same time, Endsley underscored the value of thinking about thinking, and she recommended that pilots engage in self-talk, explaining situations to themselves, examining their patterns of reasoning.

Today, many programs—from Air Force basic training to medical school programs—teach Endsley's approach, and while there's no clear way to track the impact of Endsley's work, there's little question that her efforts have helped stave off airline accidents.

At the time of the Northwest wreck, 2,000 people would die every year in plane crashes. Now it's less than 500. More exactly, over the past four decades, there has not been a single major crash in the United States due to a pilot not setting the flaps.

I'm hoping it's pretty clear that training for situational awareness bears a lot of similarity to the type of learning that we've come across in this book. Like Endsley, we've been talking a lot about the need for focused skill building—and the value of spotting relationships across different situations. Like Endsley, we've been discussing the need for metacognition—and embracing real-world uncertainty. As Endsley told me, the goal of learning—any kind of learning—is "to put information together to form meaning."

In many ways, this is the science of learning. Math or reading, biochemistry or gaming, playing the piano or knitting a sweater, there are proven ways to improve our skills and knowledge, and even something that seems at first glance as vague and ill-defined as situational awareness can be developed.

For her part, Endsley has mapped out three stages of situational awareness—perception, comprehension, and projection—and the stages are not too different from the steps that we've been discussing throughout this book.

Here are the steps of learning to learn again, and you'll see that targeting isn't that different from perception, that comprehension isn't that different from relating. In the end, both ideas strive for a type of mastery.

> **Value.** It's impossible to learn if we won't want to learn. To gain expertise, we have to see the skills and knowledge as valuable. What's more, we have to create meaning. Learning is a matter of making sense of something.
>
> **Target.** In the early part of gaining mastery, focus is key. We need to figure out what exactly what we want to learn and set goals and targets.
>
> **Develop.** Some forms of practice make people more perfect than others. In this stage of learning, people need to hone their skills and take dedicated steps to improve performance.
>
> **Extend.** At this point, we want to go beyond the basics—and apply what we know. We want to flesh out our skills and knowledge and create more meaningful forms of understanding.
>
> **Relate.** This is the phase where we see how it all fits together. After all, we don't want to know just a single detail or procedure—we want to know how that detail or procedure interacts with other facts and procedures.
>
> **Rethink.** When it comes to learning, it's easy to make mistakes, to be overconfident, and we need to review our knowledge, to reconsider our understanding, and learn from our learning.

These steps don't always occur sequentially. Sometimes we need to simply hone our skills. On other occasions, motivation is plain. If you're studying for an exam—or checking your flaps—the rethinking stage is always going to be central.

At the same time, we often get ahead of ourselves. One reason that hands-on learning doesn't work in many schools and colleges is because it's introduced too early. Same with practice: Too often, people try to develop their skills without knowing what exactly they're developing, without any sort of goals or targets.

This brings us to another idea we've come across before: Learning is a process, a method, a system, and in the end, people can get better at gaining expertise. Once we know how to learn, we can hone expertise in just about any field. If we're mentally engaged, if we're strategic and deliberate, if we practice and extend, if we relate and rethink, we can develop mastery.

Early in my research, I visited with Barry Zimmerman, who helped kick-start the field of learning to learn in the 1980s. A professor at the City College of New York, Zimmerman had worked with Anastasia Kitsantas on the dart study in the all-girls school in New York City, which we discussed in the first chapter, the one in which the young women on Team Method did so much better than the ones on Team Performance or Team Conventional Wisdom.

When I met Zimmerman, he had retired from teaching. He had recently been diagnosed with Parkinson's disease. We met in an empty room. In a strained, shaky voice, he talked about his work on learning, how learning requires a type of "feedback" loop, in which people track their outcomes. We discussed some of his major studies, which showed how a sense of self-efficacy was central to achieving any sort of mastery. Zimmerman discussed how people need to "select and organize" what they want to know.

But perhaps most of all, Zimmerman stressed how people need to direct their learning. Everyone needs to become "masters of their own learning processes," he argued, and that, I hope, is what I've encouraged with this book.

Almost ten years ago, the US Department of Education released a document that should have revolutionized how people learn. Some of the nation's leading learning scientists developed the report, and behind each recommendation, there was a bookcase worth of evidence, outlining the "consensus on some of the most important concrete and applicable principles to emerge from research on learning and memory."

POP QUIZ #32

True or false: People often have difficulty figuring out if they really understand what they've learned.

The report's conclusions were dramatic, at least relative to the behaviors of most people who aim to learn anything. The document underscored the value of quizzing. It talked about the value of spacing learning out over time. It argued for more "explanatory questioning," and the value of seeing "connections" across different examples.

Like so many government reports, there weren't many dramatic examples or interesting graphics. The text was dry, written in govern-mentese. In fact, just the title of the document could provoke an unhealthy stammer: "Organizing Instruction and Study to Improve Student Learning."

But all in all, what's remarkable is that the report had so little impact. Most teacher education programs ignored the document. Same with most schools—and corporate training programs. In the survey of the American public that I conducted, few people had heard of many of the key ideas, despite the fact most respondents described themselves as knowledgeable about education. And if not for the advocacy of a few experts like Bror Saxberg, the document might have even less visibility than it already does.

In recent years, the new science of learning has picked up steam. Scholars like Susan Ambrose, Dan Willingham, and Rich Mayer have been important evangelizers. People like Henry Roediger, Mark McDaniel, Benedict Carey, and Barbara Oakley have also written important books on the topic. In some policy circles, there's also been a strong push by experts like Ben Riley to ensure that the nation's system of schooling is grounded in high-quality research.

Yet still, learning methods have not changed. This is surprising, if only for the fact that small tweaks in learning can make an enormous difference. Some years ago, researcher Louis Deslauriers and some colleagues decided to roll out a simple intervention in an introductory college science class. If a student did poorly on the first exam, Deslauriers or one of his colleagues would meet with the students for around 20 minutes and provide some research-backed advice.

We've already covered a lot of what the researchers told the students, and they underscored the importance of mental doing. "Do not simply reread," Deslauriers would explain. "Attempt to 'do' each learning goal by generating your own explanations." As part of the meeting with each student, Deslauriers also talked about developing plans and goals, advising people to learn "in a targeted manner, to improve your ability with a specific learning goal." Finally, Deslauriers would tell students to take various approaches to engaging an idea, to make sure that they could explain a concept in various ways.

The effect of the advice was impressive. Most students saw their outcomes skyrocket, with tests scores jumping by more than 20 percentage points, or about two grade levels. What's more, the students in Deslauriers's class didn't study any longer. The new approaches didn't take any additional time. The students simply studied better.

Given this sort of research, most schools and universities often seem stuck in the Middle Ages. Stanford's Jo Boaler recently put out a guide for parents that argued that adults should "never tell kids they are wrong" in math. (It's not clear how the students would ever know that they're right.) My own daughter's teacher asked me about my child's "learning style." (Again no research on this idea.) Relatively weak approaches like underlining key points of text remain a common practice in many classrooms. (The practice doesn't add much.)

At the office, people often use highlighters (generally, not a great learning tool). *Jeopardy!* champion Roger Craig told me that he sometimes spots students studying flash cards with dozens of words on them. "I want to tell them 'you're doing it wrong!'" (Just use one word per card.) People often prepare for a presentation by rereading the text of the speech. (Unless you don't know the text at all, you're much better practicing without notes.) "If education were in the same realm as medicine, we would still be doing bloodletting with leeches," cognitive scientist Katherine Rawson told me.

The effects of better forms of learning are about a lot more than a test score. Improved educational outcomes might be the single best investment in our economic future. Better learning predicts higher income—and all sorts of other benefits like less smoking. Indeed, people who learn more also have longer, happier lives. Think of learning to learn, then, as the plastics of the twenty-first century—the one thing that no one can do without.

If you're a student or a parent or a policymaker, there's a short how-to guide for you at the end of this book. In those tool kits, you can find tailored advice on how to learn—and how to support other learners. I discuss what families and companies and governments should—and should not—do to help improve learning for all.

This effort is going to require more than advice, though. It's going to take more than a book or a guide or even a moment or two of practice. Because we all have to master the learning process—we all have to learn to learn.

TOOL KITS

Strategies for Learners

LEARNING IS A process, a method, an area of mastery, and with effort, focus, and practice, we can get a lot better at gaining expertise. Below are some of the key steps in the learning method, from setting goals to reviewing key ideas.

Find value. It's impossible to learn if we don't want to learn, and to gain expertise, people have to see skills and knowledge as valuable. So look for relevance in your learning and find ways to make expertise meaningful to you. If you're learning math and love gymnastics, for instance, then work on math problems involving rotations. If you're learning knitting, create a sweater for a close friend.

At the same time, uncover meaning in the area of expertise. Learning is often a matter of making knowledge and skills significant in some way. So don't use more passive forms of learning like rereading or highlighting. Instead, rely on more active learning strategies like self-quizzing or self-explaining. If you really want to learn a text, act it out. If you hope to really understand a concept, describe it in your own words.

For a different example, consider something known as "repeat backs." The next time a person gives you a set of detailed instructions, take time to repeat back the instructions in your own words. When you summarize the instructions, you're taking steps to generate knowledge, and you'll be more likely to remember the information.

Create targets. In the early part of learning, focus is key. People need to figure out exactly what skills that they want to learn. Think of learning, then, as a type of knowledge management, and to succeed, we need goals, deadlines, and strategies. Indeed, hundreds of studies have shown that people with clear goals outperform people with vague aspirations like "do a good job."

However, learning goals should not be vague aims. Overly ambitious learning targets can backfire because they seemed too distant. They ignore our emotional side. Instead, people are more likely to succeed if they have easy-to-accomplish benchmarks. So instead of a goal like learning to waltz, people should develop smaller targets, like attending waltz lessons once a week, which are easier to accomplish.

When it comes to targeting your learning, rigor matters a lot, too. So try and make things a little more difficult than you're used to. If you're learning art history, for instance, most people would start by reviewing some of the things that they already fairly familiar with—Rembrandt was a Dutch painter, Van Gogh was a Postimpressionist, etc.

But learning happens when people are pushed just a bit past their comfort zone, when they struggle with ideas just beyond their reach. So the more effective questions for the person learning about art history might be: Who was Alberto Giacometti? Why was Louise Nevelson such an important artist? Why is Degas considered the first modernist painter?

Develop knowledge and skills. In this stage of learning, people need to hone their abilities and take steps to improve performance. In short, people need to practice, setting aside time to develop an area of mastery.

Some forms of practice make people more perfect than others, though, and people should be sure to practice retrieving their knowledge. In one well-known study, a group of subjects who practiced recalling a passage learned a lot more than people who simply reread the passage. More concretely, you'd learn a lot more if you ask yourself questions after reading this text than simply rereading it.

What's also deeply important is feedback. We need to know what we're doing right—and wrong—and even simply monitoring performance can boost outcomes. In this regard, some people swear by learning diaries. Others believe in videos.

Helpful feedback also provides guidance. Let's say, for example, that you thought that the Spanish word for rooster was *pollo*. A weak form of feedback would have just given you the answer. ("You got that wrong; the correct answer is *gallo*.") Or, it might not provide any feedback at all. ("Please go to the next question.")

The best feedback mixes an observation with a structured way to produce the proper outcome. In the rooster example, for instance, the most effective feedback would indicate that the answer was wrong—and then would provide some slight hints. ("The correct Spanish word for rooster starts with a *g*.") If someone still doesn't provide the correct answer, then perhaps another tip ("think *ga*") until the correct answer (*gallo*).

Extend expertise. At this point in the learning process, we want to go beyond the basics and apply what we know. We want to flesh out our skills and knowledge, and people can gain a lot by expanding on a skill. Want to get better at public speaking, for instance? Do more public speaking of all kinds, from lectures to media interviews.

People can also learn a lot by explaining ideas to themselves, by asking themselves: Does this make sense? How does this work? In much the same way, people will learn a lot when they explain an idea or skill to others. This helps give a sense of why group work is often so effective: By providing instruction to their peers, individuals gain more.

Admittedly, all these approaches to learning requires cognitive struggle. They take time, effort, and hard work, and we should be sure to support our emotional side. This means measuring progress and celebrating accomplishments, however small.

Relate skills. This is the phase where we see how it all fits together. After all, we don't want to know just a single detail or procedure—we want to know how that detail or procedure interacts with other details and procedures. In short, we want to understand the underlying system of an area of expertise.

So look beyond facts and see how things hang together. Ask yourself questions that examine relationships within an area of expertise:

What's the system that exists within this area of mastery? What's the nature of cause and effect? What are some analogies? How can I make this information valuable to me?

One effective technique in this regard is hypotheticals, and if you're learning biology, for example, consider what would happen if living things didn't evolve over time. Same with reading literature. Want to better understand *Romeo and Juliet*? Then consider what would have happened if the young lovers had not died in the Shakespeare play. Would the Capulets and Montagues have continued their feud?

Concept maps are another powerful way to uncover connections in a body of expertise. When we graphically map relationships between knowledge and skills, we gain a lot more. Also be sure to mix it up. We get a better sense of relationships when our practice is varied. Want to teach yourself to build Web sites? Then mix a bit of Drupal editing with learning WordPress.

Rethink understanding. When it comes to learning, it's easy to make mistakes, to be overconfident, and we need to review our knowledge, to reconsider our understanding. So people should ask themselves as they learn: Do I really know what I think that I know?

Other people can help a lot here, and we often learn better when we're exposed to diverse ways of thinking. As political scientist Scott Page has shown, teams are more likely to succeed if they have people with diverse experiences. So if you're aiming to crack a pressing issue, ask someone with a different background to help. Want to solve a problem in your company? Invite your janitor into the brainstorming meeting.

At the same time, we need to reflect, and people should think about what they've learned. Specifically, ask yourself: How has my thinking changed? How does this material all come together? What did I learn, and what do I need to learn next?

In the end, we learn something so that we can learn the system of thought that makes up that field. So, if we study microeconomics, we're learning how to think like microeconomic experts. If we learn biochemistry, we learn how to think like biochemistry experts. As educational psychologists argue, "Think of learning as figuring out parts of an organized and intelligible system."

Strategies for Parents, Teachers, and Managers

YOUNG OR OLD, experienced or amateur, learners need support. Below I map out some ways for parents, teachers, and managers to help people gain an area of expertise.

Set expectations. There's no getting around it: Learning is hard. Gaining expertise requires struggle. For parent, teachers, and managers, this means that learners need support and encouragement, and so you should offer lots of praise and social encouragement to the people learning something.

Be sure, however, to focus on process, not outcomes, so people remain motivated. More specifically, stop using the word "smart." People who are told they are "smart" often become complacent, performing under their ability, according to work by Carol Dweck. So praise methods, not performance: "Great job working so hard." "This is going to be hard." "Keep it up."

Teachers—and parents—should also communicate rigorous norms and goals. Tell people what you expect. Even more important, be sure to model this behavior to others and show effective ways to manage struggle and overcome failures. If you make mistakes, tell yourself and others: *What a great opportunity to learn.*

Break it up. We all forget. It might take a few days—or just a few minutes. But learning often leaves as soon as it arrives. Indeed, we often forget most of what we've learned within a few hours.

We need to account for this forgetting. So encourage people to space out their learning over weeks or months so that they relearn any material that they've forgotten. It's a lot more effective, for instance, for people to study one large pile of flash cards rather than lots of smaller piles of cards because the large pile helps people revisit material. Same with homework: It's far more effective to spread it out over time rather than do it all in one evening or weekend.

Employers should take this approach, too, and instead of one-time training programs, organizations should spread out the learning out for employees. So rather than just train new employees on their first day, be sure to revisit key material periodically.

Promote focus. It's easy to get distracted. It's even easier to get distracted while learning. So create spaces where people can focus on their learning. This means spaces without music or television or loud talking. Many organizations have caught on to this trend and are doing away with distracting environments. While Google is known for its open floor plan, the tech firm now encourages employees to book a private office if they need to really focus.

Likewise, less is often more when it comes to the presentation of ideas. If there's too much information, people's working memory becomes overloaded. So when you're putting together a PowerPoint presentation, don't crowd the slides with graphics. Just have a single message on each slide. Or, if you're giving a talk, make sure you're clear about your core message, repeating it often in case the audience is distracted.

Support mistakes. For a long time, failure was a dirty word for learners. But today, we know that students need to fail in order to succeed. Part of the reason is that failure helps us understand where our thinking went wrong. Plus, errors often promote learning, helping us to remember.

Teachers, parents, and managers can encourage failure by praising failure. One example is the company SurePayroll, which offers an award for errors. SurePayroll's former president Michael Alter started the practice, offering the Best New Mistake award, giving a few hundred dollars to the winner each year.

To support mistakes, teachers and parents should also not give answers to students. Let people struggle. "What parents need to do is allow their kids to be okay with being uncomfortable, to be okay without knowing the answer," says researcher Lisa Son. "People need to do learning on their own for long-term maximum learning power."

Use analogies. Analogies often spark memories of IQ tests. (Nest is to bird, as doghouse is to _____.) But analogies often serve as true mothers of invention. Johannes Gutenberg invented the printing press after seeing a wine press, while Twitter is half text messaging, half social media.

People can use analogies to help explain new ideas. Smart marketing companies know this, and they are famous for using analogies to introduce new products. The insurance firm State Farm, for instance, has long relied on the jingle, "Like a good neighbor, State Farm is there."

Analogies can also promote innovation. Consider, for instance, how start-ups will often reference Uber to describe their services. The company Blue Apron has presented itself as the Uber for high-end cooking. The dry-cleaning company DRYV has been described as Uber for dry cleaning.

Promote review. We're all overconfident. Sometimes this is a good thing. No one would lead a company or keep up a blog without some streak of brashness. But when it comes to learning, we often think that we know more than we do, and teachers, managers, and parents should help others review what they've learned.

In her classes at Carnegie Mellon, Marsha Lovett will often give students one or two written questions after they finish a lecture to help them from being overconfident. Lovett calls the questions "wrappers." As part of the activity, students ask themselves questions: *What did I learn? What was hard to understand? What seems unclear?*

For Lovett, a lot of the benefit of wrappers is that they focus a student's thinking on misunderstandings as well as "how the students could improve their learning," she says. Lovett often recommends that students focus on the areas that give them the most difficulty. By focusing on what Lovett calls the "muddiest point," students get more out of their learning. "It's about getting in that habit of mind of thinking: 'Okay. How well do I know this?'" Lovett told me. "'Where am I feeling confused?'"

Strategies for Policymakers

LEARNING HAS BECOME a constant for just about everyone. Below are some ways for policymakers to help individuals gain better learning methods and strategies—and improve the nation's system of schooling.

Promote learning to learn. Students should learn how to learn, and policymakers should consider the following:

- Encourage schools to teach students learning strategies like goal setting, self-quizzing, and thinking about thinking.
- Improve schools of education so that they're focused on giving educators practical teaching skills based on the science of learning.
- Fund training programs that give educators a better understanding of how students gain new skills and knowledge.

Improve curriculum. The nation's education system needs better instructional materials that support richer forms of learning. There are some clear solutions, and policymakers should do the following:

- Fund programs and initiatives that make learning more active and engaging, like the use of clickers.
- Promote better textbooks and other instructional materials that support effective student learning, such as spacing out learning over time.

- Make programs of study more personalized and relevant to student interests, allowing students to learn at their own pace.

Promote smart technology use. While technology can go a long way to promote more effective ways to learn, it also can distract, reducing our ability to gain new expertise. When it comes to learning, policymakers should do more to invest in good practice, including the following:

- Encourage learning technology that provides clear academic benefits like computer-based simulations.
- Require institutions to track outcomes so that the public has a better sense of what works.
- Ensure that all students have reliable access to high-speed Internet either at home or at school.

Support the emotional side of education. Students can't learn if they don't feel emotionally ready to learn. Policymakers can help by making classrooms more emotionally supportive, including the following:

- Fund programs that give students the skills to manage their emotions like the Becoming a Man program.
- Support efforts that take a more holistic approach to learning and help schools offer free dental or child care.
- Promote better school climate and do more to make schools safe and welcoming.

Embrace social learning. Learning is often just as emotional as it is rational, and policymakers need to do more to support the social aspect of schooling, such as:

- Encourage more diversity in schools and examine housing policies that contribute to social isolation.
- Promote better school culture, including the greater use of support staff like guidance counselors.

- Encourage more parental involvement and provide parents with better tools to help their students at home.

Redesign learning environments. Most classrooms look the same as they did in the Middle Ages: a lot of passive lecturing, not so much mental doing. Policymakers should do more to spark more innovation in this space, redesigning classrooms based on the science of learning, including the following:

- Encourage—and fund—educational "start-ups," which take more innovative approaches to teaching and learning.
- Measure learning outcomes, not processes, to encourage more experimentation.
- Provide students with more opportunities to have real-world experiences like internships and externships.

REFERENCES
AND NOTES

THE BOOKS, REPORTS, studies, and other documents below served as useful general guides and resources. When applicable, I also cite these books in the notes section.

Ambrose, Susan A., Michael W. Bridges, Michele DiPietro, Marsha C. Lovett, and Marie K. Norman. *How Learning Works: Seven Research-Based Principles for Smart Teaching.* Kindle edition. San Francisco: Jossey-Bass, 2010.

Askell-Williams, Helen, Michael J. Lawson, and Grace Skrzypiec. "Scaffolding Cognitive and Metacognitive Strategy Instruction in Regular Class Lessons." *Instructional Science* 40, no. 2 (2012): 413–43. doi:10.1007/s11251-011-9182-5

Benassi, Victor A., Catherine E. Overson, and Christopher M. Hakala. *Applying Science of Learning in Education: Infusing Psychological Science into the Curriculum.* Durham, NH: University of New Hampshire, 2014. http://teachpsych.org/ebooks/asle2014/index.php

Benavides, Francisco, Hanna Dumont, and David Instance, ed. *The Nature of Learning: Using Research to Inspire Practice.* Paris: OECD Publishing, 2010.

Bourne, Lyle E. *Train Your Mind for Peak Performance: A Science-Based Approach for Achieving Your Goals.* Washington, DC: American Psychological Association, 2013.

Bourne, Lyle E., and Alice F. Healy. *Training Cognition: Optimizing Efficiency, Durability, and Generalizability.* Hove, UK: Psychology Press, 2012.

Bransford, John D., Ann L. Brown, and Rodney R. Cocking, eds. *How People Learn: Brain, Mind, Experience and School.* Washington, DC: National Academies Press, 2000.

Brown, Peter C., Henry L. Roediger III, and Mark A. McDaniel. *Make It Stick*. Kindle edition. Cambridge, MA: Harvard University Press, 2014.

Carey, Benedict. *How We Learn: The Surprising Truth about When, Where, and Why It Happens*. New York: Random House, 2014.

Carnegie Mellon University. "Teaching Excellence and Educational Innovation." https://www.cmu.edu/teaching (accessed September 14, 2016)

Carpenter, Shana K., ed. "Improving Student Learning in Low-Maintenance and Cost-Effective Ways." *Journal of Applied Research in Memory and Cognition* 3, no. 3 (2014): 121–23. doi: 10.1016/j.jarmac.2014.07.004

Center for Teaching. Vanderbilt University. https://wp0.its.vanderbilt.edu /cft/ (accessed September 14, 2016)

Christodoulou, Daisy. *Seven Myths about Education*. London: Routledge, 2014.

Clark, Ruth C. *Building Expertise: Cognitive Methods for Training and Performance Improvement*. Hoboken, NJ: Pfeiffer, 2008.

Clark, Ruth C., and Richard E. Mayer. *E-Learning and the Science of Instruction: Proven Guidelines for Consumers and Designers of Multimedia Learning*. 2nd ed. San Francisco: Pfeiffer, 2007.

Claxton, Guy. *Hare Brain, Tortoise Mind: How Intelligence Increases When You Think Less*. 1st ed. Hopewell, NJ: Ecco, 1999.

Deans for Impact. *The Science of Learning*. Austin, TX: Deans for Impact, 2015. http://deansforimpact.org/the_science_of_learning.html

Derek Bok Center for Teaching and Learning. http://bokcenter.harvard.edu /(accessed September 14, 2016)

Dharma, Jairam, and Keith Kiewra. "An Investigation of the SOAR Study Method." *Journal of Advanced Academics* 20, no. 4 (2009): 602–29.

Dunlosky, John, and Janet Metcalf. *Metacognition*. New York: SAGE Publications, 2008.

Elder, Linda, and Richard Paul. *The Thinker's Guide for Students on How to Study and Learn a Discipline: Using Critical Thinking Concepts and Tools*. Tomales, CA: Foundation for Critical Thinking, 2002.

Ericsson, Anders K., and Robert Poole. *Peak: Secrets from the New Science of Expertise*. New York: Houghton Mifflin Harcourt, 2016.

Hattie, John. *Visible Learning: A Synthesis of Over 800 Meta-Analyses Relating to Achievement*. London: Routledge, 2008.

Healy, Alice F., and Lyle E. Bourne Jr., eds. *Training Cognition: Optimizing Efficiency, Durability, and Generalizability*. 1st ed. New York: Psychology Press, 2012.

Hoffman, Robert R., Paul Ward, Paul J. Feltovich, Lia DiBello, Stephen M. Fiore, and Dee H. Andrews. *Accelerated Expertise: Training for High Proficiency in a Complex World*. Expertise: Research and Applications Series. Abingdon, UK: Taylor & Francis, 2014.

Koedinger, Kenneth R., Julie L. Booth, and David Klahr. "Instructional Complexity and the Science to Constrain It." *Science* 342 (2013): 935–37. doi: 10.1126/science.1238056

Lemov, Doug, and Norman Atkins. *Teach Like a Champion: 49 Techniques That Put Students on the Path to College.* 1st ed. San Francisco: Jossey-Bass, 2010.

Levy, Frank. *The New Division of Labor: How Computers Are Creating the Next Job Market.* Princeton, NJ: Princeton University Press, 2005.

Levy, Frank, and Richard J. Murnane. *Teaching the New Basic Skills: Principles for Educating Children to Thrive in a Changing Economy.* New York: Free Press, 1996.

Marzano, Robert J. *The Art and Science of Teaching: A Comprehensive Framework for Effective Instruction (Professional Development).* Alexandria, VA: Association for Supervision & Curriculum Development, 2007.

Marzano, Robert J., Debra Pickering, and Jane E. Pollock. *Classroom Instruction That Works: Research-Based Strategies for Increasing Student Achievement.* Alexandria, VA: Association for Supervision & Curriculum Development, 2001.

Mayer, Richard E., and Logan Fiorella. *Learning as a Generative Activity: Eight Learning Strategies That Promote Understanding.* Cambridge, UK: Cambridge University Press, 2015.

McDaniel, Mark, and Cynthia Wooldridge. "The Science of Learning and Its Applications." *Effective College and University Teaching: Strategies and Tactics for the New Professoriate,* eds. William Buskist and Victor A. Benassi, 49–60. New York: SAGE Publications, 2012.

McDaniel, Mark, Regina Frey, Susan Fitzpatrick, and Henry Roediger III, eds. *Integrating Cognitive Science with Innovative Teaching in STEM Disciplines.* St. Louis: Washington University Libraries, 2014.

Nilson, Linda, and Barry J. Zimmerman. *Creating Self-Regulated Learners: Strategies to Strengthen Students' Self-Awareness and Learning Skills.* Sterling, VA: Stylus, 2013.

Nisbett, Richard E. *Mindware: Tools for Smart Thinking.* New York: Farrar, Straus and Giroux, 2015.

Nisbett, Richard E. *Intelligence and How to Get It: Why Schools and Cultures Count.* New York: W. W. Norton, 2010.

Oakley, Barbara. *A Mind for Numbers: How to Excel at Math and Science (Even If You Flunked Algebra).* New York: TarcherPerigee, 2014.

Pashler, H., P. Bain, B. Bottge, A. Graesser, K. Koedinger, M. McDaniel, and Janet Metcalfe. *Organizing Instruction and Study to Improve Student Learning* (NCER 2007-2004). Washington, DC: National Center for Education Research, 2007. Retrieved from http://ncer.ed.gov

Schwartz, Bennett L. *Memory: Foundations and Applications.* 2nd ed. Thousand Oaks, CA: SAGE Publications, 2013.

Schwartz, Bennett L., Lisa K. Son, Nate Kornell, and Bridget Finn. "Four Principles of Memory Improvement: A Guide to Improving Learning Efficiency." *International Journal of Creativity and Problem Solving* 21, vol. 1 (2011): 7–15.

Stigler, James W., and James Hiebert. *The Teaching Gap: Best Ideas from the World's Teachers for Improving Education in the Classroom.* New York: Free Press, 1999.

Wiggins, Grant, Jan McTighe, and Jay McTighe. *Understanding by Design.* Alexandria, VA: Association for Supervision & Curriculum Development, 1998.

Willingham, Daniel T. *Cognition: The Thinking Animal.* 3rd ed. Upper Saddle River, NJ: Pearson, 2006.

———. *Why Don't Students Like School? A Cognitive Scientist Answers Questions about How the Mind Works and What It Means for the Classroom.* San Francisco: Jossey-Bass, 2010.

NOTES

In the notes below, I outline sources for my material as well as provide some additional context. If I interviewed someone, I made that clear in the text and did not provide an additional source. If a quote comes from an outside source, I noted below.

Introduction

The details from the dart study on page xiv come from interviews and from Barry J. Zimmerman and Anastasia Kitsantas, "Developmental Phases in Self-Regulation: Shifting from Process Goals to Outcome Goals," *Journal of Educational Psychology* 89, no. 1 (1997): 29.

For studies on the learning process on page xv, or what's often called "self-regulated learning," see Hester de Boer et al., *Effective Strategies for Self-Regulated Learning: A Meta-Analysis* (Gronigen: GION/RUG, 2013). Also see Kiruthiga Nandagopal and K. Anders Ericsson, "An Expert Performance Approach to the Study of Individual Differences in Self-Regulated Learning Activities in Upper-Level College Students," *Learning and Individual Differences* 22, no. 5 (2012): 597–609.

Mentioned on page xvi is Anastasia Kitsantas and Barry J. Zimmerman, "Comparing Self-Regulatory Processes Among Novice, Non-Expert, and Expert Volleyball Players: A Micro Analytic Study," *Journal of Applied Sport Psychology* 14, no. 2 (2002): 91–105; Barry J. Zimmerman and Anastasia Kitsantas, "Acquiring Writing Revision Skill: Shifting from Process to Outcome Self-Regulatory Goals," *Journal of Educational Psychology* 91, no. 2 (1999): 241. Also see Mark C. Fox and Neil Charness, "How to Gain Eleven IQ Points in Ten Minutes: Thinking Aloud Improves Raven's Matrices Performance in Older Adults," *Aging, Neuropsychology, and Cognition* 17, no. 2 (2010): 191–204.

For the survey results on page xvii, see Ulrich Boser, "Does the Public Know What Great Teaching and Learning Look Like?" Center for American Progress, forthcoming. Note that the survey was a convenience sample, which we weighted to reflect the nation as a whole. The document will be available on my Web site and the Center's Web site.

On discovery learning, page xvii, see Louis Alfieri et al., "Does Discovery-Based Instruction Enhance Learning?" *Journal of Educational Psychology* 103, no. 1 (2011): 1–18. Also Richard E. Mayer, "Should There Be a Three-Strikes Rule Against Pure Discovery Learning?" *American Psychologist* 59, no. 1 (2004): 14–19.

For research on learning styles on page xvii, see Harold Pashler et al., "Psychological Science in the Public Interest," *Learning Styles: Concepts and Evidence* 9, no. 3 (2008): 105–19. Also see Thomas K. Fagan and Daniel T. Willingham, "Do Visual, Auditory, and Kinesthetic Learners Need Visual, Auditory, and Kinesthetic Instruction?" *American Educator* (Summer 2005): 31–35.

I first came across the Betsy Sparrow research on page xvii in this article: Katherine Hobson, "Google on the Brain: How the Internet Has Changed What We Remember," *Wall Street Journal*, July 15, 2011. The full study is Betsy Sparrow, Jenny Lui, and Daniel M. Wegner, "Google Effects on Memory: Cognitive Consequences of Having Information at Our Fingertips," *Science* 333, no. 6043 (2011): 776–78.

Also cited on page xviii is Linda A. Henkel, "Point and Shoot Memories: The Influence of Taking Photos on Memory for a Museum Tour," *Psychological Science* 25, no. 2 (2014): 396–402. For the quote about the brain on page xviii, I relied on James Gleick, "Auto Correct This!" *New York Times,* August 4, 2012. http://www.nytimes.com/2012/08/05/opinion/sunday/auto-correct-this.html

Much has been written about Ötzi. For the text on page xvii, I relied on Brenda Fowler, *Iceman: Uncovering the Life and Times of a Prehistoric Man Found in an Alpine Glacier,* 1st ed. (New York: Random House, 2000). Also helpful was Bob Cullen, "Testimony from the Iceman," *Smithsonian,* http://www.smithsonianmag.com/science-nature/testimony-from-the-iceman-75198998/ (accessed September 13, 2016) and the Web site of the South Tyrol Museum of Archaeology, http://iceman.it/en/ (accessed September 20, 2016).

For the quote from educational psychologists on page xx, see Richard Paul and Linda Elder's *The Thinker's Guide for Students on How to Study and Learn a Discipline: Using Critical Thinking Concepts & Tools,* Foundation for Critical Thinking (2003). Also helpful was Lindsey Engle Richland and Nina Simms, "Analogy, Higher Order Thinking, and Education," *Wiley Interdisciplinary Reviews: Cognitive Science* 6, no. 2 (March 2015): 177–92.

For more on Levy and Murnane's work on page xx, see Frank Levy and Richard J. Murnane, *The New Division of Labor: How Computers Are Changing the Way We Work* (Princeton, NJ: Princeton University Press, 2004). Ted Dintersmith first made the point to me about Levy and Murnane's self-driving car prediction. For a more recent take on the issue, see Derek Thompson, "What Jobs Will the Robots Take?" *The Atlantic,* January 23, 2014. http://www.theatlantic.com/business/archive/2014/01/what-jobs-will-the-robots-take/283239/

The report mentioned on page xxii was Ulrich Boser, "Return on Educational Investment: A District-by-District Evaluation of US Educational Productivity," Center for American Progress, January 2011. The 50 percent figure on page xxii comes from Scott Freeman, Sarah L. Eddy, Miles McDonough, Michelle K. Smith, Nnadozie Okoroafor, Hannah Jordt, and Mary Pat Wenderoth, "Active Learning Increases Student Performance in Science, Engineering, and Mathematics," *Proceedings of the National Academy of Sciences* 111, no. 23 (2014): 8410–415; published ahead of print May 12, 2014, doi:10.1073/pnas.1319030111. Note that the Freeman analysis looked only at STEM classes.

For the testing yourself study on page xxii, see J.D. Karpicke and J.R. Blunt, "Retrieval Practice Produces More Learning than Elaborative Studying with Concept Mapping," Science 331, no. 6018 (2011).

When it comes to the idea of thinking of learning as a process on page xxiv, I'm indebted to writer Bruce Schneier, who has made a similar argument when it comes to security. When it comes to the specific steps outlined, I credit the many who've described different learning phases, including Barry Zimmerman, Bracha Kramarski, Ruth Clark, John Flavell, and Kenneth A. Kiewra. The quote about learning as a survival tool on page xxii comes from Robert A. Bjork, John Dunlosky, and Nate Kornell, "Self-Regulated Learning: Beliefs, Techniques, and Illusions," *Annual Review of Psychology* 64, no. 1 (January 3, 2013): 417–44, doi:10.1146/annurev-psych-113011-143823

Also cited

Dunlosky, John, et al. "Improving Students' Learning with Effective Learning Techniques: Promising Directions from Cognitive and Educational Psychology." *Psychological Science in the Public Interest* 14, no. 1 (2013): 4–58.

Jairam, Dharma, and Kenneth A. Kiewra. "An Investigation of the SOAR Study Method." *Journal of Advanced Academics* 20, no. 4 (2009): 602–29.

Kitsantas, Anastasia, Adam Winsler, and Faye Huie. "Self-Regulation and Ability Predictors of Academic Success during College: A Predictive Validity Study." *Journal of Advanced Academics* 20, no. 1 (2008): 42–68.

Kramarski, Bracha. "Promoting Teachers' Algebraic Reasoning and Self-Regulation with Metacognitive Guidance." *Metacognition and Learning* 3, no. 2 (2008): 83.

Kramarski, Bracha, and Tali Revach. "The Challenge of Self-Regulated Learning in Mathematics Teachers' Professional Training." *Educational Studies in Mathematics* 72, no. 3 (2009): 379–99.

Murnane, Richard J., and Frank Levy. *Teaching the New Basic Skills: Principles for Educating Children to Thrive in a Changing Economy.* New York: Free Press, 1996.

Plant, E. Ashby, K. Anders Ericsson, Len Hill, and Kia Asberg. "Why Study Time Does Not Predict Grade Point Average Across College Students: Implications of Deliberate Practice for Academic Performance." *Contemporary Educational Psychology* 30, no. 1 (2005): 96–116.

Yan, Veronica. *Learning Concepts and Categories from Examples: How Learners' Beliefs Match and Mismatch the Empirical Evidence.* University of California, Los Angeles: Pro Quest Dissertations Publishing, 2014.

Zimmerman, Barry J. "Self-Regulated Learning, an Overview." *Educational Psychologist* 25, no. 1 (1990): 3–17.

Chapter 1

Much has been written on the idea of framing, which is mentioned on page 3. My favorite study—cited here—is Aaron C. Kay et al., "Material Priming: The Influence of Mundane Physical Objects on Situational Construal and Competitive Behavioral Choice," *Organizational Behavior and Human Decision Processes* 95, no. 1 (2004): 83–96.

For citations on page 4 for relevance in learning and what's known as "utility-value interventions," see Chris S. Hulleman and Judith M. Harackiewicz, "Making Education Relevant: Increasing Interest and Performance in High School Science Classes," *Science* 326, no. 598 (2009): 1410–12. Also see Judith M. Harackiewicz et al., "Helping Parents to Motivate Adolescents in Mathematics and Science: An Experimental Test of a Utility-Value Intervention," *Psychological Science* 28, no. 8 (2012): 899–906.

On Minecraft on page 8, see Ryan Mac, David M. Ewalt, and Max Jedeur-Palmgren, "Inside the Post-Minecraft Life of Billionaire Gamer God Markus Persson," *Forbes* (March 2015), http://www.forbes.com/sites/ryanmac/2015/03/03/minecraft-markus-persson-life-after-microsoft-sale/ (accessed October 27, 2016); Tracy McVeigh, "Minecraft: How a Game with No Rules Changed the Rules of the Game Forever," *Guardian*, November 16, 2013, http://www.theguardian.com/technology/2013/nov/16/minecraft-game-no-rules-changed-gaming; and Nick Statt, "Markus 'Notch' Persson: The Mind behind Minecraft (Q&A)," *CNET* (November 2013), https://www.cnet.com/news/markus-notch-persson-the-mind-behind-minecraft-q-a/ (accessed October 27, 2016). The quote on page 8 from the biographers came from the *Guardian* article. The Persson quote came from the *CNET* article.

The idea for the Minecraft point on page 8 came from Clive Thompson, "The Sims: Suburban Rhapsody," *Psychology Today* (November 2003), http://www.psychologytoday.com/articles/200311/the-sims-suburban-rhapsody (accessed October 27, 2016).

I first came across the work of Amy Wrzesniewski on page 8 in Tom Rath, *Are You Fully Charged? The 3 Keys to Energizing Your Work and Life,* Kindle edition (Arlington, VA: Mission Day LLC, 2015). For Wrzesniewski's quotes and the quotes from the cleaning people on page 9, I relied on David Zax, "Want to Be Happier at Work? Learn How from These 'Job Crafters,'" *Fast Company*, June 3, 2013, https://www.fastcompany.com/3011081/innovation-agents/want-to-be-happier-at-work-learn-how-from-these-job-crafters (accessed September 18, 2016).

Also helpful was Amy Wrzesniewski, Justin M. Berg, and Justin Dutton, "Managing Yourself: Turn the Job You Have into the Job You Want," *Harvard Business Review,* June 1, 2010, https://hbr.org/2010/06/managing

-yourself-turn-the-job-you-have-into-the-job-you-want (accessed September 18, 2016). Also see Lora Kolodny, "The Latest Approach to Employee Training," *Wall Street Journal,* March 14, 2016, Business section, http://www.wsj.com/articles/the-latest-approach-to-employee -training-1457921560?tesla=y

On the study of student choice on page 10, see Erika A. Patall, Harris Cooper, and Susan R. Wynn, "The Effectiveness and Relative Importance of Choice in the Classroom," *Journal of Educational Psychology* 102, no. 4 (2010): 896. Note that too much choice, especially for people early in the learning process, shows limited outcomes. See Richard E. Clark, Paul A. Kirschner, and John Sweller, "Putting Students on the Path to Learning: The Case for Fully Guided Instruction," *American Educator* (Spring 2012): 7–11.

The work on seeking was pioneered by Jaak Panksepp. His quote on page 12 comes from Emily Yoffe, "Seeking," *Slate* (August 12, 2009), http://www .slate.com/articles/health_and_science/science/2009/08/seeking.html (accessed September 18, 2016).

For the discussion of situational motivation on page 13, I relied on Kenneth E. Barron and Chris S. Hulleman, "Is There a Formula to Help Understand and Improve Student Motivation?" *Essays from Excellence in Teaching* 8 (2006). Accessed August 7, 2006 from the Society for the Teaching of Psychology, http://list.kennesaw.edu/archives/psychteacher.html

Also very helpful was Suzanne Hidi and K. Ann Renninger, "The Four-Phase Model of Interest Development," *Educational Psychologist* 41, no. 2 (2006): 111–27.

When it comes to the Posse program mentioned on page 16, I relied on a number of resources, including Adam Bryant, "Deborah Bial of the Posse Foundation: Success Isn't Always about You," *New York Times,* October 4, 2014, http://www.nytimes.com/2014/10/05/business /deborah-bial-of-the-posse-foundation-success-isnt-always-about -you .html (accessed September 13, 2016).

Also helpful was "Quick Facts," *The Posse Foundation,* http://www.posse foundation.org/quick-facts (accessed September 13, 2016).

For the study on names on page 17, see David Figlio, "Names, Expectations, and the Black-White Test Score Gap," no. 11195, National Bureau of Economic Research (March 2005).

For more on the impact of social connections on learning on page 18, see C. Kirabo Jackson, "Can Higher-Achieving Peers Explain the Benefits to Attending Selective Schools? Evidence from Trinidad and Tobago," *Journal of Public Economics Elsevier* 108 (December 2013): 63–77. Also see Victor Lavy and Edith Sand, "The Friends Factor: How Students' Social Networks Affect Their Academic Achievement and Well-Being," National Bureau of Economic Research (NBER) Working Paper no. 18430 (October 2012) and "The Effect of Social Networks on Students' Academic and Non-Cognitive Behavioral Outcomes: Evidence from Conditional Random Assignment of Friends in School," University of Warwick and Hebrew University Working Paper (May 2015).

For social networks and text anxiety on page 17, see Daena Goldsmith and Terrance Albrecht, "The Impact of Supportive Communication Networks on Test Anxiety and Performance," *Communication Education* 42, no. 2 (1993): 142–58.

For the contagious study on page 18, see K. Desender, S. Beurms, and E. Van den Bussche, "Is Mental Effort Exertion Contagious?" *Psychonomic Bulletin & Review* 23, no. 2 (2015): 624–31, doi: 10.3758/s13423-015-0923-3. I first came across it in "Why Coffee Shops Boost Concentration," *Association for Psychological Science,* http://www.psychologicalscience.org/index.php/news/minds-business/why-coffee-shops-boost-concentration.html (accessed September 26, 2016).

The enthusiasm quote on page 19 comes from "WamaLTC: Club," *WamaLTC,* July 7, 2001, http://wamaltc.org/club.html (accessed September 11, 2016).

The math problem on page 20 is from K.B. Givvin, J.W. Stigler, & B. Thompson (2011), "What Community College Developmental Mathematics Students Understand about Mathematics, Part 2: The Interviews," *The MathAMA-TYC Educator,* vol. 2, no. 3, 4–18. Reprinted with permission from the authors.

I'm indebted to my sister Katharina Boser and Max McLure for tipping me off to mental abacus, discussed on page 23. For academic research on the practice, see Michael C. Frank and David Barner, "Representing Exact Number Visually Using Mental Abacus," *Journal of Experimental Psychology: General* 141, no. 1 (2012): 134–49. Also see James W. Stigler, Laurence Chalip, and Kevin F. Miller, "Consequences of Skill: The Case of Abacus Training in Taiwan," *American Journal of Education* 94, no. 4 (1986): 447–79; and N. Brooks, D. Barner, M. Frank, and S. Goldin-Meadow (under review), "The Role of Gesture in Supporting Mental Representations: The Case of Mental Abacus Arithmetic," 2016.

I quoted from Richard E. Mayer, *How Not to Be a Terrible School Board Member: Lessons for School Administrators and Board Members,* Kindle edition (Thousand Oaks, CA: Corwin, SAGE Publications, 2011). Also see Richard E. Mayer and Logan Fiorella, *Learning as a Generative Activity: Eight Learning Strategies that Promote Understanding* (Cambridge, UK: Cambridge University Press, 2015).

For citations on learning as doing on page 25, see John Dunlosky et al., "Improving Students' Learning with Effective Learning Techniques: Promising Directions from Cognitive and Educational Psychology," *Psychological Science in the Public Interest* 14, no. 1 (2013): 4–58. Note that the generation effect is not all that different from the testing effect, which is explored most recently in Peter C. Brown, Henry L. Roediger III, and Mark A. McDaniel, *Make It Stick* (Cambridge, MA: Harvard University Press, 2014) and Benedict Carey, *How We Learn* (New York: Penguin Random House, 2015).

For more on the generation effect and remembering words like "maison" on page 25, see Patricia Ann DeWinstanley and Elizabeth L. Bjork, "Processing Strategies and the Generation Effect: Implications for Making a Better Reader," *Memory and Cognition* 32, no. 6 (2004): 945–55.

When it comes learning as doing and higher order thinking, as on page 25, see Jamie L. Jensen et al., "Teaching to the Test . . . or Testing to Teach: Exams Requiring Higher Order Thinking Skills Encourage Greater Conceptual Understanding," *Educational Psychology Review* 26, no. 2 (2014): 307–29, and Luke G. Eglington and Sean H. K. Kang, "Retrieval Practice Benefits Deductive Inference," *Educational Psychology Review* (2016): 1–14.

Regarding the University of Washington on page 26, I've written about the program before. See Ulrich Boser, "Don't Hate Tests," *US News & World Report*, September 23, 2015, http://www.usnews.com/opinion /knowledge-bank/2015/09/23/testing-plays-a-key-role-in-education -accountability (accessed September 15, 2016), and I reused some of the language here.

Regarding handwriting on page 28, see Perri Klass M.D, "Why Handwriting Is Still Essential in the Keyboard Age," *New York Times*, June 20, 2016.

The idea that students need to be "thinking hard about knowledge" on page 29 comes from Dylan Wiliam's introduction to Daisy Christodoulou, *Seven Myths about Education* (London: Taylor & Francis, 2013).

For more on the idea of memory as a series of roads from page 20, see Jill Stamm and Paula Spencer, *Bright from the Start: The Simple, Science-Backed Way to Nurture Your Child's Developing Mind, from Birth to Age 3* (New York: Penguin, 2007).

The quote about connections and language attrition on page 30 is from Maureen Ehrensberger-Dow and Chris Ricketts, "Language Attrition: Measuring How 'Wobbly' People Become in their L1 [First Language]," (Baltmannsweiler: Schneider Verlag Hohengehren, 2010): 41–6. Also helpful was "Language Attrition," *Wikipedia, the Free Encyclopedia*, https://en.wikipedia.org/w/index.php?title=Language_attrition&old id=737109836.

Details regarding the new knee muscle on page 31 come from K. Grob et al., "A Newly Discovered Muscle: The Tensor of the Vastus Intermedius," *Clinical Anatomy* 29, no. 2 (2016): 256–63. Also helpful in this section was Ellen J. Langer, *The Power of Mindful Learning* (Reading, MA: Perseus Books, 1990), which provided the citation for the "meaningfulness" study.

For the Gates study on page 34, I relied on Bill and Melinda Gates Foundation, "Ensuring Fair and Reliable Measures of Effective Teaching: Culminating Findings from the MET Project's Three-Year Study. Policy and Practice Brief. MET Project," *ERIC* (January 2013), http://eric.ed.gov/?id= ED540958 (accessed September 18, 2016).

The Bill Gates quote on page 34 comes from Joe Nocera, "Gates Puts the Focus on Teaching," *New York Times*, May 21, 2012, http://www.nytimes .com/2012/05/22/opinion/nocera-gates-puts-the-focus-on-teaching .html (accessed September 18, 2016).

For additional details about Gates's interest, I also relied on Steven Brill, *Class Warfare: Inside the Fight to Fix America's Schools*, reprint edition (New York: Simon & Schuster, 2012). Note that I've done some work directly for the Gates Foundation and some of my work at the Center for American Progress is funded by the foundation.

Also cited in this chapter

Berg, Justin M., Jane E. Dutton, and Amy Wrzesniewski. "What Is Job Crafting and Why Does It Matter?" Center for Positive Organizational Schol-
arship, Michigan Ross School of Business (2008).

Bransford, John D., and Daniel L. Schwartz. "Rethinking Transfer: A Simple
Proposal with Multiple Implications." *Review of Research in Education* 24,
no. 1 (1999): 61–100.

Chi, Michelene T. H. "Active-Constructive-Interactive: A Conceptual Framework for Differentiating Learning Activities." *Topics in Cognitive Science* 1,
no. 1 (January 2009): 73–105.

Ferguson, Ronald F., with Charlotte Danielson. "How Framework for Teach-
ing and Tripod 7Cs Evidence Distinguish Key Components of Effective
Teaching." *Designing Teacher Evaluation Systems: New Guidance from the
Measures of Effective Teaching Project,* eds. Thomas J. Kane, Kerri A.
Kerr, and Robert C. Pianta. Hoboken, NJ: Jossey-Bass, 2014.

Freeman, Scott, et al. "Active Learning Increases Student Performance in
Science, Engineering, and Mathematics." *Proceedings of the National
Academy of Sciences* 111, no. 23 (2014): 8410–15.

Haskell, Robert E. *Transfer of Learning, Volume: Cognition and Instruction.*
1st ed. San Diego, CA: Academic Press, 2000.

Hyde, Thomas S., and James J. Jenkins. "Differential Effects of Incidental
Tasks on the Organization of Recall of a List of Highly Associated Words."
Journal of Experimental Psychology 82, no. 3 (1969): 472.

Panksepp, Jaak. "Affective Neuroscience of the Emotional Brain Mind: Evolutionary Perspectives and Implications for Understanding Depression."
Dialogues in Clinical Neuroscience 12, no. 4 (2010): 533–45.

Ross School of Business. "Job Crafting Exercise." Center for Positive Organizations. http://positiveorgs.bus.umich.edu/cpo-tools/job-crafting
-exercise/ (accessed September 14, 2016)

Singley, Mark K., and John Robert Anderson. *The Transfer of Cognitive Skill.*
Cambridge, MA: Harvard University Press, 1989.

Chapter 2

Details about Dillon's turnaround on page 37 come from "Success Stories:
Nothing Less Than the Best!" *Success for All Foundation* (2015), http:
//www.successforall.org/wp-content/uploads/2016/03/SFA_Success
Stories_Dillon.pdf (accessed September 29, 2016). Also very helpful was
Alan Richard, "What's Happened in the Rural School District Obama
Fought to Save," *PBS NewsHour,* http://www.pbs.org/newshour/updates
/rural-school-district-obama-fought-save/ (accessed October 6, 2016).

The Obama quote on page 37 is from Jack Kuenzie, "Obama Visits School in
SC 'Corridor of Shame,'" WISTV, http://www.wistv.com/story/6975244
/obama-visits-school-in-sc-corridor-of-shame (accessed December 11,
2016).

For more on the outcomes of Success for All, see Nick Lemann, "Schoolwork," *New Yorker* (2010), and WWC Intervention Report, "Beginning Reading: Success for All," Institute of Educational Sciences (August 2009), http://ies.ed.gov/ncee/wwc/EvidenceSnapshot/496 (accessed September 14, 2016).

For the point about knowledge management on page 39, see Paul Kloosterman, "Learning to Learn in Practice in Nonformal Education," *Learning to Learn: International Perspectives from Theory and Practice* (2014): 271. The bird quote on page 39 comes from Dorothy V. Thomas, "Longtime City Teacher," Baltimoresun.com, http://www.baltimoresun.com/news/obituaries/bs-md-ob-dorothy-thomas-20140616-story.html (accessed April 8, 2015).

On page 41, I relied on John Sweller, "Story of a Research Program," *Education Review: A Multi-Lingual Journal of Book Reviews* 23 (2016). The detail on page 42 about the interaction of online instruction with background music comes from Ruth C. Clark, *Building Expertise: Cognitive Methods for Training and Performance Improvement,* 3rd ed., Kindle edition (location 1414), Hoboken, NJ: Wiley, Pfeiffer, 2008.

For more on the role of knowledge on page 47, see Daniel T. Willingham, *Why Don't Students Like School? A Cognitive Scientist Answers Questions about How the Mind Works and What It Means for the Classroom,* Kindle edition (location 235), San Francisco, CA: Jossey-Bass, 2009.

On page 46, I quoted from Daniel T. Willingham, "How Knowledge Helps: It Speeds and Strengthens Reading Comprehension, Learning, and Thinking," *American Educator* 30, no. 1 (2006): 30. Also see Daisy Christodoulou, *Seven Myths about Education* (Abingdon, UK: Routledge, 2014).

For the material science text on page 46, I quoted from Hemant S. Betrabet, Otmar H. Boser, Robert H. Kane, Susan McGee, and Thomas Caulfield, United States Patent and Trademark Office, *Dispersion Strengthened Lead-Tin Alloy Solder,* November 19, 1991, US5066544 A.

When it comes to speed reading on page 48, see Jeffrey M. Zacks and Rebecca Treiman, "Sorry, You Can't Speed Read," *New York Times,* April 15, 2016, http://www.nytimes.com/2016/04/17/opinion/sunday/sorry-you-cant-speed-read.html (accessed September 30, 2016). I'm also indebted to Robert Pondiscio for the point on reading and knowledge.

The language about the "easiest materials" on page 49 comes from Nate Kornell and Janet Metcalfe, "Study Efficacy and the Region of Proximal Learning Framework," *Journal of Experimental Psychology: Learning, Memory, and Cognition* 32, no. 3 (2006): 609–22. Also see Janet Metcalfe, "Desirable Difficulties and Studying in the Region of Proximal Learning," *Successful Remembering and Successful Forgetting: A Festschrift in Honor of Robert A. Bjork,* ed. Aaron S. Benjamin (New York: Psychology Press, Francis & Taylor Group, 2011). Also see Metcalfe's Web site, http://www.columbia.edu/cu/psychology/metcalfe/RPL.html (accessed November 12, 2016).

Regarding Bror Saxberg on page 51, see Bror Saxberg, "TEDxSF—Demystifying the Human Mind," YouTube, https://www.youtube.com/watch?v=s

EaQRzmV-xI (accessed November 12, 2016). Also see Frederick M. Hess and Bror Saxberg, *Breakthrough Leadership in the Digital Age: Using Learning Science to Reboot Schooling* (Thousand Oaks, CA: Corwin Press, 2013).

For the section on organizing knowledge on page 54, I relied on Arthur C. Graesser and Brent A. Olde, "How Does One Know Whether a Person Understands a Device? The Quality of the Questions the Person Asks When the Device Breaks Down," *Journal of Educational Psychology* 95, no. 3 (2003): 524. Also see Daniel T. Willingham, *Why Don't Students Like School? A Cognitive Scientist Answers Questions about How the Mind Works and What It Means for the Classroom* (San Francisco: Jossey-Bass, 2010).

The Kaplan study on page 53 is Larry Rudman, John Sweller, and David Niemi, "Using Cognitive Load Theory for Improving Logical Reasoning for the LSAT," paper presented at the American Educational Research Association Conference, April 2013.

I wrote a profile of Matthew Carter and reused some of the language on pages 54 and 55. See Ulrich Boser, "A Man of Letters," *US News & World Report* 135, no. 6 (2016).

For more on Clark and cognitive task analysis on page 55, see Richard E. Clark, D. Feldon, Jeroen J. G. van Merriënboer, Kenneth Yates, and Sean Early, "Cognitive Task Analysis," *Handbook of Research on Educational Communications and Technology* 3 (2008): 577–93.

With regard to the idea of writing down what you know before learning on page 52, I relied on Robert J. Marzano, *The Art and Science of Teaching: A Comprehensive Framework for Effective Instruction*, 1st ed. (Alexandria, VA: Association for Supervision & Curriculum Development, 2007), and Natalie Hardwick, "How to Cook the Perfect Steak," *BBC Good Food*, http://www.bbcgoodfood.com/howto/guide/how-cook-perfect-steak (accessed September 14, 2016).

In the metacognition section on page 57, the text on "there's a right way and a wrong way" relied on John D. Bransford and Marcia Johnson, "Contextual Prerequisites for Understanding: Some Investigations of Comprehension and Recall," *Journal of Verbal Learning and Verbal Behavior* 11 (1972): 717–26.

Also very helpful in this section were Kimberly D. Tanner, "Promoting Student Metacognition," *CBE Life Sciences Education* 11, no. 2 (2012): 113–20, doi:10.1187/cbe.12-03-0033, and J. Girash, "Metacognition and Instruction," *Applying the Science of Learning in Education: Infusing Psychological Science into the Curriculum,* eds. Victor A. Benassi, C. E. Overson, and C. M. Hakala, 152–68 (Washington, DC: *Society for the Teaching of Psychology,* 2014), http://teachpsych.org/ebooks/asle2014/index.php

For the details on prequizzing on page 60, see Lindsey E. Richland, Nate Kornell, and Liche Sean Kao, "The Pretesting Effect: Do Unsuccessful Retrieval Attempts Enhance Learning?" *Journal of Experimental Psychology* 15, no. 3 (2009): 243.

For the emotional side of learning on page 61, I relied on Mary Helen
    Immordino-Yang's work, including for the language around emotion
    serving as a "bedrock" for learning. See, for instance, Mary Helen
    Immordino-Yang and Matthias Faeth, "The Role of Emotion and Skilled
    Intuition in Learning," *Mind, Brain & Education*, ed. David Sousa (2010),
    and M. H. Immordino-Yang, J. A. Christodoulou, and V. Singh, "Rest Is
    Not Idleness: Implications of the Brain's Default Mode for Human Devel-
    opment and Education," *Perspectives on Psychological Science* 7, no. 4
    (2012): 352–64, doi:10.1177/1745691612447308

The details about Elliot on page 61 come from Antonio R. Damasio, *Descartes'
    Error: Emotion, Reason and the Human Brain* (New York: Random House,
    2006).

For the studies on the connection between body and mind on page 62, see
    Carlo Fantoni and Walter Gerbino, "Body Actions Change the Appear-
    ance of Facial Expressions," *PloS One* 9, no. 9 (2014): e108211; Xue Zheng,
    Ryan Fehr, Kenneth Tai, Jayanth Narayanan, and Michele J. Gelfand,
    "The Unburdening Effects of Forgiveness: Effects on Slant Perception
    and Jumping Height," *Social Psychological and Personality Science* 6, no. 4
    (2015): 431–38; and Jesse Chandler and Norbert Schwarz, "How Extend-
    ing Your Middle Finger Affects Your Perception of Others: Learned
    Movements Influence Concept Accessibility," *Journal of Experimental
    Social Psychology* 45, no. 1 (2009): 123–28.

For the details on Jim Taylor on page 64, see Dr. Jim Taylor, "My Story: From
    4' 9" to World-Ranked," *Dr. Jim Taylor*, 2015, http://www.drjimtaylor
    .com/4.0/my-story/ (accessed September 14, 2016). Also see Dr. Jim
    Taylor, "Inside the Ski Racing Mind: Mental Imagery, Seeing and Feeling
    Success in Your Mind's Eye," *Ski Racing*, April 18, 2011, https://www
    .skiracing.com/stories/inside-ski-racing-mind-mental-imagery
    (accessed September 15, 2016).

For the discussion of Bandura's work and the notion of self-efficacy on page
    65, I relied on "Albert Bandura," *Wikipedia, the Free Encyclopedia*,
    September 3, 2016, https://en.wikipedia.org/w/index.php?title=Albert
    _Bandura&oldid=737561009 (accessed September 14, 2016). Also see
    "Albert Bandura Biographical Sketch," http://stanford.edu/dept
    /psychology/bandura/bandura-bio-pajares/Albert%20_Bandura%20
    _Biographical_Sketch.html (accessed September 14, 2016). I'm indebted
    to a profile of Bandura, which provided the idea that Bandura is a model of
    self-efficacy, by Christine Foster, "Confidence Man," *Stanford Alumni*,
    September/October 2006, http://alumni.stanford.edu/get/page
    /magazine/article/?article_id=33332" (accessed September 14, 2016).

For the point about project oversight on page 66, see Paul Kloosterman,
    "Learning to Learn in Practice in Nonformal Education," *Learning to
    Learn: International Perspectives from Theory and Practice* (2014): 271.

For the hundreds of studies on goal setting on page 66, see R. T. Golembiewski,
    Handbook of Organizational Behavior, 2nd ed., revised and expanded
    (New York: Marcel Dekker, 2001). Also see Thelma S. Horn, *Advances in
    Sport Psychology* (Champaign, IL: Human Kinetics, 2008).

The details—and quote—about the Pomodoro Technique on page 66 come from Francesco Cirillo, *The Pomodoro Technique* (New York: Simon & Schuster, 2014).

For more on Son's "withholding" approach on page 68, see Lisa K. Son and Nate Kornell, "The Virtues of Ignorance," *Behavioural Processes* 83, no. 2 (February 2010): 207–12, doi:10.1016/j.beproc.2009.12.005

For the work on teacher expectations on page 70, see Ulrich Boser, Megan Wilhelm, and Robert Hanna, "The Power of the Pygmalion Effect: Teachers' Expectations Strongly Predict College Completion," Center for American Progress (2014).

On my visit to Windsor Hills on page 71, I've discussed the experience before. See Ulrich Boser, "Separate and Economically Unequal," *US News & World Report*, June 17, 2015, http://www.usnews.com/opinion/knowledge -bank/2015/06/17/separate-and-economically-unequal-why-schools -need-socioeconomic-diversity (accessed September 15, 2016), and I reused some of the language here.

Also cited in this chapter

Clark, Richard, Paul A. Kirschner, and John Sweller. "Putting Students on the Path to Learning: The Case for Fully Guided Instruction." *American Educator* 36, no. 1 (2012): 6–11.

DeBoer, Harry, Roel J. Bosker, and M. P. C. van der Werf. "Sustainability of Teacher Expectation Bias Effects on Long-Term Student Performance." *Journal of Educational Psychology* 102, no. 1 (2010): 168–79.

Dunlosky, John, and Janet Metcalfe. *Metacognition.* 1st ed. Thousand Oaks, CA: SAGE Publications, 2008.

Ginns, Paul, et al. "Learning by Tracing Worked Examples." *Applied Cognitive Psychology* 30, no. 2 (2015).

Hacker, D. J. M., C. Keener, and J. C. Kircher. "Writing Is Applied Metacognition." *Handbook of Metacognition in Education,* eds. D. J. Hacker, J. Dunlosky, and A. C. Graesser (New York: Routledge, 2009), 154–72.

Hoffman, Robert R., et al. *Accelerated Expertise: Training for High Proficiency in a Complex World* (Expertise: Research and Applications Series). Abingdon, UK: Taylor & Francis, 2013.

Lee, Chee Ha, and Slava Kalyuga. "Expertise Reversal Effect and Its Instructional Implications." *Applying the Science of Learning in Education: Infusing Psychological Science into the Curriculum,* eds. Victor A. Benassi, C. E. Overson, and C. M. Hakala (Washington, DC: Society for the Teaching of Psychology, 2014).

Sana, Faria, Tina Weston, and Nicholas J. Cepeda. "Laptop Multitasking Hinders Classroom Learning for Both Users and Nearby Peers." *Computers & Education* 62 (2013): 24–31.

Veenman, Marcel V. J., Bernadette H. A. M. Van Hout-Wolters, and Peter Afflerbach. "Metacognition and Learning: Conceptual and Methodological Considerations." *Metacognition and Learning* 1, no. 1 (2006): 3–14.

Chapter 3

There's a large body of literature showing that practice doesn't make perfect. For the relevant text on page 77, see Eunsook Kim and Sung-Jae Pak, "Students Do Not Overcome Conceptual Difficulties after Solving 1000 Traditional Problems," *American Journal of Physics* 70, no. 7 (2002): 759–765. Also see E. Plant et al., "Why Study Time Does Not Predict Grade Point Average across College Students: Implications of Deliberate Practice for Academic Performance," *Contemporary Educational Psychology* 30, no. 1 (January 2005): 96–116, doi:10.1016/j.cedpsych.2004.06.001

For Mark Bernstein's story on page 79, I relied on Anders Ericsson, "Acquisition and Maintenance of Medical Expertise: A Perspective from the Expert-Performance Approach with Deliberate Practice," *Academic Medicine* 90, no. 11 (2015): 1471–86. Additional details come from Adetunji Oremakinde and Mark Bernstein, "A Reduction in Errors Is Associated with Prospectively Recording Them: Clinical Article," *Journal of Neurosurgery* 121, no. 2 (2014): 297–304.

For the Bernstein details and quote on page 81, see Mark Bernstein, "The Drop Attack," *Canadian Medical Association Journal* 172, no. 5 (March 1, 2005): 668–69, doi:10.1503/cmaj.050076, and Scellig Stone and Mark Bernstein, "Prospective Error Recording in Surgery: An Analysis of 1108 Elective Neurosurgical Cases," *Neurosurgery* 60, no. 6 (2007): 1075–82.

On page 80, I quoted from Dan Pompei, "Inside Gruden's 'Maniacal' Obsession with Football," *Bleacher Report,* May 12, 2016, http://bleacherreport.com/articles/2636358-inside-jon-grudens-maniacal-obsession-with-football (accessed September 28, 2016). Similarly, I relied on Julia Belluz, "We Spoke to 20 Experts about How to Lose Weight and Keep It Off. Here Are Their Surprisingly Simple Tips," *Vox,* May 2, 2016, http://www.vox.com/2014/11/27/7289565/weight-loss-diet-tips (accessed September 28, 2016).

Regarding the discussion of feedback on page 81, see John Hattie, *Visible Learning: A Synthesis of Over 800 Meta-Analyses Relating to Achievement* (Abingdon, UK: Routledge, Taylor & Francis Group, 2009). The rooster example comes from Bridgid Finn and Janet Metcalfe, "Scaffolding Feedback to Maximize Long-Term Error Correction," *Memory & Cognition* 38, no. 7 (2010): 951–61, doi:10.3758/MC.38.7.951; also helpful was John Hattie and Helen Timperley, "The Power of Feedback," *Review of Educational Research* 77, no. 1 (March 1, 2007): 81–112, doi:10.3102/003465430298487

Regarding the discussion of curriculum on page 81, see Ulrich Boser, Matthew Chingos, and Chelsea Straus, "The Hidden Value of Curriculum Reform: Do States and Districts Receive the Most Bang for Their Curriculum Buck?" Center for American Progress, October 14, 2015, https://www.americanprogress.org/issues/education/report/2015/10/14/122810/the-hidden-value-of-curriculum-reform/. The Gawande quote is from Atul Gawande, "The Coach in the Operating Room," *New Yorker,* September 26, 2011, http://www.newyorker.com/magazine/2011/10/03/personal-best (accessed September 28, 2016).

For the Hattie quote on page 86, I relied on John Hattie, *Visible Learning: A Synthesis of Over 800 Meta-Analyses Relating to Achievement* (Abingdon, UK: Routledge, Taylor & Francis Group, 2009).

On explanations and feedback on page 84, I relied on Andrew C. Butler, Namrata Godbole, and Elizabeth Marsh, "Explanation Feedback Is Better Than Correct Answer Feedback for Promoting Transfer of Learning," *Journal of Educational Psychology* 105, no. 2, (2013): 290–98, and Nate Kornell and Lisa K. Son, "Learners' Choices and Beliefs about Self-Testing," *Memory* 17, no. 5 (July 2009): 493–501, doi:10.1080/096 58210902832915

On Dragonbox on page 87, see Yanjin Long and Vincent Aleven, "Gamification of Joint Student/System Control over Problem Selection in a Linear Equation Tutor," *Intelligent Tutoring Systems*, 378–87, eds. Stefan Trausan-Matu, Kristy Elizabeth Boyer, Martha Crosby, and Kitty Panourgia (New York: Springer International Publishing, 2014), http://link.springer.com/10.1007/978-3-319-07221-0_47

The Willingham quote on page 88 comes from Daniel T. Willingham, *Why Don't Students Like School? A Cognitive Scientist Answers Questions about How the Mind Works and What It Means for the Classroom* (San Francisco, CA: Jossey-Bass, 2009).

With regard to repetition on page 89, see Graham Nuthall, *The Hidden Lives of Learners* (Wellington, NZ: NZCER Press, 2007). Also see Katherine Rawson and John Dunlosky, "Bang for the Buck: Supporting Durable and Efficient Student Learning through Successive Relearning," *Integrating Cognitive Science with Innovative Teaching in STEM Disciplines* (St. Louis, MO: Washington University in St. Louis, 2014), doi:10.7936/K7F769GZ

The well-cited retrieval practice study on page 91 is from Henry L. Roediger and Jeffrey D. Karpicke, "Test-Enhanced Learning: Taking Memory Tests Improves Long-Term Retention," *Psychological Science* 17, no. 3 (2006): 249–55. Also cited here was J. D. Karpicke and J. R. Blunt, "Retrieval Practice Produces More Learning Than Elaborative Studying with Concept Mapping," *Science* 331, no. 6018 (2011): 772–75, doi:10.1126 /science.1199327

Also cited on page 91 is Maria Konnikova, *Mastermind: How to Think Like Sherlock Holmes* (New York: Penguin, 2013). The retrieval practice approach regarding a pile of cards comes from Rachel Adragna, "Be Your Own Teacher: How to Study with Flash Cards," *The Learning Scientists*, February 20, 2016, http://www.learningscientists.org/blog/2016/2/20-1 (accessed September 13, 2016).

The Tarantino quote on page 90 is from Hoda Kotb, "From Video Clerk to Box Office Icon," *NBC News*, April 26, 2004, http://www.nbcnews.com /id/4817308/ns/dateline_nbc-newsmakers/t/video-clerk-box-office-icon / (accessed September 13, 2016).

For more details on Hu's work on page 93, see Yuzheng Hu et al., "Enhanced White Matter Tracts Integrity in Children with Abacus Training," *Human Brain Mapping* 32, no. 1 (2011): 10–21, doi:10.1002/hbm.20996

Lots has been written about brain plasticity in recent years. Among them is
   S. Kühn, T. Gleich, R. C. Lorenz, U. Lindenberger, and J. Gallinat, "Playing
   Super Mario Induces Structural Brain Plasticity: Gray Matter Changes
   Resulting from Training with a Commercial Video Game," *Molecular Psy-
   chiatry* 19, no. 2 (February 2014): 265–71, doi:10.1038/mp.2013.120

On page 94, I quoted from Martin Lövdén et al., "A Theoretical Framework for
   the Study of Adult Cognitive Plasticity," *Psychological Bulletin* 136, no. 4
   (2010): 659. Also see Edward Taub, "Foreword for Neuroplasticity and
   Neurorehabilitation," *Frontiers Research Topics: Neuroplasticity and Neurorehabilitation* 8, no. 544 (2014): 4–5.

Bennett Schwartz provided me with the example relating to Australia and its
   capital on page 95. Psychologists call this the "hypercorrection effect."
   For more information, see Janet Metcalfe and David Miele, "Hypercor-
   rection of High Confidence Errors: Prior Testing Both Enhances Delayed
   Performance and Blocks the Return of the Errors," *Journal of Applied
   Research in Memory and Cognition* 3, no.3 (2014): 189–97.

For details regarding Jordan Ellenberg's early life on page 96, I relied on Amy
   Goldstein, "A Sine of a True Genius," *Washington Post,* June 7, 1989,
   https://www.washingtonpost.com/archive/local/1989/06/07/a-sine
   -of-a-true-genius/a29172c8-d53f-45da-920c-4e2a407ce97e/ (accessed
   September 13, 2016). Also see Jordan Ellenberg, *How Not to Be Wrong:
   The Power of Mathematical Thinking* (New York: Penguin, 2015).

On the Flynn effect on page 97, see Lisa Trahan, Karla K. Stuebing, Merril K.
   Hiscock, and Jack M. Fletcher, "The Flynn Effect: A Meta-Analysis,"
   Psychological Bulletin 140, no. 5 (2014): 1332–60, doi: 10.1037/a0037173.
   The error quotes on page 96 are from Kathryn Schulz, *Being Wrong:
   Adventures in the Margin of Error,* Kindle edition (New York: HarperCollins,
   2010).

For the first quote from Herb Brooks on page 98, see Dave Kindred, "Born to
   Be Players, Born to the Moment," *Washington Post,* February 23, 1980,
   http://www.washingtonpost.com/wp-srv/sports/longterm/olympics
   1998/history/memories/80-kindred.htm (accessed September 16, 2016).
   There's some debate over the actual words used. See Bill Littlefield,
   "Hollywood Scores a 'Miracle' with Locker Room Speech," *WBUR,*
   June 18, 2016, http://www.wbur.org/onlyagame/2016/06/17/us-miracle
   -olympics-herb-brooks-origins (accessed September 16, 2016). For the
   second Brooks quote on page 103, see "Herb Brooks Quotes," Herb Brooks
   Foundation, http://www.herbbrooksfoundation.com/page/show/740804
   -herb-brooks-quotes (accessed September 16, 2016).

Details about the marshmallow test on page 100 come from Walter Mischel,
   The Marshmallow Test: Mastering Self-Control (Little, Brown, 2014). The
   self-talk study on page 98 is Sanda Dolcos and Dolores Albarracin, "The
   Inner Speech of Behavioral Regulation: Intentions and Task Performance
   Strengthen When You Talk to Yourself as a You," *European Journal of Social
   Psychology* 44, no. 6 (October 1, 2014): 636–42, doi: 10.1002/ejsp.2048

Also cited is Adam Winsler, Louis Manfra, and Rafael M. Diaz, "'Should I Let
   Them Talk?' Private Speech and Task Performance Among Preschool

Children with and without Behavior Problems," *Early Childhood Research Quarterly* 22, no. 2 (2007): 215–31. I came across the study via Pyschnet.

For more on Dweck from page 101, see Carol Dweck, *Mindset: The New Psychology of Success, How We Learn to Fulfill Our Potential,* Kindle edition (New York: Ballantine Books, 2008). The point about the small impact of a few words in the Dweck studies came from BBC, "The Words That Could Unlock Your Child," *BBC News,* April 19, 2011, http://www.bbc .com/news/magazine-13128701 (accessed October 4, 2016). Also cited was Kyla Haimovitz and Carol S. Dweck, "What Predicts Children's Fixed and Growth Intelligence Mind-Sets? Not Their Parents' Views of Intelligence but Their Parents' Views of Failure," *Psychological Science* (2016): 0956797616639727.

Also cited in this chapter

Brackett, Marc, et al. "Enhancing Academic Performance and Social and Emotional Competence with the RULER Feeling Words Curriculum." *Learning and Individual Differences* 22, no. 2 (2012): 218–24.

Cheryan, Sapna, et al. "Designing Classrooms to Maximize Student Achievement." *Policy Insights from the Behavioral and Brain Sciences* 1, no. 1 (2014): 4–12.

D'Mello, Sidney, et al. "Confusion Can Be Beneficial for Learning." *Learning and Instruction* 29 (2014): 153–70.

Ellenberg, Jordan. "The Wrong Way to Treat Child Geniuses." *Wall Street Journal,* May 30, 2014. http://www.wsj.com/articles/the-wrong-way-to -treat-child-geniuses-1401484790 (accessed October 7, 2016)

Ericsson, K. Anders. "Training History, Deliberate Practice and Elite Sports Performance: An Analysis in Response to Tucker and Collins Review— What Makes Champions?" *British Journal of Sports Medicine* 47, no. 9 (2013): 533–35.

Huelser, Barbie J., and Janet Metcalfe. "Making Related Errors Facilitates Learning, but Learners Do Not Know It." *Memory & Cognition* 40, no. 4 (2012): 514–27.

Klein, Gary. *Seeing What Others Don't: The Remarkable Ways We Gain Insights.* Kindle edition. New York: Public Affairs, Perseus Books, 2013.

Klein, Gary, Neil Hintze, and David Saab. "Thinking Inside the Box: The ShadowBox Method for Cognitive Skill Development." *Proceedings of the 11th International Conference on Naturalistic Decision Making.* Paris: Arpege Science Publishing, 2013.

Muenks, Katherine, David B. Miele, Geetha B. Ramani, Laura M. Stapleton, and Meredith L. Rowe. "Parental Beliefs about the Fixedness of Ability." *Journal of Applied Developmental Psychology* 41 (November 2015): 78–89.

Peary, Gerald, ed. *Quentin Tarantino: Interviews, Revised and Updated.* Jackson: University Press of Mississippi, 2013.

Protzko, John, J. Aronson, and C. Blair. "How to Make a Young Child Smarter: Evidence from the Database of Raising Intelligence." *Perspectives on*

Psychological Science 8, no. 1 (2013): 25–40. doi:10.1177/174569161 2462585

Rios, Kimberly, Zhen Hadassah Cheng, Rebecca R. Totton, and Azim F. Shariff. "Negative Stereotypes Cause Christians to Underperform in and Disidentify with Science." *Social Psychological and Personality Science* (2015): 194855 0615598378

Schmidt, Richard A., and Robert A. Bjork. "New Conceptualizations of Practice: Common Principles in Three Paradigms Suggest New Concepts for Training." *Psychological Science* 3, no. 4 (1992): 207–17. doi: 10.1111/ j.1467-9280.1992.tb00029

Steele, Claude M., and Joshua Aronson. "Stereotype Threat and the Intellectual Test Performance of African Americans." *Journal of Personality and Social Psychology* 69, no. 5 (1995): 797.

Steinberg, Laurence. *Age of Opportunity: Lessons from the New Science of Adolescence.* Kindle edition. New York: Houghton Mifflin Harcourt, 2014.

Yan, Veronica X., Khanh-Phuong Thai, and Robert A. Bjork. "Habits and Beliefs That Guide Self-Regulated Learning: Do They Vary with Mind-Set?" *Journal of Applied Research in Memory and Cognition* 3, no. 3 (2014): 140–52.

Chapter 4

When it comes to Jackson Pollock, I relied on a number of books, including Henry Adams, *Tom and Jack: The Intertwined Lives of Thomas Hart Benton and Jackson Pollock* (New York: Bloomsbury Press, 2009), Leonhard Emmerling, *Jackson Pollock* (Taschen: 2003), and Deborah Solomon, *Jackson Pollock: A Biography* (New York: Cooper Square Press, 1987).

The "workers work" quote on page 111 came from Caroline A. Jones, "Eyesight alone: Clement Greenberg's modernism and the bureaucratization of the senses," University of Chicago Press, 2005. The "controlled accident" quote came from the Emmerling biography. The "grand thing" quote on page 111 came from Jackson Pollock, *American Letters: 1927-1947* (Polity, 2011).

For the quotes from the letter from Siqueros on page 111, see Jackson Pollock and Lee Krasner Papers, "David Alfaro Siqueiros Letter to Jackson Pollock, Sandy Pollock, and Harold Lehman, 1936 Dec," Archives of American Art, Smithsonian Institution, 2016, http://www.aaa.si.edu/collections /items/detail/david-alfaro-siqueiros-letter-to-jackson-pollock -sandy -pollock-and-harold-lehman-13785 (accessed September 14, 2016). The *LIFE* magazine article on page 112 is Anonymous, "Jackson Pollock; Is He the Greatest Living Painter in the United States?" *LIFE*, August 8, 1949.

The "genius" quote on page 112 came from Naifeh Steven and Gregory White Smith, *Jackson Pollock: An American Saga* (New York: CN Potter, 1989). The "chaos" quote on the same page came from the Solomon book.

For the Smith quote on page 113, see Roberta Smith, "Review: Drips, Dropped: Pollock and His Impact," *New York Times,* December 31, 2015.

For the Taylor quote on page 114, see Jennifer Ouellette, "Pollock's Fractals," *Discover*, November 1, 2011.

For my descriptions of the making of *Kind of Blue* on page 114, I relied on Ashley Kahn, *Kind of Blue* (London: Granta Publications, 2001). On page 115, I also quoted and relied on Fred Kaplan, "Kind of Blue," *Slate*, August 17, 2009, http://www.slate.com/articles/arts/music_box/2009/08/kind_of_blue.html (accessed September 14, 2016).

The sheet music quote on page 115 is from Keith Waters, *The Studio Recordings of the Miles Davis Quintet, 1965-68* (New York: Oxford University Press, 2011).

The Davis biography quote on page 115 is from Miles Davis and Quincy Troupe, *Miles* (New York: Simon & Schuster, 1990).

To cite a few studies providing support for riffs on page 115, see Claire E. Weinstein, "Training Students to Use Elaboration Learning Strategies," *Contemporary Educational Psychology* 7, no. 4 (1982): 301-11. Also see Michelene T. H. Chi et al., "Self-Explanations: How Students Study and Use Examples in Learning to Solve Problems," *Cognitive Science* 13, no. 2 (1989): 145-82.

On Nisbett's work on page 119, see Richard E. Nisbett, *Mindware: Tools for Smart Thinking* (New York: Farrar, Straus and Giroux, 2015).

For the "sticky images" details on page 128, see Bob Harris, *Prisoner of Trebekistan: A Decade in* Jeopardy! (New York: Crown Publishers, 2006). I'm indebted to Roger Craig for this idea.

For the citation on finger dexterity on page 122, see Sian Beilock, *How the Body Knows Its Mind: The Surprising Power of the Physical Environment to Influence How You Think and Feel* (New York: Atria Books, Simon & Schuster, 2015).

On debate programs on page 118, see Briana Mezuk et al., "Impact of Participating in a Policy Debate Program on Academic Achievement: Evidence from the Chicago Urban Debate League," *Educational Research and Reviews* 6, no. 9 (2011): 622-35.

For the "young students" study on page 119, see Stephen Gorard, Nadia Siddiqui, and Beng Huat, *Philosophy for Children: Evaluation Report and Executive Summary, July 2015* (London: Education Endowment Foundation, 2015). For more details—and the slogan—from High Tech High, see Bob Pearlman, "Educational Leadership, Customizing Our Schools: Reinventing the High School Experience," ASCD, 2016. Also see Tara S. Behrend et al., "Gary and Jerri-Ann Jacobs High Tech High: A Case Study of an Inclusive STEM-Focused High School in San Diego, California," OsPrI Report 2014-03.

On page 119, I quoted from Lauren B. Resnick, *Education and Learning to Think* (Washington, DC: National Academies, 1987).

For the "holy place" quote on page 121, I relied on Ellen Maguire, "At Jackson Pollock's Hamptons House, a Life in Spatters," *New York Times*, July 14, 2006.

For the text on simulations on page 125, I relied and reused text from Ulrich Boser, "Gaming the System, One Click at a Time," Special Report: E-learning, *U. S. News & World Report*, October 28, 2002.

Also mentioned on page 126 is Kenneth R. Koedinger et al., "Learning Is Not a Spectator Sport: Doing Is Better Than Watching for Learning from a MOOC," *Proceedings of the Second (2015) ACM Conference on Learning @ Scale*, New York: ACM (2015): 111–120.

The details about Feynman and teaching on page 126 come from David L. Goodstein and Judith R. Goodstein, *Feynman's Lost Lecture: The Motion of Planets Around the Sun*, vol. 1 (New York: W.W. Norton, 1996). For the details on page 130, I relied on "Richard Feynman—Session IV," American Institute of Physics, https://www.aip.org/history-programs/niels -bohr-library/oral-histories/5020-4 (accessed September 16, 2016).

For the Protégé Effect on page 127, see J. F. Nestojko et al., "Expecting to Teach Enhances Learning and Organization of Knowledge in Free Recall of Text Passages," *Memory & Cognition*, 42, no. 7 (2014): 1038–48, doi: 10.3758/s13421-014-0416-z. Also see Catherine C. Chase et al., "Teachable Agents and the Protégé Effect: Increasing the Effort Toward Learning," *Journal of Science Education and Technology* 18, no. 4 (2009): 334–52.

On the value of uncertainty on page 130, see Marlene Schomer, "Effects of Beliefs about the Nature of Knowledge on Comprehension," *Journal of Educational Psychology* 82, no. 3 (1990): 498–504. When it came to the military on page 131, I relied on previous reporting as well as James Gibson, "Leaders First: How ROTC Is Changing for the Better," *Military1*, September 30, 2014. Also see Mark Hemingway, "Fixing ROTC: The Army Is Making Great Strides Reforming ROTC, and It's a Task Too Important to Be Neglected," *The Weekly Standard*, September 30, 2014, http://www.weeklystandard.com/fixing-rotc/article/781475 (accessed September 14, 2016). The quote on page 131 came from Rudy Chinchilla, "ROTC Curriculum Changes Will Reflect Modern Military Conflicts," *Daily Titan*, March 25, 2015, http://www.dailytitan.com/2015/03/rotc -curriculum-changes-will-reflect-modern-military-conflicts/ (accessed September 16, 2016).

I first came across Mark Runco's work, mentioned on page 131, in Po Bronson and Ashley Merryman, "Forget Brainstorming," *Newsweek*, July 12, 2010, http://www.newsweek.com/forget-brainstorming-74223 (accessed September 16, 2016). Also helpful in this section was Mark Runco, "Seven Critical Components of Creativity: Full Research Summary," *Center for Childhood Creativity* (2014): 1–19.

For more on Sawyer's work on page 133, see Keith Sawyer, *Zig Zag: The Surprising Path to Greater Creativity* (San Francisco: Wiley, Jossey-Bass, 2013).

In regard to sourcing on the tulip crash on page 133, see A. Maurits van der Veen, "The Dutch Tulip Mania: The Social Politics of a Financial Bubble," *Journal of Political Economy* 97, no. 3 (2012): 535–60; Christian C. Day, "Is There a Tulip in Your Future? Ruminations on Tulip Mania and the Innovative Dutch Futures Markets," *Journal des Economistes et des*

Etudes Humaines 14, no. 2 (2004): 151–70; and Mike Dash, *Tulipomania: The Story of the World's Most Coveted Flower & the Extraordinary Passions It Aroused* (New York: Three Rivers Press, 1999).

For the details about Scott E. Page on page 135, see *The Difference: How the Power of Diversity Creates Better Groups, Firms, Schools, and Societies* (Princeton, NJ: Princeton University Press, 2007). Also helpful in framing this specific work was Steven Johnson, *Future Perfect: The Case for Progress in a Networked Age* (New York: Riverhead Books, 2012).

Regarding Levine's work on page 136, see Sheen S. Levine et al., "Ethnic Diversity Deflates Price Bubbles," *Proceedings of the National Academy of Sciences* 111, no. 52 (2014): 18524–29, doi:10.1073/pnas.1407301111. Levine also pointed me to the academic study that's quoted on page 123: Nancy DiTomaso, Corinne Post, and Rochelle Parks-Yancy, "Workforce Diversity and Inequality: Power, Status, and Numbers," *Annual Review of Sociology* 33 (2007): 473–501.

On technology and diversity on page 137, I found helpful Chris Paris, "The Wonderful—Yet Misunderstood—World of Wikis," *Seminarium,* April 11, 2014, http://seminariumblog.org/general/semtech/wonderful-yet-misunderstood-world-wikis (accessed September 16, 2016).

The quotes about Pollock's poor painting skills on page 137 come from the Solomon and Adams books, respectively.

For the description of the wheel study on page 139, see Daniel Kahneman, *Thinking, Fast and Slow* (New York: Farrar, Straus and Giroux, 2011).

The Feynman quote on page 139 comes from Richard P. Feynman, *Surely You're Joking, Mr. Feynman! Adventures of a Curious Character* (New York: W.W. Norton, 1997). The Davis quote on page 139 is from Gerald Lyn Early, *Miles Davis and American Culture* (St. Louis: Missouri History Museum, 2001).

Also cited in this chapter

Barlow, Claire M., Richard P. Jolley, and Jenny L. Hallam. "Drawings as Memory Aids: Optimizing the Drawing Method to Facilitate Young Children's Recall." *Applied Cognitive Psychology* 25, no. 3 (2011): 480–87. doi:10.1002/acp.1716

D'Mello, Sidney, Blair Lehman, Reinhard Pekrun, and Art Graesser. "Confusion Can Be Beneficial for Learning." *Learning and Instruction* 29 (2014): 153-170.

Fiorella, Logan, and Richard E. Mayer. "The Relative Benefits of Learning by Teaching and Teaching Expectancy." *Contemporary Educational Psychology* 38, no. 4 (2013): 281–88. doi:10.1016/j.cedpsych.2013.06.001

Kuhn, Deanna. *The Skills of Argument.* New York: Cambridge University Press, 1991.

Krontiris-Litowitz, Johanna. "Articulating Scientific Reasoning Improves Student Learning in an Undergraduate Anatomy and Physiology Course." *CBE Life Sciences Education* 8, no. 4 (Winter 2009): 309. doi:10.1187/cbe.08-11-0066.

Mayer, Richard E., and Logan Fiorella. *Learning as a Generative Activity: Eight Learning Strategies That Promote Understanding.* Cambridge, UK: Cambridge University Press, 2015.

Okita, Sandra Y. "Learning from the Folly of Others: Learning to Self-Correct by Monitoring the Reasoning of Virtual Characters in a Computer-Supported Mathematics Learning Environment." *Computers & Education* 71 (2014): 257–78.

Osborne, Jonathan. "Arguing to Learn in Science: The Role of Collaborative, Critical Discourse." *Science* 328, no. 5977 (2010): 463–66.

Willingham, Daniel T. *Why Don't Students Like School? A Cognitive Scientist Answers Questions about How the Mind Works and What It Means for the Classroom.* San Francisco: Jossey-Bass, 2010.

Chapter 5

For the material on Albert Einstein on page 141, I relied on Walter Isaacson, *Einstein: His Life and Universe,* 1st ed. (New York: Simon & Schuster, 2007), and Isaacson, "The Light-Beam Rider," *New York Times,* October 30, 2015, http://www.nytimes.com/2015/11/01/opinion/sunday/the-light-beam-rider.html (accessed September 14, 2016). The Einstein quotes on pages 142 and 150 also come from the Isaacson book.

Also see John D. Norton, "Chasing a Beam of Light: Einstein's Most Famous Thought Experiment," *University of Pittsburgh,* April 14, 2005, http://www.pitt.edu/~jdnorton/Goodies/Chasing_the_light/ (accessed September 14, 2016).

For the details on the underwater experiment on page 142, I relied on John D. Bransford et al., *How People Learn: Brain, Mind, Experience, and School* (Washington, DC: National Academics Press, 2000). Also cited is Lindsey Engle Richland and Nina Simms, "Analogy, Higher Order Thinking, and Education," *Wiley Interdisciplinary Reviews: Cognitive Science* 6, no. 2 (March 2015): 177–92, doi:10.1002/wcs.1336

With regard to the Goldstone study on page 146, see David W. Braithwaite and Robert L. Goldstone, "Effects of Variation and Prior Knowledge on Abstract Concept Learning," *Cognition and Instruction* 33, no. 3 (2015): 226–56.

For a longer explanation of the answer to the king problem, Goldstone explains: "Every kingdom needs to be assigned to one daughter. There are 7 possible daughters. If there were only one kingdom, there would be seven possibilities. If there were two kingdoms, then for every one of the 7 ways of assigning the first kingdom, there would be 7 ways of assigning the second kingdom (just because Gertrude is assigned France doesn't mean that Germany can't be assigned to her too), making 7 times 7 possibilities. Every additional country that needs to be assigned to a daughter multiplies by 7 the number of possible arrangements."

Note that interleaving doesn't always show benefits, at least in the early part of the learning process. Goldstone again: "David Braithwaite and I find that variation of problems that exemplify the same deep principle isn't always a good thing. In particular, the more you know, the more you can 'withstand' variation. People with relatively poor initial understandings of the relevant math principles benefit more from training with similar problems that don't show much variation."

For studies on mixing up practice on page 149, see Dennis K. Landin, Edward P. Hebert, and Malcolm Fairweather, "The Effects of Variable Practice on the Performance of a Basketball Skill," *Research Quarterly for Exercise and Sport* 64, no. 2 (1993): 232–37, doi:10.1080/02701367.1 993.10608803. Also see Gavin Breslin et al., "Constant or Variable Practice: Recreating the Especial Skill Effect," *Acta Psychologica* 140, no. 2 (2012): 154–57.

The physics problem on page 148 is from B. H. Ross, J. P. Mestre, and J. L. Docktor, "Understanding How to Teach Physics Understanding," *Integrating Cognitive Science with Innovative Teaching in STEM Disciplines*, eds. M. McDaniel, R. Frey, S. Fitzpatrick, and H. L. Roediger (Saint Louis: Washington University Libraries, 2014), doi: 10.7936/K79G5JR7

The Steve Jobs quotes on page 150 are from Alan Deutschman, *The Second Coming of Steve Jobs* (New York: Crown Business, 2001). The Gopnik quote on page 151 is from Alison Gopnik and Caren M. Walker, "Considering Counterfactuals: The Relationship between Causal Learning and Pretend Play," *American Journal of Play* 6, no. 1 (2013): 15. Alison Gopnik, Andrew N. Meltzoff, and Patricia K. Kuhl, *The Scientist in the Crib: Minds, Brains, and How Children Learn* (New York: William Morrow, 1999).

Also helpful on counterfactuals is Robert J. Marzano, *The Art and Science of Teaching: A Comprehensive Framework for Effective Instruction (Professional Development)* (Alexandria, VA: Association for Supervision & Curriculum Development, 2007).

I first came across the idea of discussing the instruction of Steve Brodner on page 152 in Cynthia Cotts, "Top of the Class: Some of NYC's Leading Professors Share Their Secrets," *Observer News & Politics*, January 21, 2015, http://observer.com/2015/01/top-of-the-class-nycs-top-professors/ (accessed September 26, 2016). Also see Frail Fiend, "Big Interview—Steve Brodner," *Frail Fiend*, 2013, http://frailfiend.tumblr.com/post/855265 28060/big-interview-steve-brodner (accessed September 26, 2016).

On hacking, the Raymond quote on page 153 comes from Eric Steven Raymond, "How to Learn Hacking," 2014, http://www.catb.org/esr/faqs /hacking-howto.html (accessed September 16, 2016).

For the details on Facebook on page 154, I relied on Andrew Bosworth (Boz), "Facebook Engineering Bootcamp," *Facebook*, November 20, 2009, https://www.facebook.com/notes/facebook-engineering/facebook -engineering-bootcamp/177577963919 (accessed September 16, 2016). Also helpful was Mike Swift, "A Look Inside Facebook's 'Bootcamp' for New Employees," *Thestar.com*, April 18, 2012, https://www.thestar.com /business/2012/04/18/a_look_inside_facebooks_bootcamp_for_new _employees.html (accessed September 16, 2016). The Seligstein quote on page 154 came from this *Toronto Star* article.

Also see J. O'Dell, "Bootcamp! How Facebook Indoctrinates Every New Engineer It Hires," *VentureBeat*, March 2, 2013, http://venturebeat.com

/2013/03/02/facebook-bootcamp/ (accessed September 14, 2016);
Michal Lev-Ram, "What I Learned at Facebook's Big Data Bootcamp,"
Fortune, June 13, 2013, http://fortune.com/2013/06/13/what-i-learned
-at-facebooks-big-data-bootcamp/ (accessed September 16, 2016); and
Richard Feloni, "Facebook Engineering Director Describes What It's
Like to Go through the Company's 6-Week Engineer Bootcamp," *Business
Insider*, March 2, 2016, http://www.businessinsider.com/inside-facebook
-engineer-bootcamp-2016-3 (accessed September 16, 2016).

The Zuckerberg quote on page 155 comes from Epicenter Staff, "Mark Zuckerberg's Letter to Investors: 'The Hacker Way,'" *WIRED*, February 1, 2012,
https://www.wired.com/2012/02/zuck-letter/ (accessed September 16,
2016).

For the details on John Venn from page 155, see A. W. F. Edwards and Ian
Stewart, *Cogwheels of the Mind: The Story of Venn Diagrams*, 1st ed.
(Baltimore: Johns Hopkins University Press, 2004). For my very short
biography, I relied on "John Venn," *Wikipedia, the Free Encyclopedia*,
https://en.wikipedia.org/w/index.php?title=John_Venn&oldid=737
661555 (accessed September 4, 2016).

For the quote on page 156 about "visual aids," see John Venn, *Symbolic Logic*
(Macmillan, 1881).

I first came across the Venn diagram idea in Richard E. Nisbett, *Mindware:
Tools for Smart Thinking* (New York: Farrar, Straus and Giroux, 2015).

Lots of evidence supports the use of concept maps, mentioned on page 157. See,
for instance, Jack W. Berry and Stephen L. Chew, "Improving Learning
Through Interventions of Student-Generated Questions and Concept
Maps," *Teaching of Psychology* 35, no. 4 (October 21, 2008): 305–12,
doi:10.1080/00986280802373841

For information on concept-mapping-like software on page 158, see James
Fallows, "Interesting Software Update: Tinderbox How-To, Jerry's Brain,"
The Atlantic, March 9, 2015, http://www.theatlantic.com/technology
/archive/2015/03/interesting-software-update-tinderbox-how-to-jerrys
-brain/387181/ (accessed September 16, 2016). Also quoted is Steven
Johnson, *Where Good Ideas Come From*, Kindle edition (New York:
Penguin, 2010), 116.

For the Uber example on page 161, see Aaron Sankin, "Every Company
That's Like Uber but for (Something)," *The Daily Dot*, August 7, 2014,
http://www.dailydot.com/debug/its-like-uber-but-for/ (accessed
September 16, 2016) and Geoffrey Fowler, "There's an Uber for Everything Now," *Wall Street Journal,* May 5, 2015, http://www.wsj.com
/articles/theres-an-uber-for-everything-now-1430845789 (accessed
November 6, 2016).

The text regarding Mary Gordon Spence on page 161 comes from "Stump the
Chumps: Did Tom and Ray Make the Right Call? Was a Vacuum Leak
Causing Mary Gordon's Car to Sing That High-Pitched Note?" April 2,
2011, Show 201114, *Car Talk*, http://www.cartalk.com/content/stump-
chumps (accessed September 16, 2016). I also interviewed Spence.

For the quote about "everything you say" on page 161, see "Pikes Peak or Bust,"
Show 1613, *Car Talk*, http://www.cartalk.com/content/1613-pikes-peak
-or-bust (accessed October 25, 2016).

The original Vapor 3000 study on page 160 is described in Mary L. Gick and Keith J. Holyoak, "Schema Induction and Analogical Transfer," *Cognitive Psychology* 15, no. 1 (1983): 1–38. The most recent study is James R. Kubricht, Hongjing Lu, and Keith J. Holyoak, "Animation Facilitates Source Understanding and Spontaneous Analogical Transfer," *Proceedings of the 37th Annual Conference of the Cognitive Science Society* (July 2015).

On page 166, I quoted from Douglas Hofstadter and Emmanuel Sander, *Surfaces and Essences: Analogy as the Fuel and Fire of Thinking* (New York: Basic Books, 2013). The book was also a very helpful resource.

For the "three strikes" mention on page 162, see John Pollack, *Shortcut: How Analogies Reveal Connections, Spark Innovation, and Sell Our Greatest Ideas* (New York: Penguin, 2015). For the Susan Sarandon quote on page 162, see Mike McPadden, "25 Years Ago, *Thelma and Louise* Popped Culture with Feminism," *VH1 News,* May 24, 2016, http://www.vh1.com/news/262555/thelma-and-louise-pop-culture-feminism/ (accessed October 25, 2016).

The jokes on page 162 come from Amanda Green, "20 of Steven Wright's Funniest Jokes for His 59th Birthday," *Mental Floss,* http://mentalfloss.com/article/60461/20-steven-wrights-funniest-jokes-his-59th-birthday (accessed October 25, 2016), and "'What's the Deal with …': 15 Jokes from Jerry Seinfeld on His Birthday," WCBS, http://wcbsfm.cbslocal.com/2013/04/29/whats-the-deal-with-15-jokes-from-jerry-seinfeld-on-his-birthday/ (accessed October 25, 2016).

The contract study on page 164 comes from Jeffrey Loewenstein, Leigh Thompson, and Dedre Gentner, "Analogical Learning in Negotiation Teams: Comparing Cases Promotes Learning and Transfer," *Academy of Management Learning & Education* 2, no. 2 (2003): 119–27.

Regarding *Holy Blood, Holy Grail* on page 195, see Michael Baigent, Richard Leigh, and Henry Lincoln, *Holy Blood, Holy Grail* (New York: Dell, 2007).

For more on Gurpreet Dhaliwal and the superstar quote on page 168, see Katie Hafner, "For Second Opinion, Consult a Computer?" *New York Times,* December 3, 2012, http://www.nytimes.com/2012/12/04/health/quest-to-eliminate-diagnostic-lapses.html (accessed September 26, 2016).

Regarding Pólya on page 170, see G. Pólya and John H. Conway, *How to Solve It: A New Aspect of Mathematical Method,* 2nd ed. (Princeton, NJ: Princeton University Press, 2014). Also see Lee Dembart, "George Pólya, 97, Dean of Mathematicians, Dies," *Los Angeles Times,* September 08, 1985, http://articles.latimes.com/1985-09-08/news/mn-2892_1_polya-george-mathematician (accessed September 16, 2016).

On page 172, I relied on Bernard Roth, *The Achievement Habit: Stop Wishing, Start Doing, and Take Command of Your Life* (New York: HarperCollins, 2015), and Tara Parker-Pope, "'Design Thinking' for a Better You," *New York Times,* Well section, January 4, 2016, http://well.blogs.nytimes.com/2016/01/04/design-thinking-for-a-better-you/ (accessed September 16, 2016).

Also cited in this chapter

Burger, Edward B., and Michael Starbird. *The 5 Elements of Effective Thinking*, Kindle edition. Princeton NJ: Princeton University Press, 2012.

Chi, Michelene T. H., P. J. Feltovich, and R. Glaser. "Categorization and Representation of Physics Problems by Experts and Novices." *Cognitive Science* 5, no. 2 (1981): 121–52.

Cho, Young Hoan, and Kwangsu Cho. "Peer Reviewers Learn from Giving Comments." *Instructional Science* 39, no. 5 (September 2011): 629–43. doi:10.1007/s11251-010-9146-1

Fischer, David Hackett. *Historians' Fallacies: Toward a Logic of Historical Thought*, 1st ed. New York: Harper & Row, Publishers, 1970.

Foshay, Rob, and Jamie Kirkley. "Principles for Teaching Problem Solving." Technical Paper 4. Bloomington, MN: Plato Learning, 2003.

Goldstone, Robert L., and Samuel B. Day. "Introduction to 'New Conceptualizations of Transfer of Learning.'" *Educational Psychologist* 47, no. 3 (2012): 149–52. doi:10.1080/00461520.2012.695710

Hofstadter, Douglas, and Emmanuel Sander. *Surfaces and Essences: Analogy as the Fuel and Fire of Thinking*. 1st ed. New York: Basic Books, 2013.

Jee, Benjamin D., et al. "Finding Faults: Analogical Comparison Supports Spatial Concept Learning in Geoscience." *Cognitive Processing* 14, no. 2 (May 2013): 175–87. doi:10.1007/s10339-013-0551-7

Kiewra, Kenneth A. "Using Graphic Organizers to Improve Teaching and Learning." IDEA Paper #51. IDEA Center, Inc. (2012). http://eric.ed.gov/?id=ED565284

Kilpatrick, Jeremy. "Pólya on Mathematical Abilities." *The Mathematics Educator* 21, no. 1 (2011). http://tme.journals.libs.uga.edu/index.php/tme/article/view/229

Kirkley, Jamie. "Principles of Teaching Problem Solving." Technical Paper 4. Bloomington, MN: Plato Learning, 2003.

Lederman, Eric. "Journey into Problem Solving: A Gift from Pólya." *The Physics Teacher* 47, no. 2 (2009): 94. doi:10.1119/1.3072455

Nesbit, John C., and Olusola O. Adesope. "Learning with Concept and Knowledge Maps: A Meta-Analysis." *Review of Educational Research* 76, no. 3 (2006): 413–48.

Novak, Joseph D. *Learning, Creating, and Using Knowledge: Concept Maps as Facilitative Tools in Schools and Corporations*. London: Routledge, 2010.

Novak, Joseph D., and Alberto J. Cañas. "The Theory Underlying Concept Maps and How to Construct and Use Them." Technical Report. Institute for Human and Machine Cognition (2008). http://eprint.ihmc.us/5/

Paletz, Susannah B. F., Joel Chan, and Christian D. Schunn. "Uncovering Uncertainty through Disagreement." *Applied Cognitive Psychology* 30, no. 3 (2016): 387–400.

Parrotta, Pierpaolo, Dario Pozzoli, and Mariola Pytlikova. "Does Labor Diversity Affect Firm Productivity?" IZA Discussion Paper no. 6973 (2012). http://papers.ssrn.com/sol3/papers.cfm?abstract_id=2173663

Paul, Richard, et al. *Critical Thinking Handbook: 4th–6th Grades: A Guide for Remodeling Lesson Plans in Language Arts, Social Studies, and Science.* Rohnert Park, CA: Center for Critical Thinking, 1990.

Pólya, George. "On Learning, Teaching, and Learning Teaching." *The American Mathematical Monthly* 70, no. 6 (1963): 605–19.

Singh, Indra Sen, and Karren Moono. "The Effect of Using Concept Maps on Student Achievement in Selected Topics in Chemistry at Tertiary Level." *Journal of Education and Practice* 6, no. 15 (2015): 106–16.

Willingham, Daniel T. "Critical Thinking: Why Is It So Hard to Teach?" *Arts Education Policy Review* 109, no. 4 (2008): 21–32.

Chapter 6

Regarding Daniel Kahneman on page 175, see David Shariatmadari, "Daniel Kahneman: 'What Would I Eliminate If I Had a Magic Wand? Overconfidence,'" *The Guardian*, July 18, 2015, https://www.theguardian.com/books/2015/jul/18/daniel-kahneman-books-interview (accessed October 7, 2016).

On Markman on page 177, see Art Markman, *Smart Thinking: Three Essential Keys to Solve Problems, Innovate, and Get Things Done* (New York: Penguin, 2012).

On fluency on page 178, I relied on Shana K. Carpenter, Miko M. Wilford, Nate Kornell, and Kellie M. Mullaney, "Appearances Can Be Deceiving: Instructor Fluency Increases Perceptions of Learning without Increasing Actual Learning," *Psychonomic Bulletin & Review* 20, no. 6 (2013): 1350–56.

Regarding the "article with images" and a professor "enthralling" a class on page 178, see the Carpenter study and Michael J. Serra and John Dunlosky, "Metacomprehension Judgements Reflect the Belief That Diagrams Improve Learning from Text," *Memory* (Hove, England) 18, no. 7 (October 2010): 698–711.

Regarding Victory Disease and Custer on page 179, see Major Timothy M. Karcher, *Understanding the Victory Disease: From the Little Bighorn to Mogadishu and Beyond* (San Francisco: Squibd, Pickle Partners Publishing, 2015).

On the issue of overconfidence on page 178, I relied on some text from a previous article: Ulrich Boser, "We're All Lying Liars: Why People Tell Lies, and Why White Lies Can Be OK," *US News & World Report*, May 18, 2009, http://health.usnews.com/health-news/family-health/brain-and-behavior/articles/2009/05/18/were-all-lying-liars-why-people-tell-lies-and-why-white-lies-can-be-ok (accessed September 14, 2016).

Regarding inattentional blindness on page 181, see Alan D. Castel, Michael Vendetti, and Keith J. Holyoak, "Fire Drill: Inattentional Blindness and Amnesia for the Location of Fire Extinguishers," *Attention, Perception, & Psychophysics* 74, no. 7 (October 2012): 1391–96, doi:10.3758/s13414-012-0355-3

Also cited on inattentional blindness on page 182 is Christopher F. Chabris et al., "You Do Not Talk about Fight Club If You Do Not Notice Fight Club: Inattentional Blindness for a Simulated Real-World Assault," *i-Perception*

2.2 (2011): 150–53. Also Daniel Kahneman, *Thinking, Fast and Slow* (New York: Farrar, Straus and Giroux, 2011).

For details on umpires and performance on page 187, see Brian Mills, *Technological Innovations in Monitoring and Evaluation: Evidence of Performance Impacts among Major League Baseball Umpires*, Working Paper, 2015, and Ben Lindbergh, "Rise of the Machines?" *Grantland,* November 8, 2013. http://grantland.com/features/ben-lindbergh-possibility-machines -replacing-umpires/ (accessed October 7, 2016). For the Dellinger quote on page 187, I relied on Noah Davis, "Umpires Are Less Blind Than They Used to Be," *FiveThirtyEight,* August 19, 2015, http://fivethirtyeight.com /features/umpires-are-less-blind-than-they-used-to-be/ (accessed October 7, 2016).

For more on Tom Hallion, including his quotes on page 187, see Ben Lindbergh and Evan Brunell, "A Lip Reader Deciphers the Umpire-Manager Arguments of 2012." *Deadspin,* January 25, 2013, http://deadspin.com / 5978810/a-lip-reader-deciphers-the-umpire-manager-arguments-of -2012 (accessed September 15, 2016); "A Postgame Interview with Umpire Tom Hallion," *Major League Baseball,* October 26, 2008, http://m.mlb .com/news/article/3645414/ (accessed September 15, 2016). Also helpful was "Tom Hallion," *Wikipedia, the Free Encyclopedia,* May 19, 2016, https://en.wikipedia.org/w/index.php?title=Tom_Hallion&oldid=72099 5073 (accessed September 15, 2016).

The "unhappy customers" quote on page 186 is from Bill Gates, *Business @ the Speed of Thought: Succeeding in the Digital Economy* (New York: Grand Central Publishing, 1999).

The detail about Pat Metheny on page 197 comes from Gary Marcus, *Guitar Zero: The Science of Becoming Musical at Any Age* (New York: Penguin, 2012).

On changing test answers on page 197, see Philip A. Higham and Catherine Gerrard, "Not All Errors Are Created Equal: Metacognition and Changing Answers on Multiple-Choice Tests," *Canadian Journal of Experimental Psychology/Revue Canadienne de Psychologie Expérimentale* 59, no. 1 (2005): 28.

Regarding Roger Craig on page 190, I quoted from "How One Man Played 'Moneyball' with *Jeopardy!*" *NPR,* November 20, 2011, http://www.npr .org/2011/11/20/142569472/how-one-man-played-moneyball-with -jeopardy (accessed September 19, 2016). Also quoted on page 190 was Gary Wolf, "Want to Remember Everything You'll Ever Learn? Surrender to This Algorithm," *WIRED,* November 20, 2011, https://www.wired.com /2008/04/ff-wozniak/ (accessed September 19, 2016).

On forgetting and Med U on page 190, see Marcel F. D'Eon, "Knowledge Loss of Medical Students on First Year Basic Science Courses at the University of Saskatchewan," BMC Medical Education 6 (2006): 5, doi:10.1186 /1472-6920-6-5; also see Vicki Langendyk, "Not Knowing That They Do Not Know: Self-Assessment Accuracy of Third-Year Medical Students," *Medical Education* 40, no. 2 (February 2006): 173–79, doi:10.1111/j.1365 -2929.2005.02372.x

For the quote on page 191, from the website of the software Anki, see Anki, https://www.ankisrs.net (accessed September 14, 2016).

For more on forgetting on page 189, see W. Thalheimer, *How Much Do People Forget?* (April 2010). Retrieved October 19, 2011 from http://www.work-learning.com/catalog.html, and Paul Smolen, Yili Zhang, and John H. Byrne, "The Right Time to Learn: Mechanisms and Optimization of Spaced Learning," *Nature Reviews Neuroscience* 17, no. 2 (February 2016): 77–88, doi:10.1038/nrn.2015.18

For details on Verizon using spacing on page 194, see the staff-written article "Top 10 Hall of Fame Outstanding Training Initiatives," *Training Magazine*, February 4, 2016, https://trainingmag.com/trgmag-article/top-10-hall-fame-outstanding-training-initiatives-janfeb-2016 (accessed October 7, 2016).

On spacing on page 194, see M. A. McDaniel, C. L. Fadler, and H. Pashler, "Effects of Spaced Versus Massed Training in Function Learning," *Journal of Experimental Psychology: Learning, Memory, and Cognition*, advance online publication (2013), doi: 10.1037/a0032184, and Nate Kornell, "Optimising Learning Using Flashcards: Spacing Is More Effective Than Cramming," *Applied Cognitive Psychology* 23, no. 9 (December 2009): 1297–317, doi:10.1002/acp.1537

On reflection from page 196, and the quotes on page 204, see Giada Di Stefano, Francesca Gino, Gary P. Pisano, and Bradley R. Staats, "Learning by Thinking: Overcoming the Bias for Action through Reflection," Harvard Business School NOM Unit Working Paper, no. 14–093 (2015): 14–93.

The quote from Tom Magliozzi on page 196 comes from Tom and Ray Magliozzi, *In Our Humble Opinion: Car Talk's Click and Clack Rant and Rave* (New York: Perigee Trade, 2000).

On reflection as a way to learn on page 199, see Barbara Oakley, *A Mind for Numbers: How to Excel at Math and Science (Even If You Flunked Algebra)* (New York: TarcherPerigee, 2014).

On sleep and productivity on page 199, see Matthew Gibson and Jeffrey Shrader, "Time Use and Productivity: The Wage Returns to Sleep" (July 10, 2014), http://econweb.ucsd.edu/~magibson/pdfs/sleep_productivity.pdf. I also relied on Cheri D. Mah et al., "The Effects of Sleep Extension on the Athletic Performance of Collegiate Basketball Players," *Sleep* 34, no. 7 (2011): 943–50.

For sleep and learning on page 199, see Stéphanie Mazza, Emilie Gerbier, Marie-Paule Gustin, Zumrut Kasikci, Olivier Koenig, Thomas C. Toppino, and Michel Magnin, "Relearn Faster and Retain Longer: Along with Practice, Sleep Makes Perfect," *Psychological Science* 27, no. 10 (2016): 1321–30. Regarding school openings and sleep, see Ulrich Boser, Catherine Brown, and Perpetual Baffour, "Early School Start Times and Student Outcomes," Center for American Progress, forthcoming.

On the benefits of reflection and outdoors on page 201, see Ruth Ann Atchley, David L. Strayer, and Paul Atchley, "Creativity in the Wild: Improving Creative Reasoning Through Immersion in Natural Settings," *PloS One* 7, no. 12 (2012): e51474. Regarding the study on bricks, see C. Page Moreau and Marit Gundersen Engeset, "The Downstream Consequences of Problem-Solving Mindsets: How Playing with LEGO Influences Creativity," *Journal of Marketing Research* 53, no. 1 (2016): 18–30. Also cited is Jonathan Smallwood, Daniel J. Fishman, and Jonathan W. Schooler, "Counting the Cost of an Absent Mind: Mind Wandering as an Underrecognized Influence on Educational Performance," *Psychonomic Bulletin & Review* 14, no. 2 (2007): 230–36.

For more on Immordino-Yang on page 200, see Mary Helen Immordino-Yang and Kurt W. Fischer, "Neuroscience Bases of Learning," *International Encyclopedia of Education,* 3rd ed. (Oxford: Elsevier, 2010), 310–16. Also helpful is M. H. Immordino-Yang, J. A. Christodoulou, and V. Singh, "Rest Is Not Idleness: Implications of the Brain's Default Mode for Human Development and Education," *Perspectives on Psychological Science* 7, no. 4 (July 1, 2012): 352–64, doi:10.1177/1745691612447308

Regarding the company Groove on page 201, see Hunter Stuart News, "Companies Are Rethinking the Open Office and It's About Time," *Huffington Post,* http://www.huffingtonpost.com/2015/02/12/open-offices -changing-to-include-private-space_n_6669666.html. On Russell Wilson on page 204, see "Russell Wilson Benefits from Working with a Mental Conditioning Coach," ESPN.com, June 28, 2016. http://www.espn.com /blog/nflnation/post/_/id/206434

On deep work on page 204, see Cal Newport, *Deep Work: Rules for Focused Success in a Distracted World* (New York: Grand Central Publishing, 2016).

The Napolitano quote on page 205 comes from Meghashyam Mali, "Napolitano Refuses to Use Email, Calls It 'Inefficient,'" *TheHill,* March 26, 2013, http://thehill.com/blogs/blog-briefing-room/news/290311-napolitano -refuses-to-use-email

The Thompson quote on page 205 comes from Clive Thompson, *Smarter Than You Think: How Technology Is Changing Our Minds for the Better* (New York: Penguin, 2013).

Regarding checklists on page 206, see Atul Gawande, *The Checklist Manifesto: How to Get Things Right* (New York: Metropolitan Books, 2009). Also Henry S. Schneider and C. Kirabo Jackson, "Checklists and Worker Behavior: A Field Experiment," *American Economic Journal: Applied Economics* 7, no. 4 (2015).

The quote from Randall Stephenson on page 206 is from Quentin Hardy, "Gearing Up for the Cloud, AT&T Tells Its Workers: Adapt, or Else," *New York Times,* February 13, 2016, http://www.nytimes.com/2016 /02/14/technology/gearing-up-for-the-cloud-att-tells-its-workers-adapt -or-else.html (accessed October 7, 2016).

For the LeBron James quote on page 207, see Dave McMenamin, "After Many Turnovers, LeBron James Looks for a Turnaround," *ESPN,* June 7, 2016, http://espn.com/blog/cleveland-cavaliers/post/_/id/2940 (accessed October 7, 2016).

Also cited in this chapter

Bar-Eli, M., O. H. Azar, I. Ritov, Y. Keidar-Levin, and G. Schein. "Action Bias Among Elite Soccer Goalkeepers: The Case of Penalty Kicks." *Journal of Economic Psychology* 28, no. 5 (2007): 606–21.

Bjork, Robert A., John Dunlosky, and Nate Kornell. "Self-Regulated Learning: Beliefs, Techniques, and Illusions." *Annual Review of Psychology* 64, no. 1 (January 3, 2013): 417–44. doi:10.1146/annurev-psych-113011 -143823

Dunning, David, Chip Heath, and Jerry M. Suls. "Flawed Self-Assessment: Implications for Health, Education, and the Workplace." *Psychological Science in the Public Interest* 5, no. 3 (2004): 69–106.

Dunning, David, Kerri Johnson, Joyce Ehrlinger, and Justin Kruger. "Why People Fail to Recognize Their Own Incompetence." *Current Directions in Psychological Science* 12, no. 3 (2003): 83–7.

Finn, Bridgid, and Janet Metcalfe. "Overconfidence in Children's Multi-Trial Judgments of Learning." *Learning and Instruction* 32 (August 2014): 1–9. doi:10.1016/j.learninstruc.2014.01.001

Halpern, Diane F. "Teaching for Critical Thinking: Helping College Students Develop the Skills and Dispositions of a Critical Thinker." *New Directions for Teaching and Learning* 1999, no. 80 (1999): 69–74.

Huelser, Barbie J., and Janet Metcalfe. "Making Related Errors Facilitates Learning, But Learners Do Not Know It." *Memory & Cognition* 40, no. 4 (May 2012): 514–27. doi:10.3758/s13421-011-0167-z

Kallet, Michael. *Think Smarter: Critical Thinking to Improve Problem-Solving and Decision-Making Skills.* Hoboken, NJ: Wiley, 2014.

Immordino-Yang, Mary Helen, and Kurt W. Fischer. "Neuroscience Bases of Learning." *International Encyclopedia of Education,* 3rd ed. (2010): 310–16.

Immordino-Yang, M. H., J. A. Christodoulou, and V. Singh. "Rest Is Not Idleness: Implications of the Brain's Default Mode for Human Development and Education." *Perspectives on Psychological Science* 7, no. 4 (July 1, 2012): 352–64. doi:10.1177/1745691612447308

Lovett, Martha C. "Make Exams Worth More Than the Grade." *Using Reflection and Metacognition to Improve Student Learning: Across the Disciplines, Across the Academy,* eds. Matthew Kaplan, Naomi Silver, Danielle LaVaque-Manty, and Deborah Meizlish. Sterling, VA: Stylus, 2013.

Pan, Steven C. "The Interleaving Effect: Mixing It Up Boosts Learning." *Scientific American.* http://www.scientificamerican.com/article/the-interleaving -effect-mixing-it-up-boosts-learning/ (accessed September 14, 2016)

Thornton, Bill, Alyson Faires, Maija Robbins, and Eric Rollins. "The mere presence of a cell phone may be distracting." *Social Psychology* (2014).

Zimmerman, Barry. "Introduction." *Self-regulated learning: From teaching to self-reflective practice,* eds. Dale H. Schunk and Barry J. Zimmerman. Guilford Press, 1998.

Epilogue

For the description of the airline crash, including the quotes on page 209, I
relied on National Transportation Aircraft Accident Report, Northwest
Airlines, Inc. McDonnell Douglas DC-9-82, N312RC, Detroit Metropolitan Wayne County Airport, Romulus, Michigan, August 16, 1987. Also see
John Lauber, "Northwest 255 at DTW: Anatomy of a Human Error Accident," *Human Factors & Aviation Medicine* 36, no. 4 (1989). Lauber was
also the source of the blindness quote on page 210. Also see the National
Transportation Safety Board, Washington, D.C. 20594, *Safety Recommendation*, A-88-64 through -70, June 27, 1988.

I also relied on media accounts for details about the passengers on page 209,
including Bill Peterson, "The Final Moments of a Flight to Disaster,"
Washington Post, August 23, 1987. Also see Steven R. Churm, "Flight 255:
Life or Death Turned on Twists of Fate: 7 Who Died in Crash Shared Hope
for Their Future in Orange County; 3 Who Missed Plane Saved by Luck,"
Los Angeles Times, August 23, 1987, http://articles.latimes.com/1987-08
-23/local/me-3108_1_orange-county (accessed September 26, 2016).

Mike Sakal, "Spirits Live on: Arizona Remembers Northwest Flight 255
Crash 25 Years Later," *East Valley Tribune,* August 15, 2012,
http://www.eastvalleytribune.com/local/article_d74aac66-e66f
-11e1-b0e0-0019bb2963f4.html (accessed September 26, 2016).

With regard to situational awareness on page 210, see Mica R. Endsley and
Michelle M. Robertson, "Training for Situation Awareness in Individuals
and Teams," in *Situation Awareness Analysis and Measurement,* eds. Mica
R. Endsley and Daniel J. Garland (Mahwah, NJ: Lawrence Erlbaum,
2000): 349–66. Also Endsley and Daniel J. Garland, "Pilot Situation
Awareness Training in General Aviation," *Proceedings of the Triennal
Congress of the International Ergonomics Association and Human Factors
and Ergonomics Society Annual Meeting* 44, no. 11 (2000): 357–60.

For the data on plane crashes on page 212, see Lisa Mahapatra, "How Many
Planes Crash Every Year, and How Many People Die in Plane Crashes?"
International Business Times, March 10, 2014.

For the quote from Boaler on page 216, see Jo Boaler, "Advice for Parents,
from Professor Jo Boaler," youcubed.org (accessed September 26, 2016).

On the IES guide on page 214, see Harold Pashler et al., "Organizing Instruction and Study to Improve Student Learning. IES Practice Guide. NCER
2007-2004," National Center for Education Research, 2007, http://eric.
ed.gov/?id=ED498555

For the physics study on page 215, see Louis Deslauriers, Ellen Schelew, and
Carl Wieman, "Improved Learning in a Large-Enrollment Physics Class,"
Science 332, no. 6031 (2011): 862–64, doi:10.1126/science.1201783

Also cited in this chapter

Endsley, Mica R. "Expertise and Situation Awareness." *Cambridge Handbook
of Expertise and Expert Performance*, eds. K. A. Ericsson, N. Charness,

P. J. Feltovich, and R. R. Hoffman. New York: Cambridge University Press, 2006, 633–51.

Endsley, Mica R. and Michelle M. Robertson. "Team Situation Awareness in Aviation Maintenance." *Proceedings of the Human Factors and Ergonomics Society Annual Meeting* 40, no. 21 (1996): 1077–81.

Mayer, Richard. *Multimedia Learning.* Cambridge, England: Cambridge University Press, 2001.

———. "Situation Awareness in Aircraft Maintenance Teams." *International Journal of Industrial Ergonomics* 26 (2000): 301–25.

Tool Kits

The tool kits draw heavily from the main text, and besides the sources named above, I also relied on resources from the Carl Wieman Science Education Initiative. For details on SurePayroll on page 224, see Leigh Buchanan, "Rethinking Employee Awards," *Inc.com*, July 5, 2011, http://www.inc.com/magazine/201107/rethinking-employee-awards.html.ces

Quiz Answers

Here are the answers to the quiz questions throughout the book.

1. C	12. C	23. True
2. F	13. B	24. B
3. True	14. True	25. True
4. C	15. B	26. True
5. B	16. False	27. False
6. True	17. False	28. A
7. True	18. False	29. True
8. False	19. D	30. True
9. True	20. C	31. False
10. C	21. A and E	32. True
11. B	22. True	

Note that for some of the quiz questions, I relied on Paul A. Howard-Jones, "Neuroscience and Education: Myths and Messages," *Nature Reviews Neuroscience* 15 (2014): 817–24. For more information, also see an upcoming paper: Ulrich Boser, "What the Public Knows about the Science for Learning," The Center for American Progress, forthcoming.

ACKNOWLEDGMENTS

IN MANY WAYS, writing a book is a lot like learning. From the outside, both activities seem like the effort of a lone individual hunkered alone in a room for hours, reading books and articles, typing up notes and reminders. However, it turns out that both endeavors are very much a group effort.

In this regard, my first thanks goes to my wife, Nora, who has endured yet another book project with loving grace and devoted patience. My children, Leila and Sonja, were also deeply supportive, even though they were subjected to all sorts of "learning activities," from abacus training to DragonBox. I dedicate this book to my parents, who helped in ways big and small. I also owe a lot to my siblings, Markus and Katharina, and their families for their support. Indeed, it was Katharina who tipped me off to the practice of mental abacus.

Rodale was an enormous help, the best publisher that I've had the opportunity to work with. Marisa Vigilante provided thoughtful feedback and great patience, even when I misspelled her name. Kathleen Schmidt understood the book and remained supportive throughout. A special thanks to Izzy Hughes, Aly Mostel, and Kate Bittman for all their efforts. I'm also indebted to copy editor Nancy N. Bailey, who saved me from countless errors.

I'm hugely grateful to the staff at the Center for American Progress, including Neera Tanden, Carmel Martin, and Catherine Brown. I also had the support of a number of researchers including Pamela Bopp, Max McClure, Jaime Liane Dunaway, and Emma Zaballos. A number of colleagues read early drafts, including Carl Chancellor, Ken Stern, David Moldawer, and Rich Shea. A special thanks to Jeric Aspillaga, who transcribed many hours of tape.

There were many people who provided insights and interviews, whose names are not mentioned in the text or, if so, only briefly. They include Jesse Chandler, Dick Clark, Ken Knoedinger, David Daniel, Jim Stigler, David Miele, Steve Fleming, Paul Bruno, Ben Riley, Karin Chenowith, Craig Jerald, Lisa Hansel, Michael Frank, Emily Diehl, Amandna Visek, Zehra Peynircioglu, Bridget Finn, Roger Azevedo, Chris Paris, Jay Hooper, Jal Mehta, Jane Dutton, Mike Moser, Robert Pondiscio, David Trigaux, David Domenici, Angela Duckworth, Joe Reddish, Nick Antaris, Steve Flemming, Judith Harackiewicz, Mark McDaniel, Logan Fiorella, David Yaeger, Anne Marie Palincsar, Dale Shunk, Phil Winnie, Thaddeus Griebel, Dimitri Christakis, Ira Winder, Ann Renninger, Mary-Pat Wenderoth, Susan Goldwin-Meadow, Fei-yan Chen, Paul Silvia, and David Whitebread.

I appreciate the input of the many people that I spoke with at Windsor Hills, the Urban Debate Club, WAMALUG, BrickFair, and Tom Sato's Soroban classes. A devoted thanks, too, to my friends on the basketball court, who unwittingly took part in my little experiment. And finally, I'd like to express my gratitude to the law library at American University, where I wrote much of this book.

INDEX

Boldface page references indicate illustrations.

Highlighting text, 25, 27, 216
High Tech High, 123–125
Hypothetical thinking
 learning by experimentation, 151–155
 pretend play, 151
 in the scientific method, 151–152
 speculation, 149–150, 222

I

If-then plans, 101
Illusion of explanatory depth. *See* Overconfidence
Imagery
 as memory aid, 25, 122
 mental, for managing emotions, 64
Imitation, 120
Instinctive brain, 181–182
Instruction. *See* Teaching
Intelligence, 63, 96–97, 101

J

Jeopardy! competition, 190–193
Job crafting, 9–10
Jobs, Steve, 150

K

Kind of Blue jazz album, 114–115
Knowledge. *See also* Extending knowledge or expertise
 assessing before new learning, 52
 as basis of further learning, 44–49, 77, 167
 complexity inherent in, 131
 identifying feelings, 99
 mnemonics based on, 47
 networks of meaning aiding, 30
 overconfidence about, 175–180
 regrouping students by, 48–49

 systematized in expertise, 51–52
 tutoring tailored to, 46
 as uncertain, 130–131
Knowledge Effect, 46, 77, 139, 161, 167

L

Labels, 106–107
Language attrition
 meaning lost in, 30
 mind-set's effect on, 32–33
 in native speakers, 29–30
 in second language, 29
Learn crafting, 10–11
Learners, strategies for, 219–222
Legos
 BrickFair convention, 7
 learn crafting with, 11
 popularity with adults, 3
 Wolfson's Lego club, 18–19
 Wolfson's sculptures, 1–2, 3–4
Long-term memory, 47, 91–92. *See also* Memory
LSAT prep classes, 53–54

M

Magliozzi, Tom and Ray, 159–160, 163
Managers, strategies for, 223–225
Managing emotions, 99–101, 227
Marketing, analogy in, 161
Marshmallow test, 99, 100–101
Martial arts, active learning in, 28
Mastery. *See* Expertise or mastery
Meaning. *See also* Value
 created by active learning, 28–29, 219
 created by errors, 95–96
 created by the brain, 2–3
 danger of creating wrongly, 33–34

Q

Questions
arising from learning activities,
113
learning driven by, 133
metacognitive, 60
the Question, 67, 68
for relating knowledge, 143–144,
221–222
self-questioning, 133
for targeting, 39
Why? 117–118
wrapper, for review, 184
Quizzes and tests. *See also*
Evaluations
flashcards for, 194–196
internal quizzing, 53
as learning techniques, 26
LSAT prep classes, 53–54
metacognition promoted by, 60
for rethinking understanding,
187–189
self-quizzing, 90–91, 102
spaced learning encouraged by,
194
testing effect, 91
understanding aided by, 53

R

Reading retention, imagination for,
25
Reasoning
deeper, analogy as aid to, 165–167
developed by relating knowledge,
143–144
higher-order, 143
knowledge extended by, 119–120
Reflection, 196–207
in Becoming a Man (BAM)
program, 202–204
bias for action over, 203–204

as crucial part of learning, 197,
198, 222
in dynamic learning, 200
meditation for, 204
mental quiet needed for, 199,
200–202
sleep and, 199–200
solitude for, 204
by successful individuals,
205–206
talking out loud, 198
understanding deepened by, 196
writing down reflections, 197–198
Reframing for emotional
management, 100–101
Regrouping students, 48–49
Relating knowledge and skills,
141–173
analogy for, 158–167, 225
brief summary of, 213
concept maps for, 156–158, **157**,
222
deeper structures revealed by,
145–147, 149
hypothetical thinking for,
149–155, 222
learning by experimentation,
151–155
by mixing up practice, 148–149,
163–164
needed for higher-order
thinking, 143
problem solving and, 151–153
problem solving for, 167–173
questions for, 143–144, 221–222
reasoning skills developed by,
143–144
strategies for learners, 221–222
thought experiments for, 141–142
transfer of learning aided by,
142–143
Venn diagrams for, 155–156, **156**